D0463364

BURIED
TREASURES
OF THE OZARKS
AND THE APPALACHIANS

BURIED
TREASURES
OF THE OZARKS
AND THE APPALACHIANS

W.C. Jameson

Published in 1993 by

Promontory Press
A division of BBS Publishing Corporation
450 Raritan Center Parkway
Edison, New Jersey 08837

Promontory Press is a registered trademark of BBS Publishing Corporation.

Published by arrangement with August House, Inc.

Library of Congress Catalog Card number: 93-70381

ISBN 10: 0-88394-084-1
ISBN 13: 978-0-88394-084-6

Printed in the United States of America.

Contents

Buried Treasures of the Ozarks

Legends of Lost Gold, Hidden Silver, and Forgotten Caches

For my mother

Contents

Prologue

Not all of the tales included in this book were easily ac-quired. Some could be had merely for the asking; others were available from writings and literature of the area. Many of them had to be tracked down.

Some of the tracking and hunting of these tales occurred in various libraries throughout the Ozarks. Searching the dark stacks of the musty libraries is, in some ways, like pursuing a quarry in the wild Ozark mountains and forests: The quarry sometimes blends in with the surroundings and is not easily located, but the determined tracker persists and is eventually rewarded.

Many of these tales had to be tracked in the Ozark Mountains themselves, doggedly followed and occasionally cornered. A few of them got away, but many were captured. Tracking the stories in the wild meant traveling to remote parts of Arkansas, Missouri, and Oklahoma, visiting and getting to know many of the deep Ozark denizens up close and personally. In the course of this effort I have put thousands of miles on my vehicle and discovered some of the most inaccessible roads imaginable. I have leaned across many a split-rail fence talking to an Ozark old-timer who might be able to shed light on some long-obscure aspect of a particular story.

I have stared across campfires into the eyes of men who have searched for these lost treasures, listening closely as they spoke of their experiences and of their knowledge of locations, circumstances, and insights into the minds of those who buried riches lifetimes ago.

I have sat in awe in rustic log cabins while old men, in the finest Ozark storytelling tradition, related some of these tales, filling them and the listener with the wonder and magic of the unknown, of mysteries long unsolved.

I have met and visited men who have committed nearly their entire lives to the search for the wealth they believe lies just beyond the next bend or deep within the next cave.

Given a choice between prowling the libraries and stalking these tales in the wild, I prefer the latter, mainly because in so doing, one gets the stories directly from the Ozark folk themselves, from the lips of those who know the mountains and the woods, the animals and the weather, the rivers and the rocks.

In listening to these stories firsthand one receives not only the tale, but the spirit of the tale as well. That spirit is in many ways related to the spirit of the folk—a never-say-die attitude that has enabled the mountain people to survive in the remote corners of rugged and often forbidding Ozark environments. In addition to the tales, it is this spirit we wish to capture and preserve between the pages of this book.

In nearly every case where I gleaned some element of a tale from an Ozark native, I perceived in the people what I can only describe as a restless passion for the story—not just for the wealth they surely hoped to locate, but for the story itself. Many of the Ozarkers with whom I visited not only believe every word of these tales, they believe *in* the stories themselves as if the stories were icons of their Ozark existence. They believe the stories belong to them, are their property. For the most part the stories are not to be shared with a neighbor or an outsider. Handed down from generation to generation, they are the real treasures, and they are often closely guarded.

Because of that perception, many of those I visited with refused to reveal anything and would sometimes chase me away. Others, a bit more relaxed, were still suspicious and guarded, as if they thought I wanted to steal from them not only the treasures but their tales of the treasures. Very few were casual in releasing information. Some were a little more willing to disclose a few facts; others only dangled vague references before my imagination.

Many Ozarkers still search for these treasures. Some, according to their claims, actually find one. Most do not.

Even when they are frustrated at not finding wealth—no doubt much as their fathers and grandfathers were frustrated—they all retain a passion for the search and the story, a passion that is surely inherited from their elders.

Most of those I encountered were of a single type, loners and outcasts, without families and operating on the fringes of society. All were dreamers, dreaming not only of treasure but of the adventure of the search. Their dreams are what sustain them, drive them on.

All of them were men.

In getting to know them, I sometimes felt as if I were looking at the mountains themselves. The men were lined, wrinkled, and weathered like the layers of weathered limestone that make up the foundations of these hills. Many of them were bent like aged trees still clinging to precarious slopes, extending their roots deeper and deeper into the crevices in the never-ending search for water and sustenance.

Indeed, these men are a product of the land, offspring of the loins of the hills and hollows. To read these tales is to take a journey into the deep Ozarks, a journey that begins and ends with the people.

W.C. Jameson

11

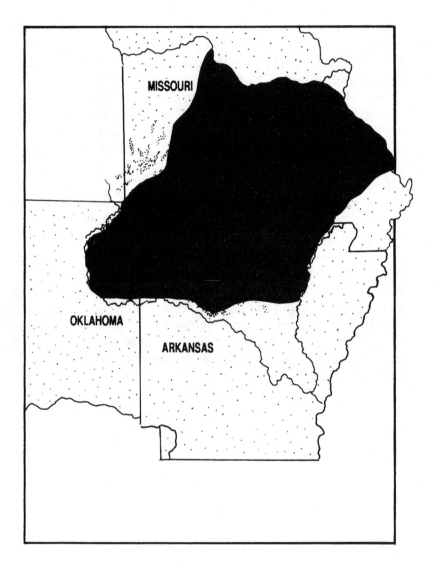

Introduction

In history, folklore, culture, and geography, the Ozark Mountains have been described as "remote," "secluded," "dark," "forbidding," "lawless," "dangerous," and "mysterious." These terms might seem inflated, but many of them are still applied today to this unique range of hills and valleys. In spite of their location near major cities, the Ozark Mountains remain in many ways dark, unexplored, and mysterious.

These grand mountains comprise significant portions of northwestern Arkansas, southern Missouri, and northeastern Oklahoma. A tiny part of the Ozarks even extends into the extreme southeastern corner of Kansas. Consisting of approximately 60,000 square miles of uplifted and dissected plateau, the Ozarks are bounded on the north by the Missouri River, on the east by the Mississippi River, on the southeast by the Black River, and on the south by the Arkansas River. The western boundary of the Ozark Mountains is less distinct, but geologists define it as where the 325-million-year-old rock gives way to younger Pennsylvanian Age rock, not so much a boundary as it is a gradual transition. Generally speaking, most investigators refer to the Neosho River in Oklahoma as the western boundary.

ORIGINS

The Ozarks had their origin in darkness, the darkness associated with the great depths of a long-ago sea. For hundreds of millions of years, the portion of the North American crust that was to become the Ozark Mountains was subjected to periodic uplift and sinking as a result of various violent forces taking place within the earth.

Approximately 280 million years ago, after the most violent of the land-forming episodes had ceased, the region that was to become the Ozarks was a flat featureless plain perched high above the seawaters that covered much of the North American continent at the time. This plain was subjected to constant erosion from rain and runoff for the next 180 million years, a process that eventually eroded the plain nearly to sea level.

There followed an episode of rising seawaters that effectively covered this low flat plain, submerging it again to great depths for the next 65 million years. During this period, more sediments accumulated upon the submerged structure, layer upon layer, and eventually hardened to form thick strata of limestone and sandstone.

About 30 million years ago the area was subjected to uplifting, and once again another flat plain was elevated several thousand feet above sea level.

The climate began to change dramatically around this time: Temperatures gradually dropped and rains fell incessantly. As the temperature cooled over the centuries, the rains turned to snow, which accumulated at the higher elevations, eventually becoming compressed, turning into ice, and forming glaciers.

After several thousand more years passed, the climate changed and the area gradually became warmer. The vast accumulations of snow and ice began to melt, and the meltwater began a headlong rush to the sea. This rapidly flowing, sediment-laden water began to carve into the soft limestone layers, removing material at a great rate and initiating the carving and sculpting of the limestone rock into many deep, narrow, steep-walled valleys that were soon to characterize this mountain range.

While the sculpting of the Ozark landscape was taking place on the surface, a different kind of sculpting was going on underground. The highly soluble limestone rock that makes up most of the Ozark range was being eaten away by the chemically active ground waters, forming vast cavern systems.

The climate entered yet another warming period and eventually stabilized about 4,000 years ago. During this time seeds of oak, hickory, and pine became established on the dissected landscapes of the Ozark uplift. Forests soon grew and prospered, and the environment took on an appearance that has remained essentially unchanged to the present. Thus the Ozark Mountains stood in relative isolation for several thousand years. The dense woods and valleys filled with many different types of wildlife. To an observer, it would have been hard to believe that processes of violent upheaval and dramatic weathering produced such a serene sylvan landscape. But serene it was, almost paradise-like. Paradoxically, while much of the rest of the North American continent was being occupied by descendants of Asians who crossed the land bridge between Alaska and Russia, the seemingly inviting recesses of the Ozark Mountains saw very little human occupation until relatively recent historical times.

EXPLORATION AND SETTLEMENT

What little we know of the Paleo-Indian populations of the Ozarks comes from the few sophisticated archaeological studies that have been conducted. Evidence suggests that the Ozarks were visited from time to time by groups of Native Americans but never significantly populated by them in historic times. Why the lush valleys of the Ozarks did not lure great numbers of Indians remains a mystery. Some have suggested that the tribes that settled on the fringes of the Ozarks held the distant dark range in awe, even fear. Many early Indians believed the Ozarks were populated by demons.

During the historic period, Osage, Illinois, Caddo, and Quapaw tribes began to move into and occupy isolated locales in the interior of the range, but their numbers were always small. The Caddo and Osage people briefly established small settlements but were subsequently removed to reservations in Indian Territory.

Spanish explorers visited the Ozarks around 1555 in search of precious metals. Evidence of Spanish occupation and mining in the area is plentiful, but their time in the region was short and they established no permanent settlements. Reports and tales of gold and silver taken by the Spanish from the Ozark Mountains are legion.

By the beginning of the eighteenth century the French had entered the Ozarks and were the first whites to establish permanent settlements in the region. By 1702, they were mining lead from Ozark rock.

The French were also instrumental in establishing trading posts along the eastern margins of the Ozarks. From these locations they often penetrated the range and entered into trade with the small Indian populations there. The French, aware of the potential of a growing fur trade, also engaged in trapping the rich beaver streams in the deep valleys.

Silver was discovered once again in the Ozarks, this time by the French, and by 1725 several mining communities had become established. The discovery of silver provided the incentive to conduct sophisticated exploration of the interior for more of this ore as well as for gold.

News of the discoveries of silver, along with the lure of rich trapping grounds, stimulated the movement of whites into the region. By 1803, this migration increased even more rapidly because of the Louisiana Purchase.

In 1818 small numbers of Cherokee Indians from southern states such as South Carolina and Georgia began migrating into the Ozarks and establishing several large farms and successful homesteads. The Cherokee intermarried with members of the other tribes already inhabiting the region. There was also some intermarriage with early white settlers as well as with slaves who had escaped and sought refuge in the remote range.

In the 1820s, the Ozarks were becoming a refuge for still other Indian tribes that were gradually being displaced from their homelands by white settlers pushing westward. Among these recent immigrants were Peorias, Miamis, Kickapoos, and Creeks, some 6,000 Indians altogether.

16

In 1838, the United States government initiated a mass displacement of the Five Civilized Tribes of Southern Indians (Cherokee, Chickasaw, Choctaw, Creek, and Seminole) into Indian Territory (now Oklahoma), a movement that was linked to the Trail of Tears and that continued throughout the early 1840s. Hundreds of Indians passed through or near the Ozarks during this migration and, when they had the opportunity, escaped into the rugged wilderness knowing they would not be pursued by the military escort.

By this time there existed a curious mix of cultures living in the Ozark Mountains: the earlier Cherokee arrivals, who had initiated flourishing farming ventures; remnant French settlers; recent arrivals of displaced Indians from Kansas and Missouri; and escapees from the Trail of Tears. These different people were competing for limited farming lands. Their cultural diversity exacerbated tensions, and the situation became volatile. Fighting and killing occurred with frightening frequency. Violence was the order of the day.

Soon more and more whites were moving into the region. Settlement was slow owing to the difficulty of travel, the remoteness, the narrow valleys, and the thin soils, but still they came, slowly but consistently, and the more that arrived, the greater the potential for competition and violence.

Many of the white newcomers resented the ownership of vast tracts of land by Indians. Having difficulty displacing the Indians by vigilante means, the whites convinced the U.S. government to remove the Cherokees to Indian Territory. As soon as this was accomplished, the whites moved in and took over the old Cherokee holdings.

Many of the Indians, however, remained in hiding in the Ozarks. Angered at the acquisition of their property by greedy whites, they reacted violently. The Indians were legally declared outlaws and were pursued by armed posses. Indian gangs continued to roam the Ozarks inflicting vengeance on white settlers.

To add to the Indians' problems, white settlers continued to migrate into the area in ever greater numbers. During the decade before the Civil War, the Ozarks experienced an influx of settlers from Kentucky, Tennessee, North Carolina, Virginia, and Pennsylvania. These newcomers were primarily of Scots-Irish descent and have been described as a restless, uneducated, adventurous frontier type. Most of them were searching for free land on which to homestead and raise their crops and families.

A wealthier group, mainly slave-owners from some of the same districts of the South, moved into and settled the better river bottoms where the slaves could be used to clear timber and plant tobacco, hemp, and corn. They were followed by capitalists attempting to take advantage of a perceived prosperity in the Ozarks. This latter group eventually became community leaders and initiators of change.

Still others arriving in the Ozarks were the so-called "poor white trash" who were run out of many of the eastern and southern states. This group included a criminal element that preferred to prey on the established settlers rather than work for themselves.

The new white arrivals added even more ingredients to an already tense and fragile mix of residents; conflict and violence became even more common.

The Civil War saw renewed interest in the settlement of the Ozarks. Some railroad construction was started as well as some timbering, commercial agriculture, and prospecting. Many of the immigrants arriving during this time were from the northern states and had badly needed capital for financing many of these endeavors.

Following the Civil War, the Ozarks became a refuge for a variety of lawless refugees from both North and South. Many of these men had nothing to return to. Their homes and villages had been burned, looted, and destroyed during the war. Many of them turned outlaw and gradually drifted toward the Ozarks, for it was generally known that the mountains were without law. The Ozarks took on a fearful reputation as the realm of predatory gangs of bandits, hostile Indians, and renegade ex-soldiers—a place for honest settlers to avoid.

Disorder and struggle in the Ozarks during this time was

becoming a way of life. Horse and cattle theft and even murder were common. The Ozark Mountains became synonymous with violence and death. Travelers gave the range a wide berth. Many honest God-fearing farmers, frightened of the growing lawlessness, moved from the isolated interior of the mountains—where hills and hollows offered the greatest sanctuary to outlaws—to more protected settlements near military outposts. The mountaineers who remained were clannish, isolated, and wild.

A third phase of settlement began with World War II, and the population grew steadily—though always slowly—from then on. The region continued to be perceived as a barrier as a result of poor or nonexistent roads, impassable valleys and rivers, limited agricultural potential, and isolation. Though more populated, the mountains were home to people who were as clannish and violent as ever. It has been said that the rugged and hostile land of the Ozark Mountains has shaped the people, and, until recently, the people have not had much success in shaping the land. Elements of a twentieth-century frontier culture can still be found along the few back roads that penetrate the remote hollows of the dark Ozark range.

Despite improvements in modern transportation, much of the Ozarks remains tucked away far from the mainstream of contemporary civilization. As the twenty-first century draws near, more and more of the younger Ozark natives are lured by the urban areas. Once they have begun careers and enjoyed the cultural diversions of the cities, they are loath to return to the hollows. Thus, in parts of the Ozarks the population is decreasing and many old homesteads are being abandoned in the isolated wilderness.

WEALTH IN THE OZARKS

The potential for discovering gold and silver in the Ozarks has fascinated people for centuries. De Soto's soldiers, on a mission from the Spanish royalty, explored and prospected the region in search of precious ores, carrying away enough to fill a treasury. The silver mines of the French and those of other later arrivals flourished for a time and then faded.

But there is wealth of another kind to be found in the Ozark Mountains—the wealth of a wonderfully rich folk tradition that includes music, dance, food, language, architecture, and tales. Interwoven through this rich tapestry of folk culture and history are many exciting tales about the search for lost mines and buried treasure. The Ozark Mountains inspire such stories. The history, the culture, and the geography all combine to generate an environment of wonder, magic, and tradition that give rise to awesome narratives of the place and the time.

The lure of buried treasure is powerful; hundreds have succumbed to it over past generations. Tales of lost and buried treasure in the Ozarks descend from the days of Spanish explorers, French traders and miners, Indians, and outlaws. Many who inhabit the Ozark Mountains today are descended from these very people.

While many of the farms and homesteads in the Ozarks did not flourish, the stories did. Some of the poor possessionless few who survived the rugged environment searched for, and occasionally found, hidden treasures in the remote hills and valleys of the range. Most of them aspired to wealth that eluded them. Most were unlucky, some fared better, many died trying.

People come and go, but the tales live on. The stories tell of lost and buried fortunes and of the ancient mines; they tell of ingots of pure silver and gold; they tell of the eternal quest for that which lies just out of sight beyond the next bend or just under a few feet of earth.

ARKANSAS

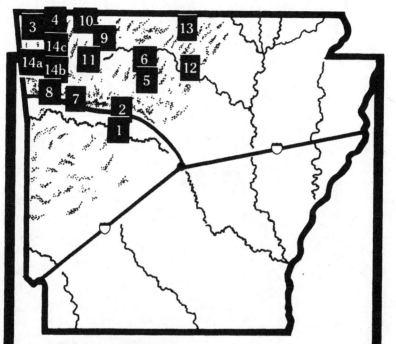

1. Tobe Inmon's Silver Bullets
2. The Mystery of the Turtle Rock
3. The Cave of Spanish Gold
4. The Madre Vena Ore Cache
5. Spanish Silver in Searcy County
6. The Lost Tabor Mine
7. Lost Aztec Mine in Franklin County
8. The Lost Tunnel of Gold
9. King's River Silver
10. The Buried Treasure of Mill Ford Cave
11. Lost Silver Mine near Huntsville
12. Stone County Silver
13. Old Man Napier's Hidden Treasure
14. Civil War Treasures
    a. The Lost Payroll
    b. Buried Arms at Cross Hollow
    c. Hidden Treasure on Callahan Mountain

Tobe Inmon's Silver Bullets

During the last two decades of the nineteenth century, there was significant westward migration from Kentucky, Tennessee, Virginia, and Alabama. Many of the migrants made it as far west as the rich agricultural and mining fields of California, but some got no farther than the Arkansas Ozarks, where they were lured by the promise of decent land.

All had reasons for leaving their homes in the East—a sense of adventure, the potential wealth awaiting them in the California gold fields, or simply desire for a better way of life. Some migrants had been chased out of their home area for one reason or another; they too found their way to and settled in the Ozark Mountains. Shunned, even persecuted, by cliquish neighbors and referred to as "poor white trash," most of those who abandoned the Appalachian valleys were humble, uneducated, and used to scraping out a meager living from the land and subsisting on very little.

Tobe Inmon was a resident of one poor valley in western Kentucky who managed to eke out a precarious existence for himself and his family by growing some corn on a rocky hillside and raising hogs and chickens in the bottoms. Inmon and his family did not get along well with their neighbors, and he earned a reputation as a recluse, neither needing nor wanting the company of others.

When Inmon was accused of stealing a neighbor's livestock and threatened with his life, he packed his few possessions, loaded his wife and two young boys onto a wagon, and left Kentucky. They headed west, driving their few hogs ahead of them as they traveled. They had no idea of their destination as they followed a long and arduous journey over country that offered little but mud, swamps, and misery.

One day Inmon somehow got off the main trail, got lost, and in searching for a way through the mountains found a little valley that immediately appealed to him. It was rather narrow with a running stream in the bottom and plenty of floodplain for a crop of corn. There appeared to be forage for his hogs and abundant timber for a cabin, some pens, and firewood. Another element of the valley that was attractive to Inmon was that the nearest neighbors lived over two miles away.

Deciding that setting up residence here was more appealing than continuing the tiring journey, Inmon went about the task of constructing a one-room log cabin and some pens for his livestock. When he had time he planted some corn at the flat area near the creek. Life was beginning to look good.

The nearest settlement of any importance was Dover, a small town some twelve miles south of Inmon's Moccasin Creek Valley farm, an important stop along the old road to Fort Smith. Occasionally Inmon would haul some chickens or a hog into Dover and trade for staples like flour, sugar, and coffee. The residents of Dover considered him a curious figure. He rarely spoke except to conduct what little business he had, and even then he was quite surly, preferring to conclude his affairs and leave town as soon as possible.

Inmon dressed in little more than rags and always appeared unclean. The few times he brought his family into town, they too looked wretched and ragged. Those who chanced by Inmon's homestead in the valley remarked at the squalor in which the family lived, claiming the log cabin had large open chinks that let in the cold air and appeared to offer only a little more shelter than the hog pen.

One day during the autumn of 1903, Inmon rode into Dover and asked for a doctor. His youngest son had come down with fever and was unconscious. Inmon was directed to Dr. Benjamin

Martin, the only doctor in town, who agreed to follow him out to Moccasin Creek. Martin was an affable man in his late forties, was well-liked by the community, and had delivered virtually every child in the town and the surrounding area under ten years old. The doctor was appalled at the primitive conditions in which the Inmon family lived, but he agreed to remain at the youth's bedside until he was out of danger.

Finally the fever passed and Martin prepared his horse and carriage for the return trip to Dover. As he was hitching the animal to the trace, Inmon appeared from around one corner of the cabin and asked the doctor about his fee. Aware of the man's poverty, Martin told Inmon he could just settle up when times got better and not to worry about it until then. Inmon was insistent, however, and finally offered the doctor a small canvas sack containing about thirty bullets for a large-caliber rifle.

During this time bullets were scarce. Most people who had need of them were happy to get them when they could. Martin examined the bullets and found them to be well-made, and as he was an enthusiastic hunter and sportsman, he accepted them gratefully as payment.

As the doctor packed the little sack of shells away in the carriage, he asked the farmer where he had gotten such fine ammunition. Inmon explained that he had made the bullets himself with lead he extracted from "an old mine back in the hills not too far from the cabin." Martin thanked him again, climbed onto his carriage, and returned to Dover.

At home Martin placed the sack of bullets on a shelf in his study, intending to use them on his next deer hunt. Over the next few weeks, however, he stayed busy treating the sick and delivering babies, and as a result his autumn deer hunt had to be postponed. He gradually forgot about the sack of shells lying on the shelf of his bookcase.

A full two years passed before the doctor remembered the bullets. While readying his equipment for a deer hunt, he located the sack of bullets on the shelf and placed them on the desk in his study so he would not forget to take them along the next morning. That evening, while reading at his desk, he

25

picked up one of the bullets and turned it over and over in his fingers. Presently he scratched the tip of the bullet, trying to pick off some of the black residue. As some of the surface coating was removed, he noticed a peculiar color beneath.

On a hunch the doctor canceled his deer hunt. The next day he went to Russellville, a larger settlement a few miles south of Dover, and took the bullets to a friend knowledgeable about minerals. He discovered, to his astonishment, that they were made of pure silver. Martin sold the sack of shells for seventy-two dollars.

On returning to Dover that evening, Martin made plans to depart for the Inmon homestead the first thing in the morning to try to convince the poor farmer to show him the location of his so-called lead mine.

At sunrise the next day, Martin flogged his poor horse the entire trip to Moccasin Creek Valley. His carriage bounced along the seldom-used road until it seemed it would fall apart.

When the doctor arrived at the Inmon home he found it deserted; the site had apparently been unoccupied for several months. He drove the carriage to the farm of the nearest neighbor, asked the Inmons' whereabouts, and was told they had packed up and departed for Texas six months earlier. No one knew exactly where in Texas they had gone.

With what little light there was left in the day, Martin climbed the low hill just behind the Inmon cabin and wandered through the woods, inspecting every rock outcrop he encountered for any evidence of mining. He searched until darkness prevented him from continuing and he finally had to return to Dover.

The next morning found Martin busily outfitting himself with camping gear and provisions for an extended stay out at Moccasin Creek Valley. On this trip, he stayed for two and a half weeks, living in the deserted ramshackle cabin and exploring the hills and woods in search of the lost silver mine. After exhausting his food supply, he was forced to return to town.

Immediately on arriving home, Martin busied himself with preparations for an even longer stay at the valley in search of the ore. As he bustled around town, people remarked on his unshaven and filthy appearance and thought he acted strangely. He refused to tell people what he was doing and ignored pleas for his medical services. He was consumed with finding the fortune in silver he firmly believed existed in some hidden shaft in the Ozark Mountains near the old Inmon farmstead.

Over the next two years Martin continued to make forays into the hills behind the old Inmon cabin in search of the mine. Each time he was disappointed. Back in Dover, his patients gave up on him and sought another doctor to treat them.

Eventually Martin ran out of money and had to sell his home and practice in order to finance his search for the elusive silver. Finding the mine had become his all-consuming passion. Many residents of Dover were convinced the man had gone insane.

More years passed, and the long and unsuccessful search for Tobe Inmon's silver mine left Martin broke, broken, and disheartened. He finally moved in with a sister living in Russellville. His health began to deteriorate rapidly, and he died of complications from pneumonia.

On learning the story of Tobe Inmon's silver bullets, several Dover residents took up the search. During the years after Martin's death, many treasure hunters combed the hills and valleys around Moccasin Creek Valley. Some of them discovered ancient tools that were later identified as being of Spanish origin, thus giving rise to the belief that the early Spanish explorers in Arkansas under the leadership of De Soto had mined the region. Aside from the tools nothing else was found.

Could it be that Tobe Inmon had stumbled onto a long-lost Spanish silver mine? It is likely that this was the case. Poor Tobe. With all his poverty, he apparently had his hands on a fortune in silver, but he did not recognize it for what it was. And poor Dr. Martin: he recognized what it was but could never locate the source of the wealth.

In the summer of 1951, a Cherokee Indian named Lawrence Mankiller brought a large nugget into Fort Smith, where it was identified as a piece of high-grade silver. Mankiller stated that he had found the nugget on the floor of an old mine shaft while deer hunting in Moccasin Creek Valley. He had sought shelter from a rain shower in the convenient shaft, and while sitting just inside the entrance, he poked around in the rubble on the floor of the shaft and found the nugget.

Mankiller received an offer of several hundred dollars from a group of men who wanted him to lead them to the old shaft. Mankiller agreed to the proposition, pocketed the money, and promised to take them to the shaft the next morning. That night, however, Lawrence Mankiller disappeared and was never seen again.

Piney Page, the late Ozark folklorist, was raised in and around the Moccasin Creek Valley. He told the story of a relative who, while plowing a corn field on the floodplain where Moccasin Creek joins Shop Creek, paused in his labors to take a drink from the cool stream. While young Grover Page was lying on his stomach sipping creek water, he spied an object on the bottom that looked different from the rest of the stream gravel. On retrieving it, he discovered it was a silver nugget the size of a man's big toe.

The Page family had the nugget assayed and, on the encouragement of the evaluation, began to explore the creek area for the source of the ore. Some distance up the narrow valley through which runs Shop Creek, a thin seam of silver mixed with lead was discovered on a west-facing outcrop. The Pages invested in some mining equipment and blasted and drilled the weathered limestone rock in pursuit of the vein of ore. Considerable effort was expended and initially a large amount of silver was extracted, Page recalled, but the seam was soon lost. The Pages continued to work the small mine intermittently over the next six years, but the return was discouraging and ultimately they turned their attention back to farming.

A man who lives near Moccasin Creek Valley claims that on dark overcast nights associated with the waning moon, strange lights appear on the ridges adjacent to the valley, "dancing along the ridge crests." Mexicans and Indians have long believed that mysterious lights such as these appear above pockets of gold and silver. They explain that the lights represent spirits of the dead whose mission is to guard the ore and protect it from those who are not worthy, for anyone who removes the ore for selfish profit will be cursed. If one believes in such folklore, then the presence of the dancing lights in Moccasin Creek Valley may indicate that the silver is still there, still protected by the spirits, as elusive as it was to Benjamin Martin over seventy-five years earlier.

Perhaps someday the spirits will decide to relinquish their hold on the silver treasure that lies in these hills and smile upon the searcher who stumbles onto Tobe Inmon's lost mine.

The Mystery of
the Turtle Rock

Piney Page was the source of another tale of buried trea-
sure in Pope County. Growing up in the rural part of the county,
he heard many stories about lost and buried Spanish gold and
silver in the area of Piney Creek between Pilot Rock Mountain
and Ford Mountain, but the one that fascinated him most was
the one an uncle told him concerning the mysterious turtle rock.

Around 1910, as Page recalled it, an old-timer named Mose
Freeman went out to gather his corn crop from the bottoms
adjacent to Big Piney Creek where it makes a horseshoe bend
between the two mountains. When he arrived, he noticed two
men camped in the wooded area next to his field. Freeman
intended to go talk to the two men after he picked his corn, to
see if they carried any news from the bigger settlements in the
southern part of the county. Visitors were scarce in this valley
and Freeman always looked forward to having company.

But the two men seemed to be trying to stay out of his sight.
One of them was a short mean-looking half-breed with a scar
that traversed the entire length of his face, and the other was tall
and gangly and appeared to take orders from the short man.

Presently the two men came out of the woods and furtively
approached Freeman, saying they wanted to ask him some
questions. They wanted to know if he was aware of any old
carvings of snakes or turtles on the exposed rock in the area.

Freeman thought this was a strange question but he allowed
as how he had never seen anything like this. On hearing his

reply, the two men showed no interest in continuing the conversation and promptly returned to their camp in the woods. Freeman went back to picking corn. He decided that he did not like the looks or manner of the pair and would have little or nothing to do with them. One morning a few days later, the two strangers were observed leaving the vicinity, riding a wagon that was piled high with camping gear and pulled by two sickly-looking horses. They appeared to be in a hurry to leave and acted nervous if anyone approached them. Both men carried rifles and displayed them aggressively when anyone ventured too close to the wagon.

The day following their departure, Mose Freeman and one of his sons went down to the deserted camp in the woods to look around. The camp was a poor one and they saw nothing of significance. Out in the woods a short distance from the camp, however, Freeman discovered several holes that had been dug around a large beech tree. On the tree was an old and weathered figure of a snake carved into the trunk. The snake was about three feet long, curving up the trunk of the tree, and its head was pointed downward. History records that the Spaniards used images of snakes and turtles to indicate the locations of buried treasure. The reptile's head was supposed to point toward the hidden wealth.

About twenty paces north of the old beech tree, Freeman found a large rock that appeared to have been recently dug up, turned over, and then set back down in its original location. With the help of his son and some poles they used as levers, he turned the rock back over. There, on the newly exposed side of the large limestone slab, was the carved image of a turtle. The rock had been laid over a freshly excavated hole about two feet deep, and in one corner of the excavation Freeman found a pot-sized hole from which a container had evidently been removed. Whatever the two strangers had unearthed during their search will probably never be known, because they were never seen again.

Stories of carved images of turtles on the limestone rock in Pope County are common. Several natives of the area have seen them, and a few have associated them with tales and legends of buried Spanish treasure. Most believe they are just that, tales and legends, having nothing to do with buried gold or silver. But historians point out that everywhere the Spanish have engaged in mining, both in North and South America, such carvings are quite common.

In 1976, a geology professor associated with a small college in Missouri was conducting a field studies class through the foothills of the Ozark Mountains. The professor and his students spent several days in Pope County examining the unique stratigraphy and collecting fossils from the Ozark limestone. The students were required to record their discoveries in a field journal and to keep a photographic record of their observations and collections. After eight days in the field, one of which was in the Big Piney Creek area, the professor and his students returned to Missouri.

One afternoon several days later, the professor, seated in his office, was going over the journals and photographs turned in by the students. One photograph in particular attracted his attention. It was a picture of a large flat piece of limestone rock, on the top of which could be seen the dim outline of a turtle. The only visible landmark in the photograph was an oak tree that looked very old.

The professor, who had heard legends of buried treasure in Pope County and of its association with carved images, became quite excited about the photograph. When he contacted the student who had taken it, however, she was unable to remember the location of the rock.

The professor has returned to the same area with other classes several times, but so far he has been unable to locate the turtle rock. Could it have been the same one found by Mose Freeman? Or could it be a different one, one that points to the existence of some long-hidden Spanish treasure? The search continues.

The Cave of
Spanish Gold

In Benton County, Arkansas, between the towns of
Gravette and Sulphur Springs near the Missouri border, lies a
cave associated with a fascinating legend of hidden gold. Originally called Black Cave, it is now a minor tourist attraction,
advertised on a nearby billboard as "The Spanish Treasure
Cave." Not too many years ago, residents of Benton County
were eager and curious to know exactly what the cave contained.

One Ozark legend relates that some representatives of the
Spanish army made exploratory forays from deep in Mexico up
through Texas and into the Oklahoma-Missouri-Arkansas border
area. Along the way they robbed and pillaged Indian villages,
eventually amassing a large fortune in gold. They arrived in
what is now Benton County in midwinter and sought shelter in
one of the many limestone caverns found in the region.

The party of nineteen soldiers finally succeeded in locating a
cavern that was large enough for both men and horses and
faced an area that provided plenty of firewood. Here they would
be content to wait out the cold weather as long as necessary.
While they remained close to the mouth of the cave, they noted
that a passageway ran deep into the mountainside and the light
from their modest campfire was not able to penetrate its depths.

A party of about thirty Indians had been trailing the Spaniards
for several days. It is believed the Spaniards, after raiding the
Indian camp about a week earlier, had stolen several of the

tribe's women. Intent on revenge and recapturing their women, the braves had dogged the Spaniards' trail ever since.

During a heavy snowfall one afternoon, one of the Indian scouts spotted the smoke from the soldiers' campfire as it exited a natural vent in the rock above the cave. After scouting the area thoroughly, the Indians made elaborate plans during the night. When dawn broke, they launched a ferocious attack, and for several hours they battled until all the Spaniards were killed. Before they died, however, several of the soldiers carried the gold deep into one of the passageways of the cave and cached it within.

Nothing more was heard of this incident until early in the fall of 1885, when an old Spanish gentleman arrived in Sulphur Springs. He was carrying three ancient parchment maps, each of which contained involved directions on how to reach the cave in which the Spaniards had concealed the gold.

The old man was precise and mannerly in his dealings with the Benton County citizens, and while his command of English was poor, he managed to communicate details of the lost Spanish gold.

He said that a second detachment of soldiers was sent north to ascertain the fate of the first group. They encountered many Indian villages along the way and heard descriptions of raids made by the soldiers as well as of their taking gold and women and killing many warriors. Eventually the second group of soldiers came upon the cave and found the skeletons of their comrades, victims of the Indian massacre. The soldiers explored the cave and discovered a great fortune in gold cached at the back of one of the many long passageways. Since they lacked extra horses or mules to transport the gold, they decided to bury it deep within the cave until they or others could return for it. They spent days filling the chambers and passageways of the cave with dirt in order to discourage others from entering.

The old Spaniard hired two local men, one named Callister and the other named John Harwick, to guide him into the woods in search of the cave. For several days they searched, with no luck.

One day the Spaniard was able to make the two guides understand that the cave they were looking for had positioned at its entrance a large rock with the image of a deer hoof carved on it. After several more days of searching and talking with people who lived in the area, they located a squatter far back in the woods by the name of Rufus Wetzel. Wetzel and his family, which consisted of nine children and a very skinny, tired-looking wife, lived in a poorly constructed log cabin in a remote part of the Ozark Mountains not far from the town of Gravette.

Wetzel said he was aware of such a rock and had seen it many times while hunting in the woods. But he declined to show the men the rock's location and kept asking why they wanted to know. The Spaniard feared that if the mountain man was told information about the treasure in the cave he would try to retrieve it for himself. They tried to bargain with the squatter, offering him unheard-of sums of money for the information, but the more they offered him the more suspicious he became.

One day when Wetzel had disappeared into the woods to hunt deer, Mrs. Wetzel, anxious for the intruders to be on their way, agreed to show them the stone they sought. She led the men deep into the woods about a mile from the cabin and pointed it out.

As they approached the rock, the Spaniard became quite excited. Without a doubt this was the stone described in the ancient Spanish documents. It was very large and required the assistance of several more men before it could be removed from the opening of the cave.

Once the great rock was removed, they saw that the interior of the cavern was indeed filled from bottom to top with dirt that had apparently been carried in. The Spaniard hired the same men to excavate the fill dirt from the passage. Eager for wages, the men set to the task. After several days of work that they had removed only a small portion of the dirt, but they were happy to continue their labors, for the Spaniard was paying them well.

As dirt was removed from the passageway, the diggers found bits and pieces of Spanish armor and weapons, lending credence to the notion that the Spanish had indeed visited this cave at an earlier time.

The days passed into weeks and still the men continued to dig. The more fill dirt they encountered, the more convinced they were that some great treasure was concealed at the end. Why else would anyone go to so much trouble?

During the excavation, the Spanish gentleman came down with a serious fever and had to be confined to a pallet. For a time he lay in the shade of a nearby tree, directing the excavation, but it soon became clear he was suffering from a severe case of pneumonia and it did not appear he would live much longer. Eventually he informed the diggers that he needed to go south to Texas where the climate was much warmer and more hospitable to a man in his condition. He left enough money to pay the men for their continued digging, and as he rode away he told them he would make contact with them as soon as possible.

The old man gathered up his maps and, along with all the old pieces of armor and weapons that had been removed from the cave, packed them into his wagon. Before leaving, he explained to the men that once they broke through the fill dirt they would find that the cave branched out into several corridors, each heading in a different direction, and that the treasure was supposed to be concealed in one of them. He reassured the diggers that when he was well he would return and they would all share in the treasure. With that, he departed.

The men continued to dig for several more days but soon tired of the labor. They divided the money that had been left and promised each other they would resume the excavation if he ever returned. The Spaniard was never heard from again, and the story of the lost Spanish gold cached in the old cave passed into Ozark folklore.

In 1922, a Benton County man named Parkins traveled to Oklahoma to search for work. His journey took him to the little settlement of Paul's Valley in the south-central part of the state, where he found employment as a carpenter. He soon made friends with a fellow worker who asked him many questions about Arkansas.

Eventually the talk turned to caves in the Arkansas Ozarks,

36

and the new friend told Parkins he knew a story about an old Spanish treasure cave up near the Arkansas-Missouri border. Parkins, having been raised on the local folklore of the Spanish cave, asked the man how he came to know of the legend.

The friend told Parkins that during the winter of 1886, a very sick old Spanish gentleman stopped at Paul's Valley on his way to Texas. The man was seriously ill and was taken in by the friend's father, who intended to nurse him back to health. He became sicker and it was soon clear that he would not live much longer. On his deathbed he confided to the family that he had some old maps that showed the way to a Spanish treasure in a cave in Arkansas. If anything happened to him, he asked, could they please send the maps to an address in Madrid, Spain? The family agreed, but the man died before he was able to provide them with the address.

The friend took Parkins out to the old Paul's Valley cemetery and showed him the Spaniard's grave. A rotted wooden marker bore the barely readable inscription "Age Unknown. A Traveler From Spain."

When Parkins inquired about the maps, the friend said that they had remained in the family's possession for a long time but that he no longer knew where they were.

Sometime around 1900, one George Dunbar arrived in Gravette from somewhere in the East. Dunbar claimed to have yet another set of Spanish maps and documents that identified the same cave as one that contained a great Spanish treasure. He also said his information stated exactly where the gold was concealed inside the cave.

Dunbar thought it would be a simple matter of going to the cave, following the map, retrieving the gold, and walking out. He did not reckon with the many tons of fill dirt stuffing the passageways.

He examined the cave and observed the work of previous diggers. He was amazed at the number of small passageways that extended out from the main corridor in various directions, many of them still filled with dirt, but he thought the job of removing the fill was only a temporary barrier between him and the vast fortune in Spanish gold he knew to be awaiting him.

Dunbar hired a crew to continue the excavation of the cave. When he thought the work was proceeding too slowly, he had his men install small-gauge railroad tracks through many of the passageways, tracks on which ran ore carts to speed the removal of the dirt. He excavated farther and farther into the many branches, only to find more openings filled with yet more dirt.

He awoke each morning believing that day would be the one in which he located the gold, but each evening he went to bed disappointed. For several years he supervised the excavation of the cave until he eventually ran out of money. Never healthy, Dunbar allowed his failure and subsequent depression to weigh heavily on his mind and within a matter of weeks he died, an old, broken man who was never able to realize his dream.

Within a year after Dunbar's death, a W.W. Knight picked up the excavation of the cave. He employed an even larger crew and extended the tracks deeper into the cave. His men often worked round-the-clock, but even with that Knight came no closer to the gold than any of the others who searched. He quit his excavation in 1918. Over the next few decades men tried to take up the excavation where others left off, but all were unsuccessful.

Longtime residents of the Gravette area can recall their grandparents and great-grandparents telling of a great earthquake that shook the region in 1812. The tremor fractured much of the thinly-layered limestone rock that makes up this portion of the Ozark Mountains, and as a result many of the caverns in this area are prone to cave-ins. Some suggest that this is what happened in the old Spanish Cave in Benton County—that a cave-in collapsed portions of the cavern system, forever concealing the Spaniards' gold deep within the interior. Many also believe that much of the dirt that was excavated had not been placed in the cavern by the Spaniards, but filtered in from above through the many fractures in the rock.

Over the years fortunes have been spent in attempting to locate and retrieve the hidden gold of the Spaniards, but the treasure remains hidden, concealed deep within the mysterious cave.

The Madre Vena
Ore Cache

One of the most talked-about lost treasure caches in the
Arkansas Ozarks is associated with the Madre Vena Cave.
Though some of the stories refer to the "Madre Vena Mine," it is
probably not a mine at all but a natural cavern in which gold
and silver ore was concealed over 130 years ago. In any case,
many firmly believe that somewhere in some deep subterranean chamber in the Ozark Mountains lies a fortune waiting for
the searcher who can locate it.

The legends and tales of Spaniards operating gold and silver
mines in the Ozark Mountains are numerous, and so much
evidence has been discovered that that notion is hard to disre-
gard. The Spanish explorers, under the leadership of De Soto,
virtually littered the Ozark landscape with tools, weapons, armor, and other artifacts of their culture.

During the peak of the Spanish exploration and mining in the
Ozark Mountains, great quantities of the gold and silver taken
from the mines would be loaded onto mules and burros and
transported out of the mountains toward the southeast. A large
company of well-armed soldiers would escort this ore-laden
pack train to Florida, where it would in turn be shipped to the
motherland. At other times, great caravans carrying remarkable
fortunes in precious minerals would travel from deep in the
Ozark Mountains to the seat of government in Mexico. The
Spanish royalty who resided in Mexico, after receiving such a
load of wealth from remote Arkansas, would normally organize

another expedition to return for more of the same. These return expeditions would be amply outfitted and often supplied with hundreds of Mexican laborers.

As the years passed and Spanish influence in the New World decreased, the mines in the Ozarks were abandoned and the soldiers and most of the miners returned to Mexico. Some, however, remained in the Ozark Mountains and continued mining gold and silver. Many took Indian wives, and for several generations they and their descendants continued to dig ore from the intrusive rock formations hidden beneath the thick layers of Ozark limestone. As late as the mid-nineteenth century, small groups of Mexicans were believed to be still working in the mines in some of the more remote sections of the Ozarks.

One such group, a foursome led by a man named Manuel Alarcón, had small but continuous successes excavating gold and silver from several different locations in the mountains. After several years of mining, they had accumulated an impressive fortune, but as they transported their wealth from mine to mine and camp to camp on their mules, they came to believe this practice was unwise because of the numerous bandits who frequented the area, and decided to cache their fortune while they mined for more. They searched for a site that was remote and would offer security.

Finally they came upon a cave in northwestern Arkansas close to where the Arkansas-Missouri border is now. Researchers believe the cave is approximately ten miles north of Bentonville and that, while the entrance is in Arkansas, the underground passages extend beneath the border into Missouri.

The four Mexicans examined the cave, explored its many and intricate passageways for two days, and finally located a large chamber that seemed adequate for storing their fortune. Legend claims that the passageway into this chamber was especially low and narrow, and that the four men had somehow managed to wedge a huge oval limestone slab into the entrance, effectively sealing it. In front of the slab they stacked rocks and dirt from the cavern floor, thus further disguising the opening from anyone who chanced to enter and explore the cave. Following this,

41

the Mexicans camped outside the entrance to the cave for several days as they discussed plans to journey to a distant site to mine for more ore. One of the men suggested they name the cave *Madre Vena*—"mother lode." They agreed.

During the evening meal of the second day after caching the ore, Manuel Alarcón proposed that they make a map to the cave. The men carved detailed directions into a thin, wide slab of limestone they found nearby. Included on the map were prominent landmarks in the vicinity, important trails, and the location of the Madre Vena Cave. Unable to agree on where to hide the map, they finally turned in for the night.

Just before dawn the next day, Alarcón arose from his bedroll and slew his three comrades. By the light of the moon, he dug three graves and buried the bodies—lowering the limestone map into one of the graves along with the corpse. Carefully and efficiently, he filled each of the three graves, piled stones across the top of them, and erected wooden markers, each one carved with the name of a dead comrade.

Then he prayed aloud over the graves and conducted a brief funeral service for his former partners.

What possessed Manuel Alarcón to murder his three lifelong friends has puzzled people for many years. Some say he wanted all the gold and silver for himself and the only way he could get it was to eliminate those with whom he would otherwise have to share. Some say he was simply crazy.

With the sun high in the heavens, Alarcón gathered up the horses and supplies and rode away. He paused at a nearby ridge to regard the final resting place of his fellows. Some distance beyond the graves and in the woods, he could discern the entrance to the Madre Vena Cave.

Alarcón was not seen again for thirty years. It has been said that he roamed the Ozarks, a semi-crazed man who was never able to sleep at night, that he became a hermit and shunned all contact with civilization, and that he continued to work small mines in the Ozarks to add to his already large cache of gold and silver buried within the Madre Vena Cave.

He surfaced three decades later in Pierce City, Missouri, a

small community about twenty miles southeast of Joplin. Alar-cón was on his deathbed, suffering from a terrible fever, and could breathe only with great difficulty. While he was being treated by a doctor in Pierce City, he related the entire story of the gold and silver cache in the Madre Vena Cave and told of killing his three friends and burying the map on the stone slab in one of the graves. As best he could, he provided directions to the graves and to the cave. The next morning Manuel Alarcón was dead.

News of the Mexican's ore cache spread throughout the Ozarks during the following weeks, and people came from several states to search for the great wealth in the cave. The Ozark hills and mountains near the Missouri-Arkansas border were crawling with hopeful treasure-hunters for several months, but nothing was ever found.

A few years later, a man familiar with the Madre Vena Cave story undertook a search in a rather remote valley and one that had not received the attention of previous searchers.

After two days of exploring the area, the man discovered three graves in a little glade near the edge of a thick oak and hickory forest. He spent the next few days scouring the woods but was unable to locate a cave that matched the description provided by the dying Alarcón. Presently he returned to the glade and started to dig up the graves. In the second one he discovered the limestone slab with the map chiseled into the surface.

With great difficulty the man raised the stone slab from the grave. Realizing the slab was too large to transport, he copied the map onto a piece of paper. Then he demolished the stone so others could not use it, threw the pieces back into the grave, and refilled it.

Even with the map, the man had no luck in locating the Madre Vena Cave. After two weeks of searching in the area, he abandoned it, never to return.

Several years later, the man passed the map along to a friend named Vanwormer who lived in Afton, Oklahoma. Vanwormer made one or two halfhearted searches for the Madre Vena Cave but never had any luck. Several years later he gave the map to his son, Frank.

Frank Vanwormer was considerably more enthusiastic about the Madre Vena treasure than his father and made several determined forays into the Arkansas Ozarks in search of it. Though he was unsuccessful, he was nevertheless convinced that the treasure was real and that it was only a matter of time before he located it.

Vanwormer eventually learned of the interest of another man from Afton who had also been searching for the Madre Vena treasure for many years. His name was John Koch, and he claimed to have reliable evidence that the cave was in a certain little valley in another remote part of northwest Arkansas.

Vanwormer, Koch, and a third man joined forces and systematically combed the countryside. One day they came upon the graves of the three men killed and buried by Manuel Alarcón. They dug up the graves and discovered the shattered pieces of the stone map. In trying to reconstruct the stone map, they found that several of the broken parts were missing, giving an incomplete picture of the area. It was useless.

Being familiar with Alarcón's story, and knowing that the graves were supposed to be close to the entrance of the lost Madre Vena Cave, the men concentrated their search in a small area east of the three graves.

On the afternoon of the second day they discovered a cave along a low bank of limestone outcrop not far from the graves. The entrance had apparently been disguised with rocks and dirt piled in front of it. In the years since this was done, small trees and shrubs had grown up in the debris, causing it to blend in with the surrounding forest. This was undoubtedly why the opening had been so difficult to detect for so many years.

With some effort the men removed the trees, shrubs, rocks, and debris and found themselves looking into a dark passageway that continued laterally into the side of the hill.

They soon discovered that retrieving the cache was to be no easy task. The cave had numerous passageways—some of them dead ends and others appearing to extend into the mountain forever. The men estimated there were several miles of passage-ways in the cave.

They searched the interior of the cave for a week, but were no closer to retrieving the treasure than they were the day they discovered the opening.

They returned to their homes in Oklahoma for a time to attend to personal business. When the search was resumed several weeks later, the third man elected not to return to the Ozarks, saying he did not believe the treasure existed and that he had neglected his farm long enough.

Vanwormer and Koch continued to explore the cavern. One day while examining a new passageway, they discovered a large, somewhat circular stone slab wedged into what they believed was the opening into a natural chamber. They deter-mined that the stone could not have been placed there naturally and that it must have required the labor of several men to move it.

Using crowbars and levers, they tried to pry the great stone out of the opening, but were unable to dislodge it. On a return visit to the cave, they carried several bundles of dynamite with them. The first charge they set off did nothing but scar the face of the large slab and did not move it at all. They decided to set a larger charge, which also failed to move the slab, but did cause a portion of the roof to weaken and crumble. They then tried an even larger charge of explosive.

Flying rock debris from the third charge struck Koch, injuring him severely. He had to be dragged from the cave and trans-ported to a doctor.

While Koch was recovering, Vanwormer returned to the Ma-dre Vena Cave to examine the results of the latest charge of dynamite. More of the cavern roof had been destroyed, but the stone was still wedged in the same position.

With his injury and the disappointing news about the stone slab, Koch became disheartened and declared he was abandon-ing his search. Vanwormer, depressed that his partner did not wish to continue, made a few more halfhearted attempts to remove the large stone slab from the hidden passageway but eventually gave up.

As Vanwormer quit the cave, he purposely set off several more dynamite charges, which caused a portion of the cavern roof to collapse and fill in much of the main passageway. His intention was to discourage other searchers.

Around 1915, a man named Enoch Hodges rediscovered the Madre Vena Cave and reportedly began digging through the collapsed rubble that resulted from Vanwormer's dynamite charges. Hodges worked intermittently for five years trying to clear a passageway through the dirt and rock but eventually gave up.

Since the 1920s other attempts to reach the Madre Vena ore cache have been organized, but all have ended in failure.

Today, according to researchers, a small landslide that occurred in the region sometime during the mid-1960s has covered the entrance to the Madre Vena Cave. Once again trees and brush have grown up in the debris that covers the opening, making it difficult to detect. Beyond the covered entrance and the collapsed rubble in the main passageway of the cave, a fortune in gold and silver ore may still be gathering dust in the dark chamber.

Spanish Silver
in Searcy County

During the first decade of the twentieth century a man named Herndon spent considerable time doing some exploratory mining near Silver Hill in Searcy County. Throughout this prospect area he occasionally found traces of silver ore, but never enough to justify any serious large-scale mining.

One day, however, he located a vein of silver that held some promise. Herndon was encouraged to the point of filing a claim and employing a surveyor to locate and mark property lines. The surveyor was a local man, very knowledgeable about the history of the region. As they were walking around the area of the claim, the surveyor told Herndon that not far from where they stood was some evidence of ancient Spanish mining. Intrigued, Herndon asked the surveyor to lead him to the location. About twenty minutes later they arrived at a clearing consisting mainly of exposed bedrock. In the center of the open space was a crater-like excavation ringed by several large mounds of rock debris that had apparently been removed from it. Trees growing out of the old mounds of excavated debris testified to their age.

Sixty years earlier, the surveyor said, a man who identified himself as a Mexican priest had arrived in the area. He claimed he was an emissary from a church in Mexico in which was discovered an aged Spanish map purporting to show the location of a fabulous silver mine in Arkansas. The priest produced the map from a well-made leather case and showed it to several area residents. The map was of heavy parchment on which was crudely sketched a system of trails and the outlines and descriptions of several mountains and hills. Many of the residents recognized the landmarks as being consistent with the Silver Hill environment.

The priest said the information given to him by church officials suggested the map had been constructed by a soldier who had served with De Soto, and indicated a site where a very rich silver deposit had been extensively mined centuries earlier. The map gave the location of the mine in precise degrees of latitude and longitude and was dated 1580.

The brief written description on the ancient map told how great quantities of silver had been taken from a deep shaft carved into the limestone rock of the mountain and smelted down into ingots for ease of transportation back to the Spanish homeland.

The Spaniards were forced to cut short their mining however, because of continued threats from hostile Indians. Recurrent raids and occasional killings reduced the force of Spaniards until they believed it was not safe to remain in the region. For several nights, under cover of darkness, the Spanish miners systematically filled in the shaft. Then they loaded as many of the silver ingots as possible onto mules and abandoned the site. One legend suggests that the Spaniards were overtaken by Indians and all were killed. Another legend says they were pursued for several days by the Indians and battled them often but finally escaped. The existence of the map in the church archives in Mexico suggests there may be some truth to the second legend. In any case, the Spanish apparently never returned to rework the silver mine in the Ozark Mountains.

The surveyor told Herndon that the Mexican priest offered a group of area residents half of the silver remaining in the shaft if they would excavate the many tons of rock the Spanish had used to fill it. An agreement was made, and several men neglected their farms while they pursued the dream of a fortune in silver.

As the excavation commenced, it became evident that the men were digging into an old vertical mine shaft that had been filled in. After several days of digging, they had removed about twelve feet of fill from the wide shaft. Soon thereafter, they encountered a huge limestone slab that had somehow been wedged into the shaft and firmly secured, preventing any further penetration into the old mine. The diggers judged that it must have taken twenty men to place the large rock in that position. After several unsuccessful attempts at removing it, they finally blasted through the slab using several charges of dynamite.

Once the debris from the blasted rock was cleared away, the men could see that the shaft leveled off to a more horizontal angle, and on its floor they found numerous mining tools of Spanish origin. The workers also discovered several molds into which hot metal had evidently been poured to form ingots. However, even after searching thoroughly, they found no seam of silver. A curious question presented itself—if all of the silver had been mined, why was the long shaft so elaborately sealed?

A mining engineering firm from Kansas City was hired to examine the site and decide the potential for the existence of silver. Like the diggers before them, the consultants had no luck in locating a vein of ore in the shaft. They did find evidence that this had indeed been a working silver mine at one time, but they still could not resolve the question of why the shaft had been filled in. On this same consulting visit, the Kansas City company discovered several small veins of silver in the hills nearby, and started mining operations that lasted for several years.

The Mexican priest, discouraged at not being able to locate any of the wealth alluded to in the ancient document, returned to his home country.

Herndon continued to prospect for and mine some small amounts of silver, but he also eventually abandoned the area.

As the years passed, the other silver mines in the region were worked out and the Kansas City company closed them and moved away. Shortly thereafter, an old man named Grinder moved into one of the abandoned mine buildings, squatting on the land on which the old Spanish mine was located.

Grinder was an eccentric who had lived in the nearby hills all his life and survived mostly by hunting and trapping. He occasionally did odd jobs for some of the local farmers, but most people considered him a little crazy, and because he was rather coarse and unkempt, shunned him. Soon, however, the talk around the county was that old man Grinder was digging in the old Spanish shaft in the hope of locating the lost vein of silver. Laughter and jokes directed at the old man were the usual response to his mining, for no one seriously believed the old coot would find anything.

After working in the shaft for several weeks, Grinder ordered and paid for some mining equipment that was delivered from Little Rock to the Silver Hill site. Area citizens were baffled as to where Grinder obtained money to pay for what amounted to thousands of dollars' worth of sophisticated machinery.

Shunning the town, Grinder spent all his time out at the mine, apparently working intently in the deepest part of the shaft for many hours at a time. Visitors to the old mine were ordered away at the point of a shotgun.

Within a year, Grinder abandoned his mining endeavor and sold all the equipment. To the surprise of many, he shortly thereafter purchased a 120-acre farm in a neighboring county, stocked it with a large herd of fine cattle, and paid for everything with cash.

Those who ventured into the old Spanish shaft after it was abandoned by Grinder told of how a completely new passageway had been opened and penetrated deep into the rock for several dozen yards.

Had old man Grinder discovered the long-concealed vein of silver ore that the Spaniards had gone to so much trouble to hide? Evidently he found something that encouraged him to dig and remove tons of rock singlehandedly. Whatever he found, old man Grinder was not telling, and he apparently took his secret to his grave.

The Lost Tabor Mine

Tabor was a poor man who lived a hermit's life in the woods and mountains near the town of St. Joe in Searcy County. Slightly crippled and inflicted with a speech impediment, he was well known to the townsfolk. The few times he would come into town to purchase provisions, he always paid for them with pure silver ore. When asked about the origin of the silver, Tabor would cackle a toothless laugh and his tall skinny frame would launch into an awkward dance while he teased the locals that they would never be able to locate his mine.

Sometimes people tried to follow Tabor back into the hills where he lived, but he always managed to elude the trackers after leading them for miles in circles through the dark woods.

Near the end of 1865, Tabor was no longer seen around St. Joe, and as he was an elderly man, people assumed he had met his end alone in the remote and often hostile wilderness of the Ozark Mountains. Now and then somebody would venture into the Tomahawk Creek region in search of Tabor's silver mine, but no one ever claimed to have found it. Most who entered the region returned telling stories of the dark, close forest that seemed to be haunted. People searched for the silver mine off and on for nearly fifty years, but the story of the eccentric old man and his wealth was eventually forgotten.

Hulce Taylor owned some land along Tomahawk Creek and managed to earn a respectable living by farming the bottoms and raising some cattle. One morning in 1924 he took his young daughter with him as he set out in search of two cows that had strayed from the main herd.

After about half a day of searching, the farmer and daughter found themselves walking alongside a remote stretch of overgrown trail that paralleled Tomahawk Creek. Taylor had never been to this part of the woods before and he proceeded cautiously. Here the forest of tall oak and hickory was very dense, and the trail was more like a tunnel than a passage through the woods. Little light penetrated the thick forest canopy to reach the ground. There was moisture everywhere and the area had the pungent smell of rotting vegetation. Just beyond their range of vision, deep in the woods, small unseen forest creatures skittered through the underbrush.

The little girl told her father she was frightened and wanted to return home, but Taylor coaxed her into going on. The farther they walked the narrower the little valley became, until it seemed as if the very walls would close in on them. Thick dense vines grew from the forest floor up to the tops of the sheer limestone cliffs.

Presently they arrived at a portion of the valley where several large trees had been blown down, making further passage difficult. Taylor presumed the toppled trees were a result of a violent storm that had struck the area a few days before.

Just as Taylor decided to return back up the trail, he noticed that the dense vines that had covered one portion of a cliff had been torn away, probably by high winds. There, near the center of the recently exposed cliff, was the entrance to an old mine.

He later described the mine as containing a rich vein of silver ore so pure it could be easily dug out with a pocketknife. When neighbors began to ask too many questions about the mine and the silver, Taylor resorted to silence. Soon he refused to speak of the mine in front of anyone, even his own children.

Taylor's farm continued to prosper, even when other farmers were having hard times, and many neighbors believed he was secretly mining the silver from the old shaft. No records exist to verify whether he did, and Taylor's descendants have been unable to provide any information.

From the geographic location and description of the shaft Taylor accidentally happened upon, it is likely the Lost Tabor

Mine. In any case, it has apparently been lost again and, in spite of several organized attempts to relocate it, remains lost.

Lost Aztec Mine in Franklin County?

In legends of lost mines and buried treasures in the Ozarks, one sometimes hears vague references to gold mines operated by the Aztec Indians. This notion is remarkable, because the Aztecs' homeland is hundreds of miles south in Mexico. It seems unlikely that members of that Meso-American tribe would make the long journey to the Ozarks to mine gold, but the legends and folktales persist. Many dismiss the stories as so much nonsense, saying there has never been any physical evidence of the presence of Aztec Indians in the Ozarks.

However, for years mysterious petroglyphs have been discovered in remote portions of the Ozarks. The origins of these writings on the stone are clearly prehistoric, and several scholars suggest that they bear some similarity to Aztec symbols, but, they hasten to point out, that is mere conjecture and not to be taken as proof.

In 1986 a remarkable discovery was made on Wolverton Mountain, a flat-topped narrow sandstone ridge in northern Conway County. Several farmers and ranchers living on the mountain were battling a fire and had plowed a firebreak between the forest and a grass field. As a plow cut through a shallow layer of soil, it kicked up a small carved stone figure of a human being. Its style was unmistakably Meso-American, strikingly similar to that of carvings unearthed in ancient Aztec excavations in Mexico. Several experts who have seen the stone figure have tentatively identified it as being Indian, most likely

Aztec.

While this stone carving may not prove Aztec visitation in the Ozarks, it certainly opens the door to speculation that such an event might indeed have occurred.

One man who resides in Franklin County has reason to believe that the Aztecs visited that region long ago. O.P. VanBrunt, a septuagenarian who lives in Mulberry, has been searching for a lost gold mine in the Ozark Mountains for many years. He has been passionately pursuing the notion that there is a fortune in gold hidden away in a tunnel in a hill in the northeastern part of the county.

VanBrunt's father also searched many years for the tunnel, starting in 1918. Like other residents of the area, he always referred to it as the Lost Spanish Mine and associated it with the mining of Spanish explorers who visited this region with De Soto.

Arkansas legend says that the Spanish encountered Aztec Indians mining gold in the region when they arrived. Some claim that the Spaniards drove the Indians out, while others believe all of the Aztecs were slain by the conquistadores. In either case, the Spanish apparently took over the rich mining operation that was begun by the Aztecs and worked it for several years.

It is told that the Spanish remained in the area until the war with France broke out and that there was a possibility it might extend to the Americas. Fearing their mine and gold would be seized, the Spaniards stored the wealth of several years of mining deep in the excavated tunnel, sealed it, and left mysterious writings and symbols on cliff faces and rock outcrops in the region to guide them back to the mine when they were able to return. They never did.

The story of the mine, however, lived on in the oral tradition, and when this region was being settled in the latter part of the last century, occasional forays into the Ozarks in search of the mine took place.

In 1915, a local physician named Tobe Hill became fascinated with the stories about the lost Aztec mine worked by the Spanish. Hill once related a story about an interesting encounter with an aged Spaniard traveling through the Ozarks. The old man, obviously tired and hungry, stopped by the Hill residence asking directions. Hill invited him to stay for dinner and learned that he was seeking the Lost Spanish Mine. The Spaniard said that he learned of the mine's existence from relatives in his homeland who had provided him with information about the symbols and writings that were supposed to lead to the site of the hidden mine. As he sketched several of these symbols, the physician recalled seeing such drawings and scrawlings on many limestone outcrops several miles north of his farm.

The next morning the Spaniard thanked Hill and bade him farewell as he walked off into the mountains. He was never seen again in the Ozarks.

In 1918, Hill formed the Louisiana Mining Company and, with several associates, sought the legendary mine for four years.

O.P. VanBrunt, whose father was associated with the Louisiana Mining Company, remembers traveling with his father by covered wagon to a remote part of the Ozarks as a six-year-old. He and his father lived at the site for two weeks, digging in likely places for the opening to the elusive tunnel. At one point in their digging, the elder VanBrunt found a rock speckled with gold. He recovered enough ore from the rock to fashion two wedding bands.

VanBrunt lacked the opportunity to return to the diggings during the succeeding decades, but his interest in the Lost Spanish Mine never waned. In 1973 he resumed searching for the cache on McElroy Mountain in the northeastern part of Franklin County. Many caves and several man-made tunnels have been found in the mountain, and VanBrunt is convinced that the stored wealth of the Spaniards and Aztecs lies concealed within.

Jesse Jones, who owns most of McElroy Mountain and leases the digging rights to VanBrunt, is also convinced of the existence of the mine and the hidden treasure. Jones, in fact, believes he actually discovered the entrance to what he calls the "Doc Hill Mine." He said it is on the western side of the mountain near the

Mulberry River. The tunnel, according to Jones, measures six feet by six feet and penetrates the mountain to a depth of nearly 150 feet. Here and there in the tunnel can be found the remains of ancient timbers once used for shoring.

Jones claims to have found a small wheel fashioned from gold near the mountain. He said he sent it with a man to have it assayed but it never came back. Jones also claims to have panned gold flakes from a small stream that flows close to the entrance of the tunnel.

Both VanBrunt and Jones are convinced that the ancient writings found on the bare rock walls in the area tell of the gold's location, but no one has yet been able to interpret their meaning.

VanBrunt said McElroy Mountain is remarkably different from other mountains in the area. The rock layers of McElroy Mountain have a rusty tinge, and when the sun is at a certain angle they take on a coloring as red as blood. According to local legend, the mountain was stained forever by the blood of the slain Aztecs and is cursed, never to give up its fortune in gold secreted deep within.

The Lost Tunnel of Gold

One warm summer afternoon in the mid-1960s, Ralph Mayes paid his daily visit to his father-in-law, who was recuperating in the Washington County Hospital. He brought a small bag of items his father-in-law needed from home as well as a paperback western to read while he was laid up.

Mayes's father-in-law shared his hospital room with a man named Alvin Bishop. Bishop was recovering from a heart attack, and as he had come to know young Ralph Mayes, he also looked forward to his visits.

Today Mayes asked Bishop what had brought on his heart attack and heard a remarkable story of a lost gold mine in the Boston Mountain region of the Ozarks.

Alvin Bishop said that he had come into possession of a very old parchment map that purported to show the location of a hidden tunnel wherein large, thick veins of pure gold could be found. The map had been given to his grandfather by local Indians many years earlier and was handed down to his father and then to him. It was full of cryptic figures and symbols and the writing was definitely Spanish. Though the map was difficult to interpret, Bishop, along with his father, recognized many of the landforms indicated on it and decided to search for the treasure.

The two men hiked many miles through the Ozarks over the next few years in search of the hidden tunnel. While many of the landmarks noted on the map matched those in the territory through which they searched, the men remained frustrated at not being able to understand many of the symbols, which allegedly showed the exact location of the tunnel.

Then in 1963 they found it. They drove to the old Sunnydale schoolhouse some three miles east of the town of Winslow on State Highway 71 and from there followed an old, seldom-used dirt road in a more or less southerly direction. The road ended at a ridge known locally as Piney Point, where the men had to leave their vehicle and walk a narrow trail, eventually coming into a valley on the west side of the ridge. They followed a small stream in the valley for some distance, looking for a large flat rock near a large oak tree shown on the old map. The entrance to the tunnel was supposed to be beneath the rock.

With great difficulty, Alvin Bishop and his father succeeded in shifting the rock just enough to reveal the opening of a vertical tunnel, which had obviously been excavated with primitive mining tools centuries earlier. The shaft was square, and along two opposing walls thick veins of gold ran into the shaft as far as the two could see.

Alvin Bishop had exhausted himself in moving the huge rock and, before taking a much-needed rest, he decided to climb into the tunnel in order to evaluate the wealth that lay before him. With great difficulty he lowered himself into the vertical tunnel and, bracing his back against one wall and his feet against the other, started to descend the shaft. As he exerted himself, he suffered a heart attack, and it was only with great difficulty that his father was able to remove him from the ancient mine and bring him to the Washington County Hospital.

Mayes was fascinated by Bishop's story and determined to learn more about the old Spanish mine. Each day he looked forward to visiting with Bishop, and soon the two men entered into an agreement to go to the mine, extract the gold, and share in the wealth. Bishop would provide directions to the mine, and Mayes would provide the labor.

Mayes and Bishop talked several more times before Bishop regained his strength and was discharged from the hospital. Several more meetings at the Bishop home resulted in a plan to journey to the isolated valley west of Piney Point and from there to the tunnel of gold.

While Bishop was preparing equipment for the expedition he suffered another heart attack. He was dead before he was able to receive medical attention.

Several weeks after Bishop's death, his widow turned the old Spanish map over to Mayes. Since Bishop never explained the meanings of the various signs and symbols on the map, Mayes could not interpret any of it. Furthermore, as he was totally unfamiliar with the Ozark Mountains east of Winslow, he had no idea what to look for. To compound the problem, he could find no geographic designation of a Piney Point. Baffled and frustrated, he soon lost the desire to search for the tunnel of gold.

Though unable to find it, Ralph Mayes firmly believed in the existence of the tunnel. He was convinced that Alvin Bishop had located the shaft and had actually entered it. Mayes believed that not being able to locate the tunnel had likely cost him the opportunity of becoming a millionaire. For Alvin Bishop, finding the tunnel ultimately cost him his life.

King's River Silver

Prior to the Indian removal initiated by the United States government in the 1830s, the Ozark Mountain region in the northwestern part of Arkansas was home to several tribes who lived in relative peace and harmony. They grew corn, beans, and squash along the river bottoms and ran cattle and horses where good grazing could be found. This agricultural bounty was supplemented with hunting and fishing from the abundant woods and streams. The King's River region in what is now Carroll County offered an abundance of such good living, so it is little wonder that when a few white settlers moved into the area the Indians welcomed them openly and fully.

Jasper Combs and his family were among the first whites to share in this bounty. Around 1820, Combs established a small farmstead along one side of the river and began to grow crops and raise livestock. He became good friends with the Indians he met in the area. They occasionally shared meals and engaged in trade. Combs and the Indians hunted and fished together and helped each other build cabins, plow fields, and cooperate in the raising of livestock. Combs's children played with the Indian children, and life in the valley was good.

During Combs's many dealings with the Indian residents of the valley, he noticed that several of them wore arm bands, necklaces, and other jewelry that appeared to be fashioned from pure silver. He asked where they found the metal but they always steered the conversation toward other topics. Once, when having dinner with an Indian family, Combs noticed that even some of the cooking utensils were made from silver.

61

With the passing months Combs's curiosity grew keener. One afternoon as he and one of the tribe elders were returning from a hunting trip, he asked again where the silver came from.

The elder explained to Combs that the source of the silver was an old mine whose location was well known to the Indians but was kept a carefully guarded secret from others. Any member of the tribe who revealed the location of the mine would be dealt a swift and certain death at the hands of his fellows.

Having great respect for the traditions of the Indians as well as placing a great value on them as friends, Combs promised never to concern himself with the matter again.

Around the beginning of the 1830s, the federal government undertook a project to remove the Native Americans from their farms and homesteads in the Ozark Mountains and resettle them on lands in the West. When the people of the King's River area were being moved, an arrangement was made with United States government officials to hold a certain parcel of land in their name and to let them return to it from time to time. The Indians claimed it was holy ground and that their ancestors were buried on it, but Jasper Combs believed it was the site of their silver mine.

Jesse Combs, a son of Jasper Combs, recalled times when the Indians returned to the area. Arriving from the Oklahoma settlements in horse-drawn wagons, they would stop at the Combs' homestead to await more arrivals and then proceed to the assigned parcel of land, where they would remain for several days before returning to Oklahoma Territory. When they left, their wagons were loaded down with pure silver.

According to Jesse Combs, the Indians made regular trips to the area until the Civil War. As a result of the hostile presence of Union and Confederate soldiers throughout this part of the Arkansas Ozarks, the Indians stayed away, and by the time the Civil War ended they had ceased coming to the King's River area.

Lester Combs, a son of Jesse and grandson of Jasper, was a longtime resident of Springdale, Arkansas, and liked to tell a story he had heard from his father. He said his father, Jesse, once

62

met a young Indian while working in a sawmill near Kingston, just up the King's River from the old Combs farmstead. The boy was knowledgeable about the special parcel of land allotted to the Indians during the removal phase during the 1830s and said that his elderly grandfather, who lived on an Indian reservation in Oklahoma, probably knew the whereabouts of the ancient silver mine that was believed to be on the Indian land.

Jesse Combs, intrigued by the potential existence of wealth in the area, arranged for the boy to bring his aged grandfather to the area to see if the old silver mine could be located.

When the grandfather arrived, Combs and the young boy took him to the Indian allotment. The old Indian pointed out many familiar landmarks he remembered as a youth nearly sixty years earlier. He reminisced about people, places, and events from which he had long been separated by time and geography, but his recollections convinced Combs he was indeed intimate with the area.

He finally asked about the silver mine. The aged man thought quietly for several minutes. Slowly, he turned toward Combs and told how, as a young boy, he helped dig silver out of the ancient mine and load it into leather packs. He recalled how they had to crawl on hands and knees far into a tunnel in the side of a mountain to retrieve the silver. They had to carry several torches because it was a long way to the silver and they stayed in the mine most of the day.

The old Indian then repeated the penalty for exposing the location of the sacred mine. At that point, he seemed to hesitate about trying to locate the silver, but finally decided it was time for the wealth to be used for the good of the Indians. He agreed to show the mine to Combs.

For several weeks they explored the area and found many strange carvings and signs on the rocks and trees. The old man continued to find familiar landmarks but appeared to be disoriented with regard to distance and direction.

Combs was growing impatient and tried to push the Indian to remember, but the old man finally gave up and said he wished to return to the reservation in Oklahoma. At first Combs believed

63

the old Indian was reluctant to reveal the location of the silver mine because he feared the punishment awaiting him should he tell. But eventually he came to believe that the old man simply could not remember.

In the years that followed, Combs explored the area of the old Indian land allotment many times in search of some indication of the silver mine, but he was never successful.

The Buried Treasure of
Mill Ford Cave

The year was 1825 and the last of a large group of Indians was being removed from their communities around what are now Benton, Madison, and Carroll counties in northwestern Arkansas. Mounted United States soldiers were overseeing the removal and providing escort for the caravans of Indians to resettlement points a few days' ride to the west.

The Indians consisted primarily of members of the Cherokee, Choctaw, and Osage tribes, and their removal was brought about as a result of complaints from some of the more affluent landowners in the area who claimed that the Indians represented a threat to decent, hard-working white settlers. They lobbied government authorities to remove the Native Americans to the newly established territory that was to become Oklahoma. Other white settlers in the Ozarks—those who had lived in friendship with the Indians for many years—correctly viewed the removal as an attempt by wealthy landowners to procure the newly vacated farms and homesteads. In any case, Vice President John C. Calhoun orchestrated a treaty that determined the eventual removal of hundreds of Indians from the area.

Many of the white settlers helped their Indian friends during the move. From throughout the hills and valleys of the Ozarks came entire families who participated in the packing and loading of wagons and driving livestock to their friends' new home in the West.

On their way through the Ozarks, the caravan of Indians, white settlers, and soldiers arrived at Mill Ford, a well-known crossing on the White River. The ford, near the present boundary between Benton and Carroll counties, is now covered by the waters of Beaver Lake.

As a large herd of cattle was being driven across Mill Ford, an old Indian watched from astride his horse on a nearby bank. On the horse next to him was one of the white settlers helping in the move, a longtime friend of the old Indian.

As the last of the cattle entered the river, the old Indian pointed to a high bluff some distance downriver and told his friend an intriguing tale of buried treasure that was connected with it.

Many generations earlier, he related, a large detachment of Spaniards was traveling through this portion of the Ozarks. All of the Spaniards were soldiers and they were escorting several ponderous oxcarts, each filled with silver ingots. Indian legend tells that the Spaniards were transporting silver they had mined somewhere deep in Texas to a river port on the Mississippi from where the wealth was to be rafted to the Gulf, loaded onto a sailing vessel, and from there carried to Spain.

The Spaniards had great difficulty crossing the rugged Ozarks during the rainy season. Many of the creeks were too swollen to ford; the trails were muddy and slick; the huge and heavy oxcarts, so efficient in crossing the prairies, were clumsy and hard to handle in the uneven terrain of the mountains. They often got stuck in the deep mud, and many hours were wasted in extracting them. To add to these problems, the Spaniards became lost in this new country and had been roughly circling the same area for several days.

One rainy afternoon while trying to cross at Mill Ford, the Spaniards were attacked by a large band of Indians that seemed to appear out of nowhere. Though greatly outnumbered, the Spaniards defended themselves fiercely, but the outcome was inevitable: most Spaniards were killed outright during the fighting, and the few who survived the onslaught were subjected to horrible tortures and killed, and their bodies were thrown in the river.

The Indians gathered up the vast fortune in silver ingots, crossed the river, and proceeded downstream to the high limestone bluff, heading for a cave whose narrow entrance was behind the bluff. Once there, they carried the ingots inside and stacked them along one wall near the entrance. The low narrow opening was sealed and covered over with forest debris.

The old Indian relating the story said that many years passed and the Indians forgot about the cache of silver bars in the cave. As far as he knew, he said, the bars were never removed; it is believed they are still stacked along one wall just inside the low entrance. The story of the hidden treasure thrilled young Indians in the area for generations, and the white settlers accepted the tale as part of local folklore.

In the early 1920s, however, something happened that caused area residents to take the old tale a bit more seriously.

Two young men were traveling along the old trail that passed close to the area in which the hidden entrance to the treasure cave was believed to exist. It had been raining hard all day and all the previous night, and the men were having difficulty negotiating the slick path. Not wishing to continue walking along the muddy trail and anxious to get out of the rain, the two found temporary shelter under a nearby tree.

As they huddled there, one of the men pointed toward two dull, gleaming objects just barely sticking out of the ground some twenty yards beyond where they were crouched. When the rain finally subsided, they walked over to the curious objects and discovered them to be two silver ingots partially buried in the soil.

The men dug the silver bars out of the ground and within the week carried them to nearby Fayetteville, where they were assayed. The men were told the two bars displayed an "exceptionally good grade" of silver ore.

Believing they might have accidentally discovered the long-lost treasure cave of the Indians, the two men returned to the area. Unfortunately, the heavy rains of the previous week had eroded away much of the soil from one part of the hillside and deposited it in another, completely rearranging the topography. Several trees, including the one the men had huddled under the week before, had been uprooted and carried down the slope to be deposited in a narrow gully below. For several days the two men searched for the entrance to the cave but were never able to locate the exact point where they dug up the silver ingots.

News of the discovery of the silver bars spread throughout the area, and soon the bluff fronting the White River downstream from the Mill Ford was alive with treasure hunters. Several enterprising individuals tried to sink shafts from the top of the bluff in the hope of penetrating the cavern they knew to exist somewhere deep in the rock, but none was successful.

On the face of the steep bluff overlooking the river a cave opening can be seen. This is known locally as Mill Ford Cave. It is believed that this entrance leads to the back side of the bluff where the treasure is believed to be cached. Several people have entered this cave, but a jumble of rock debris in one of the passages, resulting from an ancient cave-in, has impeded them.

The elusive rear entrance to Mill Ford Cave is still searched for today. It is believed the rising lake waters did not cover it. A group of treasure hunters recently spent several days in the area using metal detectors in the hope of locating some evidence of the cache of silver ingots, but their sensitive instruments remained silent.

Lost Silver Mine near Huntsville

In 1936, one of the most bizarre trials ever to be held in the state of Arkansas took place at the Madison County courthouse in Huntsville. Two local men were being tried for counterfeiting hundreds of dollars' worth of silver coins and passing them throughout the area. The counterfeiting scheme was discovered only when a sharp-eyed banker noticed that a coin given to him by one of the men was slightly thicker than one from the United States mint.

Huntsville is in the northwestern part of Arkansas in the southern Ozarks. Deep, shaded canyons and densely wooded mountains have long made this area a haven for outlaws, bootleggers, and whiskey still operators. These days, one finds mostly pulpwood loggers and farmers, and while stories of lost or buried treasures will come up in conversation occasionally, most residents of this county have little memory of the counterfeiting trial of nearly sixty-five years earlier.

The two Huntsville counterfeiters were arrested without incident. When the time arrived for them to make their statements during the trial, they both freely admitted that they had, in fact, been involved in the making of bogus silver dollars from ore they extracted from a secret mine. The story they told generated one of the most intensive searches for a lost silver mine ever to occur in the state of Arkansas, a search that continues today.

The two men claimed they had initially learned of the existence of the silver mine many years earlier from an old man named Elliot. Elliot was not living at the time of the trial but it is believed he took the two men to the mine and showed them how to retrieve the ore. Several Huntsville residents said that old man Elliot was himself known to have counterfeited silver dollars during the Civil War in this area, and passed his skills on to the two Huntsville men. He showed the two how to fashion the wooden molds used in forming the images on the fake coins.

Both men stated they dug pure silver from an old mine within a half-day's walk from the Madison County courthouse. They carried the silver ore in canvas packs to a secluded site in Bear Creek Hollow, some ten miles northeast of Huntsville and near the small community of Forum. Bear Creek Hollow was remote enough that it was seldom visited by anyone, except possibly the whiskey still operators and customers rumored in local folklore. The hollow seemed like an ideal location for the counterfeiters' activities.

Some students of Arkansas history believe that the men actually mined the silver from somewhere in Bear Creek Hollow and made up the story of its location near Huntsville to throw searchers off the trail. They point to an obscure historical reference to the fact that silver was, in fact, discovered in Bear Creek Hollow in 1886.

Once the men had accumulated a sufficient amount of the ore, they melted it down and rolled it out into thin sheets about the width of a coin. Then they set a mold atop the sheet of silver and hammered it with a mallet, forming a coin and imposing an image on one side. They turned over the coin, hammered another image onto the other side, grooved the edges of the newly made coin by hand, and shortly thereafter placed it into circulation.

Those who have claimed to have seen the wooden molds used by the two Huntsville men testified they were well-made and that the images stamped onto the counterfeit coins were difficult to distinguish from real ones. An analysis of the silver content of one of the coins revealed that they contained a higher quantity of silver than those minted by the United States government!

Several times during the trial, attempts were made to get the men to reveal the location of the silver mine they claimed was nearby, but both of them adamantly refused. One of the men claimed there was enough of the silver ore remaining in the mine to pave every road in the state of Arkansas.

Both men were convicted of counterfeiting and sentenced to several years at Cummins prison farm southeast of Little Rock. The Madison County sheriff visited the men several times during their prison term and tried to persuade them to reveal the location of the silver mine, but still they refused. Attorneys for the two men also tried to learn where the mine was, saying that their sentences might be reduced if they were to provide the information, but they continued to be silent on the subject.

Several Huntsville residents anticipated the release of the two men and their subsequent return to Madison County so that they could tail them to the lost mine. According to relatives of the two, they left immediately for California upon being released from Cummins prison and neither of them ever set foot in Madison County again.

To this day people continue to search for the long-lost silver mine supposedly located near Huntsville, hoping to stumble upon the rich lode the counterfeiters used to make their silver coins. The mine has never been reported found. As far as the residents of Madison County are concerned, it is still lost.

Stone County Silver

Cow Mountain near Timbo in Stone County is reputed to have an ancient silver mine somewhere at the top. Longtime residents of the area believe silver was mined by Indians as recently as the latter part of the last century. Jimmy Driftwood, a three-time Grammy Award winning singer and songwriter and a resident of Timbo, relates this story of the lost silver mine that he heard from his father.

Many years ago, when Stone County was being settled by whites moving into the area, the Native Americans were slowly but most certainly being driven out. One old Indian who frequented the area was not inclined to leave. One day he was chased and caught by a group of farmers who informed him he must vacate the county. The Indian remained steadfast and stoically disregarded their threats. He knew he was too old to fend for himself alone in the wild and rugged portions of the Ozarks that lay to the west, and as he was used to begging food and clothing from the white settlers, he decided he had nothing to lose by resisting.

Presently one of the farmers threw a noose around the old man's neck and dragged him to the nearest oak tree with the intention of hanging him. Seeing the men were determined to kill him, the old man begged for his life and promised his captors that if they spared him he would show them a rich mine atop Cow Mountain. He told the men there was enough silver in the old mine to make them wealthy for the rest of their lives and they could have it if they would just let him live in peace in the area.

His captors agreed to the proposition and on the morning of the next day they followed the old Indian to the mountain. As they approached the ridge, he insisted on blindfolding the men for the remainder of the trip, telling them that it was the Indian way of doing things and that the blindfolds would be removed once they reached the mine. Reluctantly the men agreed.

After a long ride to the top of the ridge along a switchback trail, they arrived at the site of the ancient mine and were allowed to remove their blindfolds. True to his word, the Indian showed them a nearly vertical shaft that extended deep into the mountain. Next to the shaft were several large piles of broken rock that had apparently been dug out of the mine and three smaller piles of loose rock. The Indian pointed to the smaller piles and told the men they would find silver ore mixed in with the rock. The farmers scrambled from their horses and sorted through the small accumulations, filling their pockets and saddlebags with as much of the silver-embedded rock as they could carry.

When they had loaded as much as they could, the Indian reapplied the blindfolds and led the men back down off the mountain.

Two days later the old man disappeared, never to be seen again. It was said that the other Indians who lived nearby had captured and killed him because of the arrangement he had made with the farmers. Carrying his body to the old mine shaft atop Cow Mountain, they threw him in, refilled it, and disguised the entrance so that no one could ever relocate it. Another version of the legend claims that the old Indian learned of the plot to kill him and fled the country.

The farmers made several efforts to find the mine on top of Cow Mountain but never succeeded.

Old Man Napier's Hidden Treasure

During the Civil War, an elderly resident of Mountain Home in Baxter County was reputed to have amassed a substantial fortune that he converted into gold coin. Old man Napier had the reputation of being a cranky tightwad who negotiated the price of everything he purchased. While he made a great deal of money, he had never been known to spend any of it on himself or his family.

Napier always walked everywhere he went, dressed in the same black suit and hat, and carried a cane. He owned and operated several small farms in the region and lived in a well-cared-for two-story house in town.

In the hills outside Mountain Home lived a small band of outlaws who frequented the road into town and preyed on travelers. Robberies were common and the local law enforcement officials seemed ineffective in dealing with the bandits.

One day this group of outlaws rode onto Napier's property in town, barged into his house, and attacked him and his family. Napier, his wife, and his children were bound hand and foot, and the outlaws threatened to kill them all if the old man did not reveal the location of his gold. He refused. The outlaws also tried to get the wife and children to tell, but it was clear they had no idea where the gold had been hidden.

After several minutes the outlaws applied hot irons to Napier's bare flesh, but still he refused to cooperate. The family was dragged out into the front yard and subjected to beatings—all in vain, for Napier refused to talk. As the family and neighbors looked on, the outlaws set fire to the house and barn before mounting up and riding away.

Napier remained under a doctor's care for several weeks while his burns and bruises healed. His family moved into a house on one of his farms, but he remained in town, often visiting the site of his former home and drawing water each day from the brick-walled well between the ruins of the burned-out house and the road.

Within the decade, old man Napier died without ever having revealed the location of his hidden wealth to his wife or children. A man named Bucher purchased the old Napier property and built a fine new house on the site of the one that had been burned down. Bucher chose to ignore Napier's old well and sank a new one closer to the new house, but he kept his milk and butter cool by storing them in the old one.

Stories soon reached Bucher about old man Napier's wealth and the possibility that it was buried somewhere on the property. Bucher dug in promising locations around the house and the old barn but never found anything.

Around 1920, one of old man Napier's granddaughters returned to Mountain Home to visit friends. While there, she decided to ride out to view the old home and property. None of the original buildings was left standing; the only thing remaining that she remembered from her grandfather's home place was the old brick-walled well down by the road.

The granddaughter confirmed the oft-told stories of the huge wealth that was supposedly concealed on the property but said no one in the family ever had any inkling of where the old man hid it. None of the money ever fell into the hands of the relatives, so she presumed it was still hidden—most likely, she said, near the site of the old house or barn.

Several years later, around the time when automobiles were becoming more numerous in Baxter County, a stranger stopped at the old Napier home place. He had been driving across the rough roads of the Ozarks and had sprung a leak in his radiator. He managed to plug the leak, and was now in search of water to refill it. The residents of the old Napier place told the stranger he was welcome to draw as much water as he needed from the old well down near the road.

On the second drawing of the bucket up from the well, the stranger found a gold coin in the bottom of the container. News of the discovery quickly spread around the small community, causing a great deal of excitement among the residents. At last, they believed, Napier's hidden gold had been found.

With the consent of the owners of the property, an attempt was made to enlarge the opening of the well with dynamite so that a man could be lowered to the bottom to retrieve the cache of coins presumed to lie hidden there. On the second effort to widen the shaft, the explosion caused the walls to collapse, filling in the well and perhaps forever burying Napier's hidden gold.

Civil War Treasures

The Lost Payroll

The five Confederate soldiers rode uneasily through the densely wooded area of a remote portion of the Ozark Mountains in northwestern Arkansas. The sergeant, a veteran of several skirmishes, peered into the shadowy foliage all around, ever watchful, ever listening. From time to time he looked back at his detachment—one corporal and three privates—and wished he had been provided with some seasoned soldiers instead of raw recruits. He had been given the responsibility of delivering a large payroll to the Confederate encampment near Prairie Grove, a few miles southwest of Fayetteville. Before he left he was informed by his commander that Union troops were in the area, but as there was a shortage of men, he had to travel without the normal contingent of guards.

As they traveled north along the old military road, the sergeant regarded his four charges. The corporal was barely more than a boy but had proven himself an eager and competent soldier. He had been entrusted with leading the pack horse on which were strapped the bags of gold coin to pay the soldiers at Prairie Grove. Like the sergeant, he was scanning the woods for any sign of the enemy. The three privates were all under seventeen years old and were visibly nervous about the assignment.

The sergeant had turned in his saddle to instruct the corporal to check the fastenings on the payroll bags when a shot rang out from the trees to the left of the detachment. The bullet pene-

77

trated the chest of the sergeant, and as he fell from his horse he yelled, "Ambush!"

Several more shots were fired in rapid succession and two of the privates fell from their mounts and were dead before they hit the ground.

The other private was also hit but managed to hang onto his saddle as he spurred his mount up the trail toward Prairie Grove. His wound was bad and he eventually passed out and fell from his horse.

The corporal never had an opportunity to draw his revolver to return fire—he was trying to control his own excited mount as well as maintain a grip on the reins of the pack horse transporting the payroll. Finally, amid the shooting and shouting, the corporal succeeded in turning his horse around and spurring it back in the southerly direction from which the detachment had come. Fearing pursuit, he ran the horses at top speed until it seemed they could go no farther.

Stopping to rest the animals and listen for sounds of pursuit, the corporal spotted a deep crevice in the limestone wall of a cliff rising just off the trail. Quickly he dismounted, retrieved the payroll sacks from the pack horse, and stashed them into the crevice at the base of the cliff. He stuffed rocks, branches, and leaves into the opening to make it look like the rest of the forest floor. He then mounted his horse and, leading the pack horse, returned to his company to report the attack.

When he arrived, he found the camp in a turmoil. Men were rushing around, securing rifles, ammunition, and provisions, and preparing their horses for a forced ride. He sought out the company commander and told him of the attack on the payroll detachment, of escaping the ambuscade, and of concealing the gold along the trail on his return to the camp.

The commander informed the corporal that they would have to attend to the matter of the payroll some other time, because for now they were preparing to go into battle with a force of Union soldiers at Prairie Grove. In a short time, the entire Confederate force was on the march back up the trail.

The Prairie Grove fight was one of the major Civil War battles to take place in Arkansas. The corporal, along with many other Confederate soldiers, was killed during the battle that followed. A few of the troops who were familiar with the story of the corporal and the hidden gold payroll tried to find the cache in later years but without success. The sacks of gold coins are believed to lie concealed in a deep limestone crevice just a few miles south of Prairie Grove along the old military road.

Buried Arms at Cross Hollows

During November 1861, Confederate General Ben McCulloch led an army of 12,000 soldiers into Cross Hollows, a small settlement that had been established some twenty years earlier about ten miles north and slightly east of Fayetteville. Here they were to set up a winter headquarters and serve as an arms and ammunition depot for the war effort.

Several wooden barracks were erected in two long rows that extended about a mile along the valley. Over a period of time, supplies of arms and ammunition were delivered to this location and stored in several frame buildings erected for that purpose. In addition to rifles and pistols, a number of cannons were stored at the Cross Valley location.

One day McCulloch received word that a large contingent of Union troops under the command of General Curtis was approaching the valley. A quick assessment by McCulloch determined he did not have the manpower to withstand an assault by this large Union force, so he gave orders to his men to conceal the arms, destroy the buildings, and abandon the area.

While several men were given the job of burning down all the barracks and supply buildings, the rest hauled rifles, pistols, ammunition, and cannons up an adjacent hill. On a ridge above the valley a long trench was quickly excavated and all the war materials dumped in. The trench was hastily covered, and the men fled the valley.

Several hours later when Curtis and his army arrived at Cross Hollows, all they found were burned buildings and scattered remnants of the Confederate camp. They found no sign of arms and assumed the Confederate soldiers carried everything with them as they retreated toward the south. It never occurred to General Curtis to search the adjacent ridge for the hastily concealed arms.

During the close of the Civil War, many Confederate soldiers who were involved in burying the arms supply on the ridge at Cross Hollows related the tale to others. Several mentioned they would return to the area after the war and retrieve the materials, but none ever did. By the time the war was over, no one seemed to remember exactly where the arms were buried.

Today Cross Hollows is a ghost town. None of the original buildings remain, and there is little to suggest that the site was home to 12,000 Rebel soldiers. Somewhere atop one of the ridges that surround the valley, hundreds of Confederate rifles and pistols along with several cannons still lie buried.

Hidden Treasure on Callahan Mountain

Callahan Mountain is an impressive limestone structure that can be seen just west of Highway 71 between Springdale and Rogers in Benton County.

Many of the people who live near Callahan Mountain are descendants of pioneers who settled in the area before the Civil War, and the following story has been attributed to some of the old-timers who remember hearing it from their parents and grandparents.

During the Civil War, a ragged and depleted company of Confederate soldiers was fleeing a regiment of Union troops. The chase had lasted for nearly two days. As the Rebels' horses were tiring, the men sought a place to hide and defend themselves against the imminent attack.

Spying the gentle slopes of Callahan Mountain, the soldiers climbed it and selected a position that would be defensible against the enemy should they decide to continue the fight.

Before long, the Confederates saw Union troops ascending the

80

slopes behind them. Realizing the battle would soon commence, the contingent of Rebels, about thirty-five in all, elected to hide all their gold, money, watches, and other valuables so that the Yanks would not get them should they prevail.

They quickly dug a hole, placed the valuables into it, refilled it, and rolled a huge stone onto the top. Supposedly it took twenty-one of the soldiers to move the stone into position!

Once the troops engaged, there was an exchange of gunfire that lasted for about two hours. During a lull in the battle the Confederates escaped by descending the western side of Callahan Mountain, intending to return sometime in the future to retrieve the valuables.

Unfortunately, every member of the Rebel company lost his life in the famous Battle of Pea Ridge, which was fought not far from Callahan Mountain just a few days later.

Other Tales of Treasure in Arkansas

Baxter County Gold

During the early 1940s, a number of men living in the Ozarks earned a meager living hunting and trapping. One such man was named McChord, a congenial fellow who was often seen driving around Baxter County in an old pick-up truck.

Gordon Lambrecht, another Baxter County resident, met McChord. The two struck up a friendship born of their mutual enjoyment of hunting and the outdoors, and spent many hours together exploring remote parts of the Baxter County Ozarks.

After about three months of friendship, McChord asked if Lambrecht would like to accompany him to a secret place he knew of where they could dig for gold. Intrigued, Lambrecht agreed to go along.

The two men rode together in McChord's pick-up truck to the town of Cotter, where they borrowed a small boat from a man who ran a commercial boat dock. They transferred some supplies from the truck to the boat and started upstream. After about a half-hour of travel upriver, McChord turned the small boat into a side stream and followed it for approximately five hundred feet until it got too shallow for them to proceed. McChord banked the craft and unloaded the supplies, and the men walked another six hundred feet up to the top of a hill along a trail that McChord claimed he hacked out himself.

At the top of the hill was an outcrop of rock and evidence of some recent excavation. McChord told Lambrecht that this was his gold mine and instructed him to dig in one certain area.

After an hour of digging, the men returned to the small stream where they panned for ore along the banks. McChord showed Lambrecht how to recognize the small flecks of gold in the bottom of the pan.

Lambrecht was impressed with McChord's knowledge of mining and geology and did as he was instructed. After several hours of labor, the two men had accumulated a small sack of what McChord said was gold ore.

They returned to the boat dock around sundown. Later that evening, McChord cashed in the sack of ore and paid Lambrecht twenty dollars for his labor.

Jesse James in Arkansas

In addition to the extraction of native ore from the rock of the Ozark Mountains, many legends have been passed along concerning such valuables as coins, bills, jewelry, and other items of wealth being secreted in hiding places throughout the range.

Jesse and Frank James and their gang of desperadoes were regular visitors to the Arkansas Ozarks and were known to conceal money from holdups at several different locations. Near the Hickory Creek boat dock on Beaver Lake lies Nelson Hollow Cave, a favorite hiding place for the James gang, where many residents of the area believe some of their loot may be cached.

Another story involving the James gang concerns a bank robbery in Missouri. Frank and Jesse, along with the Younger brothers, took a total of $34,000. They reportedly fled to another favorite hiding place just east of Springdale, Arkansas, and buried the money in a rock crevice at the base of a reddish stone bluff found there.

Mystery Mine In Crawford County

Around the turn of the century a group of men was cutting walnut timber in the vicinity of White Rock Mountain in Crawford County. They spent several days at a time at this endeavor and had established a camp adjacent to Hurricane Creek.

One evening as they were preparing their supper, the timber-cutters were surprised to see a large party of Mexicans ride up. The Mexicans requested permission to camp alongside the creek, and the timber-cutters welcomed them. The group was composed of two elderly men, about twenty-five younger ones, and several women. The caravan consisted of about a dozen light wagons pulled by teams of burros. Most of the younger men rode fine horses.

As the Mexicans set up camp, they unloaded mining tools. Curious, one of the timber-cutters entered the Mexican camp and struck up a conversation with them. In broken English, one of the leaders of the group of Mexicans explained that they had a map and directions to a gold mine in this area that had been worked by their ancestors. They had traveled for many days from far away in Mexico to the Ozarks, intending to find the mine and extract the remainder of the ore.

Over the next few days, several of the younger men struck out into the mountains in search of the mine. One evening they announced they had found it and moved their camp from the creek up into a steep-walled canyon.

For the next several weeks, the timber-cutters heard the sounds of dynamite blasts. Once a day several of the women would drive one of the wagons to the creek to fill water barrels. They told the timber-cutters that the men had found the ancient mine and were excavating the gold.

Eventually, the sounds of blasting were no longer heard. Several of the timber-cutters ventured up into the canyon and discovered that the Mexicans had left. They found the mine shaft easily. A large amount of rock had been removed from it and deposited at the opening of the tunnel. An inspection of the mine revealed no gold whatsoever, and the men decided that

84

the visitors had extracted all that remained and returned to Mexico.

The Lost Snowball Mine

Around 1910 a farmer who lived near Snowball, Arkansas, returned home from a hunting trip with a bucket half full of pure silver ore.

He told his family that he had met some Indian friends in the woods who told him of a silver mine that had been used by the tribe for several generations. They agreed to take the farmer to the mine but insisted on blindfolding him first. When they reached the mine, they showed him a vein of silver about four feet wide running along one wall of the shaft and allowed him to take as much as he could. The farmer cut several large chunks of the pure silver with his hunting knife and placed them in an old bucket he found nearby.

Before they blindfolded him and led him out of the mine and back through the forest, they made him promise never to search for the mine on his own. He agreed.

Many years later he told his son about the trip to the mine, and the son searched for the secret silver mine until he died. The mine has never been found.

MISSOURI

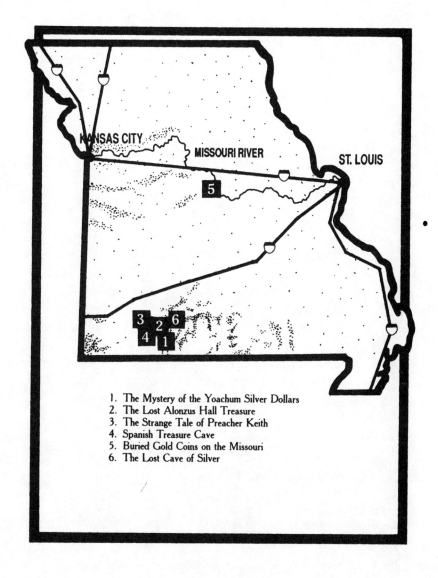

1. The Mystery of the Yoachum Silver Dollars
2. The Lost Alonzus Hall Treasure
3. The Strange Tale of Preacher Keith
4. Spanish Treasure Cave
5. Buried Gold Coins on the Missouri
6. The Lost Cave of Silver

The Mystery of the
Yoachum Silver Dollars

One of the most enduring legends of lost and buried trea-
sure ever to come out of the Ozarks concerns the Yoachum
silver dollars. That the silver dollars existed there can be no
doubt—government records clearly substantiate their existence
and several collectors have examples of them. The origin of the
silver and the circumstances involved in the manufacture of the
dollars are still being debated, but the search for the coins and
the mysterious cave from which the silver was allegedly taken is
still going on today.

This story has its beginnings in the year 1541, when Spanish
explorers under the leadership of De Soto penetrated the rugged, isolated valleys of the Ozark Mountains in search of mineral
wealth. Their intention was to locate gold and silver, extract the
ore, smelt it, and ship it back to Spain to fatten the coffers of the
motherland.

A large party of Spaniards explored much of the Ozark Mountain country in southwestern Missouri. The first indications of
ore must have been promising enough to encourage them to
establish a small settlement in the area while the mines were
being developed. They constructed a large log fortress atop
Breadtray Mountain, near the mouth of the James River where
it flows into the White River. The mountain is approximately
three miles northwest of the present town of Lampe, Missouri,
near Table Rock Lake.

The Spaniards were especially delighted with some prospecting near their log fortress. While inspecting an ancient shelter cave long used by Indians, they discovered numerous passageways, one of them containing a thick vein of silver ore. They enslaved several local Indians and put them to work in the cave digging the ore and smelting it into ingots. In no time at all the miners were excavating a tunnel as they followed the vein of silver ore, all the while extracting silver, forming it into eighteen-inch-long ingots, and stacking them against one side of one of the cavern passageways until they could be loaded onto mules and transported to the Mississippi River. From there the ingots were rafted downriver to the Gulf of Mexico, where they were loaded onto a sailing vessel bound for Spain.

The Spaniards treated the Indian laborers cruelly, whipping them if they didn't work at a pace satisfying to the overseers and chaining them at night to prevent their escape. From time to time other Indians were seen observing the fortress and the entrance to the mine from high atop neighboring ridges. Their menacing demeanor made the Spaniards double and triple their nighttime guards.

Hunting parties sent out to find fresh meat often ran into Indians. In some of the confrontations, Spaniards were killed or injured. A few hunting parties sent out never returned.

Increasingly nervous at the growing presence of the hostile Indians, the Spaniards began to discuss the possibility of taking what silver they had accumulated and abandoning the area.

Early one morning a few days later, however, the Indians launched a vicious raid on the fortress and the mine simultaneously. Hundreds of Indians streamed out of the woods and attacked the Spaniards, killing most of them. At the mine all of the overseers were slain and the Indian captives released. A few of the Spaniards escaped, but the silver they had accumulated remained stacked along one wall of the dark cavern.

With the Spaniards gone and the Indians once again dominant in the area, the silver mine remained inactive for over two and a half centuries.

Choctaw legend relates that the cave remained undisturbed until around 1809. During a violent spring thunderstorm, a small hunting party of Choctaws sought shelter in the cave. While waiting out the storm they explored the many passageways that penetrated deep into the mountainside and in this manner discovered the large cache of silver ingots and the old man-made shaft that followed the thick vein of silver ore. They also found several skeletons, no doubt Spanish casualties in the Indian raid over two hundred and fifty years earlier.

The Choctaw traditionally had little use for silver save for the fashioning of ornaments, but contact with white trappers and traders in the area had taught them that they could trade the shiny metal for such supplies as blankets, weapons, and horses. At the entrance of the cave they conducted a two-day ceremony that was intended to drive out the evil spirits they believed resided there.

For many years thereafter, the Choctaw made regular trips to the cave and returned with just enough silver to make jewelry and conduct trade. They carried the silver as far as St. Louis to barter for goods.

One afternoon a Choctaw scout reported a party of Mexicans riding toward the cave along a trail that paralleled the White River. The leader of the Choctaw, accompanied by three armed warriors, rode out to meet the Mexicans and asked the reason for their presence in the Indian homeland.

The leader of the party of Mexicans explained that they were searching for a silver mine that had been excavated over two hundred years earlier, which and they believed was nearby. He unrolled a large sheepskin map replete with Spanish writing and symbols, and the Choctaw chief recognized several prominent area landmarks inscribed on the leather.

After examining the map the chief told the Mexicans that there was no such silver mine in the area and encouraged them to leave.

Fearful that the Mexicans might return and discover the old mine, the chief ordered the entrance to the mine sealed and the area abandoned until he deemed it safe to return. The cave remained closed until a few years later, when other Indians arrived in the valley.

After the War of 1812, the Delaware Indians were relocated into the Ozark Mountains. Originally occupying lands that encompassed parts of Ohio, Indiana, and Illinois, the Delaware were evicted and became involved in a trans-Mississippi migration that landed most of them in the James River area of the Ozarks in southwestern Missouri before 1820. Here they were joined by some Shawnee, Kickapoo, Potawatomi, and Seneca, all likewise evicted from their traditional homelands in the East.

Around this time the Yoachum family also moved into the James River valley and established a farm. The name has been listed in the literature under several different spellings: Yocum, Yokum, Joachim, Yoakum, Yochum, and Yoachum. Most researchers believe the members of the family who settled this area spelled the name "Yoachum."

James Yoachum was born in Kentucky around 1772. A year later his brother, Solomon, was born, and two years after that a third brother arrived, his name being lost to history. While the brothers were still young the family moved to Illinois and tried farming. James had a wanderlust and was not content to work on the family farm. As soon as he turned eighteen, he left the farm and a pregnant wife and decided to seek his fortune trapping in the Ozark Mountains in southwestern Missouri.

James had considerable success in this venture and decided to return to Illinois to get his brothers to accompany him back to the mountains. On arriving at the homestead, he discovered his wife had died in childbirth, leaving him with a son. The boy, named Jacob Levi, was being raised by Solomon and his wife.

James remained in Illinois for several years but still had difficulty adapting to the tedium of farming the flat expanses of the Illinois prairie. Eventually he decided to return to the Ozark Mountains and his trapping enterprise, with the agreement that his two brothers along with their families and Jacob were to join him soon.

On his second trip to the Ozarks, James met and married a Delaware woman named Winona and settled near the confluence of the James and White rivers. Historians claim that the James River was named for James Yoachum, for he developed a very productive farm along the river.

Because of family concerns, the brothers' move to the Ozarks was delayed and they were not able to join James on his farm until 1815. By this time, James Yoachum had planted a large part of the bottoms in corn and squash and had acquired handsome herds of cattle and horses. Most of his neighbors were Delaware Indians, a peaceful people who often brought gifts of food to the new settlers. In return, the Yoachums shared much of their harvest with their new friends, and occasionally presented a gift of a fine horse to a selected member of the tribe.

The Yoachums noticed that the Delaware, as well as members of many of the other tribes living nearby, wore jewelry and ornaments of high-quality silver—long beaded necklaces, arm bands, and hair fixtures. When James inquired about the origin of the silver, the Delaware explained that many years ago an aged Choctaw told them of the existence of a great fortune in silver bars, stacked shoulder-high to a man, in a cave deep in the Ozark forest. A Delaware friend of the Yoachums related the ancient tale of the old cave and the Spanish mine. When James asked if he could see the cave, the Indian told him that it would violate a pact made between the Choctaw and the Delaware tribes never to reveal the location of the silver.

And so it remained for several years, until the federal government initiated an Indian removal process wherein many Native Americans were evicted from their homelands in the Ozarks and resettled on reservations in Indian Territory several miles west in what is now Oklahoma.

As their Indian friends were packing their belongings and loading them onto wagons, the Yoachum brothers arrived to help. They brought gifts for their friends, including blankets, cooking utensils, and horses. In gratitude, several of the Delaware leaders agreed to reveal to the Yoachums the location of the cave from which came the silver. Within days after the departure of the Indians, the Yoachum brothers located the cave. The three men vowed never to reveal the site, and with one exception apparently carried the secret with them to their graves.

When the brothers needed silver from the cave they would ride out from the farm, stay gone for two or three days, and return with several of the ingots that they claimed were taken from a stack of hundreds they found along one wall of the cave. In time they accumulated an impressive pile of silver bars.

As more and more settlers arrived in the Ozarks, and as more and more trading posts became established, the brothers became involved in the commerce of the day. The largest establishment in the area was the James Fork Trading Post, which was managed by a man named William Gilliss. Even though the Yoachums had one of the largest and best farms in the region, they continued to hunt and trap and trade their furs at the James Fork Trading Post for coffee, sugar, flour, and other staples.

The trading post was owned by the business firm of Menard and Valle, operating out of the town of Ste. Genevieve, Missouri. Colonel Pierre Menard, for a long time a good and established friend of the Indian tribes in the Ozarks, watched closely over the trading.

Menard was also very protective of the interests of French trappers in the region. Since the Yoachums were considered outsiders, he told Gilliss to insist that they and others in the area always purchase their supplies with cash. The medium of exchange, thereafter, was no longer to be furs or even gold and silver, but federally issued coin and currency. The Yoachums, though rich in silver, were poor by other standards. They had no money.

In order to remedy this situation, the brothers, under the leadership of James, decided to make their own money. Using simple blacksmith tools, they made some dies, melted down the ingots, rolled the silver out into sheets, and stamped out their own coins. The coins were a bit larger that the ones issued by the government. On one side they bore the inscription "Yoachum" and the date "1822." On the other side was stamped "United States of America" and "1 Dollar."

Over a period of several months thousands of these coins were stamped out and placed into circulation by the brothers. Soon most of the residents of this part of the Ozarks used the coins for any and all kinds of purchases. Gilliss, the manager of the James Fork Trading Post, examined the coins and judged them to be of the purest silver, eagerly accepting them as a legitimate medium of exchange. The Yoachum silver dollars soon became more available in the remote Ozarks than the government-issued money.

This economy worked well for many years. No one outside this remote part of the Ozarks had ever heard of the Yoachum dollars, but residents of the area were happy with the way things were going.

In 1845, however, something occurred to bring the Yoachum dollar to the notice of the federal government. When the lands around the James and White rivers, formerly Indian lands, were opened for purchase by non-Indians, the government sent a surveying crew to establish section lines and county boundaries. During this time the settlers in the area were also notified that they would be required to abide by certain homestead laws relative to securing title to the property on which they lived. Part of the requirement was to pay a filing fee at the government office in Springfield.

Dozens of James River residents intent on paying their filing fee, along with others who wished to purchase some of the newly available Indian lands, arrived at the office in Springfield and tried to pay with the Yoachum silver dollars.

The government agent on duty refused to accept the Yoachum dollars, citing an 1833 regulation that required federally issued coin. He told the settlers that unless they paid in legitimate United States money they could not have official titles to their land.

Enraged, as well as tired from the long journey into Springfield, several of the men pointed loaded guns at the agent and told him that the Yoachum currency meant more to residents in this part of the country than government money and that he had better accept it or suffer the consequences. Fearful for his life, the agent accepted the Yoachum silver dollars and presented each man with a valid certificate to his land.

The agent, being an aggressively dedicated public servant and loyal employee, immediately forwarded the Yoachum dollars along with an explanation of what had occurred to authorities in the nation's capital. Once the coins arrived at Washington, D.C., they were assayed and found to be composed of almost pure silver. In fact, they contained much more silver than the government-issued coin.

Federal authorities did not consider the dollars counterfeit because there was no attempt to duplicate United States government minted coins. Still, they were concerned about the proliferation of non-federal money in the region. They wired the Springfield office and ordered the agent to confiscate Yoachum dollars and to ascertain the location of the silver mine.

Within a few weeks the government agent found his way to James Yoachum's house and announced that he had come to have a look at the silver mine. At gunpoint, Yoachum ordered the agent off his property.

Properly intimidated, the agent left. He returned a week later in the company of eight other federal agents, all well-armed and menacing-looking. This time he explained to James Yoachum the official position of the United States government relative to the locally cast silver dollars and told Yoachum that he was being discouraged from manufacturing and distributing said coins.

Yoachum, considered by many to be a law-abiding and patriotic sort of man, stated he never willfully intended to break any laws. He agreed to stop making the dollars but refused to reveal the location of the silver mine. Discussions continued into the evening with both parties refusing to change their positions. Finally the stalemate was broken when the government agents agreed not to prosecute the Yoachum brothers if they agreed to halt the manufacture and circulation of the coins. The location of the old Spanish mine remained a secret.

Several more years passed, and James Yoachum died. There are two versions of his death. One is that he was taken with a fever and died in his sleep. The other version is that he and his wife, Winona, were killed in a cave-in at the mine on a trip there to retrieve some of the silver. The year was 1848.

After Yoachum's death, the two remaining brothers decided to abandon the Ozarks and go to California. The gold fields were just opening up and the brothers, possessing a strong sense of adventure, were determined to try their luck in a new place. The story has it that before leaving, the brothers gave the dies used in casting the silver dollars to one of the family members who owned a grist mill in the vicinity. Historical records verify that a nephew of James Yoachum owned and operated the largest grist mill in the Ozarks at that time.

The brothers loaded their wagons and left with their families, never to be seen in the Ozarks again. While their fate may never be known, it was told around the James River valley for many years that the brothers, along with their families, died crossing the Rocky Mountains on their way to California. With their death the secret of the location of the old Spanish cave was gone.

Jacob Levi, James Yoachum's son, related a story to his son, Tom, that his father told him after the visit by the government agents. He said that all three brothers went to the cave and sealed it so no one could find it. Jacob often heard his father describe the country around the cave, and he searched for but was never able to find the cave himself. He related this knowledge to Tom, who lived for many years in Galena. Tom, like his father, was never able to find the silver mine.

The legend of the Yoachum dollar has been told and retold many times during the past 160 years and, as with most legends, each retelling is likely embellished. There are, in fact, different versions of the manner in which the brothers located the mine. In addition to the version related above, another claims the Yoachum brothers clandestinely observed local Indians carrying silver bars from the cave. The brothers allegedly killed the Indians who made repeated visits to the cave, concealed the entrance against discovery by others, and altered the trail so that it no longer led to the cave.

Another version of the legend claims that the brothers had no silver mine at all and that the silver used in the Yoachum dollar was simply recast government-issued coin. Before the arrival of

97

the three Yoachum brothers and their families in the James River portion of the Ozarks, the federal government program of relocating the Delaware Indians had long been in place. In addition to the lands assigned, each Indian family was given an annuity of four thousand dollars in silver currency. The Yoachums, greedy for the silver, began making and selling liquor to the Delaware—which was against the law. Not wishing to be caught in possession of the Indian money, they melted it down and recast it using their own handmade dies. To cover their illegal activities, the story goes, the brothers claimed the silver came from a lost Spanish mine they had discovered back in the mountains. The reason the Yoachums were so reluctant to reveal the location of the silver mine, according to researcher Lynn Morrow, was that such a mine never existed.

The above version of the legend suggests that the Yoachum brothers manifested certain outlaw tendencies. This is supported by some documents located in the Missouri Historical Society Archives. A man named John Campbell, who was appointed Indian agent for the James River region, was constantly on the lookout for unscrupulous white settlers who might take advantage of the Delaware. In 1822, Campbell prepared a list of such men. The list includes the name of Solomon Yoachum and suggests he was involved in selling liquor to the Indians. It also suggests that Solomon, James, and the third brother were evicted from the Delaware country for not paying a filing fee on the land.

One version of the Yoachum legend claims that the brothers resettled just outside of the Indian lands near the mouth of the Finley River, where they operated brandy and whiskey stills. It was also said that the Yoachums manufactured the finest peach brandy in the country.

Morrow further contends that the Yoachum brothers knew their silver coin scheme was to be short-lived. When the Delaware were moved out of the Ozark Mountains and relocated farther west in Indian Territory as a result of the James Fork Treaty of 1829, the Yoachums' source of silver left with them. Morrow also noted that after the Indians left the area the Yoachum dollar became scarce.

Whichever version of the legend one chooses to accept, the fact remains that the Yoachum dollar did exist, and that thousands of them were manufactured.

Homer Johnson, a longtime resident of the southwestern Missouri area around Breadtray Mountain, often told a Yoachum silver dollar story that concerned his grandfather, Jefferson Johnson. Jefferson's boyhood friend was Robert Yoachum, a son of Jacob Levi Yoachum, and the two often played together as children. One afternoon the two boys were saddling some horses in the Yoachum barn when Jefferson spied a barrel nearly filled to the top with Yoachum dollars. He estimated there must have been several thousand of the coins in the barrel.

Some of the Yoachum silver dollars have been found: An unidentified man from St. Louis reported in 1974 that, while metal detecting near Branson, he discovered a cache of 236 large silver coins. He described them as being two inches in diameter, roughly cast, and each bearing the inscription "Yoachum" on one side.

Many more of the Yoachum dollars have been recovered and are now in the hands of collectors. It is estimated that many more are yet to be found.

Treasure hunters and coin collectors have long wondered what became of the original dies used for casting the silver dollars. The dies were presumed lost until a remarkable discovery occurred in 1983. On March 11 of that year, J.R. Blunk of Galena was digging near a riverbank on some property near the site of the original Yoachum settlement on the James River. He unearthed a large mass of what appeared to be wax. He broke open the ball of wax and inside found two short sections of iron rod. Scraping wax from the end of one of the rods, Blunk noticed the reverse lettering of the word "Yoachum." On the other rod he was able to discern "1 Dollar."

Excited at his discovery, Blunk spent the next several months researching the Yoachum silver dollar legend and turned up the names of several collectors who owned samples of the original dollars. Through one of the collectors he obtained a Yoachum

99

dollar and, on close examination, realized that it had indeed come from the dies in his possession.

The dies and coin were examined by a professional numismatist named Fred Wineberg who opined that the coins were indeed formed from the dies in Blunk's possession.

But what of the thousands of other Yoachum dollars? What of the barrel full of coins seen in the Yoachum barn by Jefferson Johnson? How many of the coins were hidden away or otherwise disposed of when the government forbade their circulation? How many of the legendary Yoachum dollars are lying forgotten in some moldy old trunk in a dusty attic somewhere deep in the Ozark Mountains?

The Lost
Alonzus Hall Treasure

Alonzus Hall was one of several notorious outlaws who roamed, robbed, and murdered throughout the Ozark Mountains during the Civil War. He has been described as a handsome young man, tall, with deep blue eyes and a charming and disarming smile. A charismatic person, he had little trouble making friends. He was a favorite of the ladies in any settlement he visited, and his confident demeanor and self-possession made it easy for him to assemble a band of followers to help him perpetrate his criminal ways throughout the Ozarks.

Hall was clever and crafty and had a strong sense of adventure and danger. The combination of being high-spirited and mercenary inspired him and his gang to attempt many daring holdups.

One such spate of criminal activity led to Hall's undoing and eventually cost him his life. But before he died, Hall admitted to burying a large fortune in gold coins, a fortune that apparently still lies concealed today in a small cave that is now beneath the waters of Table Rock Lake near the Missouri-Arkansas border.

Alonzus Hall and his gang were well known and feared throughout much of the Ozarks. They primarily ranged from just north of Springfield southward into Arkansas. Because law enforcement was not very sophisticated in this wild land, the bandits raided and pillaged at will, spreading terror throughout the ridges and valleys.

Early in April 1862, the gang was particularly active. The

intrepid Hall led his band of six cutthroats into the settlement of Centralia, Missouri, and at gunpoint robbed the bank of $52,000 in gold coin. Riding from town, the outlaws escaped southward into the hills. The townsfolk were reluctant to pursue them, for they were ill-equipped to chase well-armed and desperate outlaws into the wild, isolated regions where the criminals knew every trail and hiding place.

As the outlaws rode south, they stopped at two small farmsteads. After asking for and receiving food for themselves and grain for their horses, they robbed each of the farmers. At one farm they took $4,000 and at the other $6,000. Then they rode deeper into the secluded mountains.

Captain W.F. McCullough (sometimes spelled *McCulla)* was in command of a company of Union soldiers temporarily encamped near the Frisco Railroad tracks about twenty-five miles west of Springfield when he received word of the bank robbery at Centralia. McCullough had been following the Hall gang for several months, and now was ordered to search for them and to try to capture them at any cost.

The day after the bank robbery, McCullough received word that the outlaws had been seen traveling south along the old Wilderness Road and were last spotted in Greene County. He immediately ordered his men to pursue the bandits. The soldiers rode twelve hours straight without a break, hoping to overtake them within the next day or two. The outlaw trail led the soldiers through Greene County, into Christian County, and finally into Stone County and to the White River.

On the evening of the second day, one of the army scouts reported to McCullough that he had spotted the outlaws camped under a ledge near the bank of the White River about a mile away. At the same time, one of the outlaws who had been posted as a lookout had spotted the approaching soldiers and immediately alerted the others.

On receiving the news of the approaching army, Hall and another of the outlaws gathered up the gold coins and other money and carried it to a nearby cave. They divided the loot into four equal piles, stuffed each into a buckskin bag, and

102

hastily scraped out a shallow trench in the floor of the cave into which they placed the sacks. They covered the site with rocks and debris to conceal any traces of digging. By now Hall and his companion could hear gunshots coming from the campsite and knew that the soldiers had engaged his men in a battle. Hall and his companion raced toward the campground to join in the fight.

McCullough had launched a vicious attack on the desperadoes, who were heavily outnumbered and out-armed. The fighting was brief, lasting only about five minutes. By the time it was over, three of the Union troops and six of the outlaws were killed. Alonzus Hall had been shot through the stomach and was in poor shape when the soldiers found him.

Hall was bandaged, loaded into a wagon, and transported to a temporary bivouac area along the White River near present-day Reeds Spring. He suffered terribly throughout the night and the next day was taken to the Union Army General Hospital at Springfield.

The attending surgeon summoned to examine Hall's wound was Dr. Boucher (sometimes spelled *Bushay* and *Busha*). After looking at Hall's wound, Boucher deduced that a musket ball had penetrated his lower intestines, doing irreparable damage. He predicted Hall would not live for more than a day or two.

Several hours later Hall regained consciousness and Boucher informed him of his condition. Hall appeared silent and moody but resigned to his fate.

The next morning, however, he called Boucher to his bedside and asked if he could make a confession. As the surgeon was the ranking officer in the camp at the time, he agreed to take Hall's statement. Securing a hospital journal, he scribbled copious notes as the outlaw leader related the story of the recent robbery spree.

Hall told Boucher all that had transpired from the time of the Centralia Bank holdup until the attack by the Union soldiers at the campground on the White River. He said that the $62,000 was buried in a cave near the old ferryboat crossing where the Wilderness Road met the White River. He also asked Boucher to make certain the money he took from the farmers was returned to them.

Boucher took explicit notes of the confession, filling several pages of the journal. The next morning when he went to visit Hall, he found the patient had died.

Boucher was confused about what to do with Hall's information. His military training told him he should immediately file it with his superiors, but the potential wealth lying buried in a shallow cave less than a day's ride from the camp tempted him greatly. With dreams of riches awaiting him, Boucher hid the journal, expecting someday soon to be able to travel to the intersection of the Wilderness Road and the White River to retrieve the gold.

All too soon, however, the surgeon was transferred to a more active military post in the East. He left the journal hidden among some files in the hospital at Springfield, hoping to return for it.

There is no record that Boucher ever returned to Springfield. Hospital personnel discovered the journal a few years later.

By the turn of the century several people had read the notes in his journal. The descriptions of the robbery and subsequent flight of the outlaws through the Ozark Mountains were quite vivid, as were the accounts of the encounter with the Union soldiers and burying the $62,000 in gold coin and other money in the shallow cave.

The journal contained a thorough description of the cave in which the gold had been buried. Hall had said the cave was not very far from the overhanging ledge where they encountered the soldiers, because once they buried the loot it was only a very few minutes until the outlaw leader and his companion returned to the fray. The cave was described as being slightly illuminated as a result of sunshine beaming through a narrow crack in the limestone roof. The men buried the loot in the cave floor at the approximate center of the shaft of light.

It is an easy task to locate the point at which the old Wilderness Road intersects with the White River—it is quite apparent on the many maps of the region. It would also seem easy to locate the overhanging ledge under which the outlaws camped, as well as any small caves in the area. An overriding problem in the search for Hall's treasure, though, is that the rising waters of Table Rock Lake are believed to have completely submerged this site.

Near where the loot is thought to have been buried, the Kimberling (sometimes spelled *Kimberly)* Bridge has been built. Some say the construction of the bridge may have obliterated any traces of the overhang and the cave. Others claim that the site is intact but lies under several feet of lake water.

There is no evidence that the gold and money buried by Alonzus Hall were ever recovered. The consensus of most researchers of this event in Ozark history is that the treasure still lies in a shallow excavation in a small cave somewhere beneath the waters of Table Rock Lake.

The Strange Tale of Preacher Keith

One of the most bizarre tales ever to come out of the Ozarks involves an itinerant preacher and the strange way he hid his wealth. Residents of the Ozark Mountains in southwestern Missouri still talk about Preacher Keith. A few of his relatives who still live in the region maintain that the legends of this eccentric man and his lost fortune in gold are all true.

W.M. Keith arrived in the Missouri Ozarks around 1830. It is believed that he came from the Red River Valley area of Oklahoma, near where that great and muddy river was crossed by the Chisholm Trail. No one has an explanation for why he left Oklahoma and traveled east to the Ozarks. He arrived carrying only the clothes on his back and a well-worn Bible.

Shortly after Keith came to Missouri, he constructed a rude cabin near Reeds Spring. From the moment of his arrival, his neighbors regarded him as a bit odd. A tall and gangly man of Lincolnesque stature and profile, Keith had a habit of talking aloud to himself as he walked for miles up and down the area roads from dawn until dusk with no apparent destination in mind.

He survived well by living off the land, hunting, trapping, and performing seasonal jobs for area farmers. In spite of his odd manner, he was regarded as a competent worker and was generally well-liked.

After Keith had been in the area for several months, he proclaimed himself a preacher and filled his Sundays with visiting outlying areas and holding church services for any and all who would come to hear him. He loudly interpreted the Bible to the many hill folk who came to listen, conducting services in barns or under the shade of a convenient tree.

Soon he met and married a young girl whose name was Lee. Keith and his bride moved into the cabin near Reeds Spring and began to raise what ultimately became a large family.

Keith provided well for his family. In addition to the few coins passed on to him for his preaching and what he made from hunting and trapping, he planted the hillside near his cabin in corn. As his family grew he added extra rooms to the rustic cabin. He seemed to be a good husband and father.

In 1849, Preacher Keith heard about the discovery of gold in California. The lure of wealth waiting to be found in that far-away land was irresistible to him and, bidding his wife and children goodbye, he set out for the Golden State with the hope of striking it rich. And strike it rich he did.

Keith had great success in the California gold fields. After a year of panning the clear cold streams of the Sierra Nevada Mountains, he had accumulated a relatively large fortune. He converted his ore into gold coins, purchased passage on a steamer, sailed around the horn of South America, and eventually landed in New Orleans. There he bought two mules, onto which he loaded several leather sacks filled with his gold coins. He and the mules walked the entire distance from New Orleans back to the Ozark Mountains, where his family held a joyous reunion.

News of the preacher's fortune soon spread throughout this part of the Ozarks, and Keith became visibly annoyed that so many of his neighbors were aware of his wealth. He grew suspicious of all who chanced by his cabin and assumed that everyone was intent on taking his gold away from him. He threatened many visitors with his rifle and was known to stay awake nights guarding his property.

After several weeks of worrying about the security of his fortune, Keith loaded the gold onto the mules and carried it out into the woods beyond the cabin. Far from the prying eyes of his neighbors and family, he hid it in a location that remains secret to this day.

For reasons he never explained, Keith refused to reveal to members of his family the location of his wealth. His relatives claim he undertook and completed the task of hiding the gold in no longer than one hour, so it is assumed the fortune was stashed close to the old log cabin. Some believe the sacks of gold coins were secreted in one of the many limestone caves in the area.

Others who have researched the legend of Preacher Keith believe the eccentric fellow buried the gold somewhere near his orchard of apple, peach, and cherry trees, a source of pride for him. He spent many long hours pruning the trees and tending to the grove, which was a short distance from the cabin just beyond the immediate woods. Some say that when Keith needed a little cash, he would disappear into the woods in the direction of his orchard and reappear a few minutes later carrying a single twenty-dollar gold piece. He always laughingly informed people that the gold coins grew on the trees in his orchard.

Another strange twist to the Preacher Keith legend is the belief that he walled up the front of one of the caves in a nearby mountain and stashed his gold within.

From time to time Keith was observed hauling slabs of rock back into the woods some distance from the cabin. He would be gone for several hours, sometimes shooing away any who came near. When he returned to his cabin at the end of the day he had mortar splashed across the front of his overalls. Occasionally he would mention a "room" he was building in which he was going to hide his gold where no one could ever find it.

Keith also told of fashioning a large wooden door for the rock enclosure. He claimed the door was eight feet tall and four feet wide and made of heavy oak timbers that he cut and planed himself. Supposedly the huge door was fastened shut with a stout lock.

As if this were not strange enough, rumor also circulated that Keith had built a casket inside the small room of the walled-up cave! He claimed to his family one day that he had constructed a long casket from hand-riven pine boards. He said that when he was ready to die he would go to the walled-up room, lock the door, and lie in the casket surrounded by his wealth to wait for his Maker's call.

Preacher Keith visited his private hoard at least once a week for many years. During all that time his family had no inkling of the location of the cave or his treasure and, in spite of constant questioning, he refused to tell them.

As he grew older his behavior became more erratic and unpredictable. Fewer and fewer people showed up for his Sunday services, and most of the area residents believed the old man was touched.

None of this bothered Keith. He continued with his hunting and trapping and growing corn on the bare soil of the Ozark hillsides, providing for his family, and, despite the diminishing attendance at his services, preaching his Sunday sermons.

One morning Preacher Keith announced to his family that he was going hunting. He left the cabin after breakfast, walked out into the woods carrying his rifle, and was never again seen alive.

People in Reeds Spring just presumed Preacher Keith went to his mysterious cave and laid himself down to eternal rest in his homemade casket, surrounded by the twenty-dollar gold pieces he had hoarded so effectively for so long. They combed the woods near his cabin for several weeks after his disappearance but found neither the man nor the cave. Several people focused their search around the orchard, still believing that the wealth was concealed nearby, but they had no luck. Eventually the search was halted.

About two months after the disappearance of Preacher Keith, a local man was out hunting one evening when he discovered a badly decomposed corpse in an abandoned orchard in a hollow about four miles south of the Reeds Spring settlement. The body was seated on the ground and leaning up against the bole of a cherry tree. A rifle lay across its lap.

The hunter went for help and returned with three companions. They examined the body thoroughly but could find no wounds. Figuring the man must have died from a heart attack, they buried the body beneath the tree where it was found.

The men noticed that several large holes had been dug throughout most of the orchard, as though someone had been searching for something—what, they could not determine.

When word of the dead man reached Reeds Spring, several members of the Keith family went to see the hunter who had made the grisly discovery. He described the clothing and boots worn by the corpse and produced the rifle that was with it. The family agreed that the dead man must have been W.M. Keith.

What actually happened to Preacher Keith will probably never be known. Some believe that the old abandoned orchard in which he was found held the secret to his gold and that his cryptic comments about his gold growing on trees referred not to the orchard behind his cabin but to the one in which his body was discovered. The many holes in the abandoned orchard remain a mystery.

To this date the walled-up cave in which the eccentric old preacher was supposed to have hidden his gold has never been discovered.

And the empty casket must still lie in the dark room amidst the piles of gold coins, forever waiting for the owner who will never return.

Spanish Treasure Cave

Few legendary buried treasure locations in the Ozarks have received more attention than a mysterious cave about four miles north of Reeds Spring in Stone County.

There is little doubt among researchers that a fabulous wealth in gold and silver lies concealed deep within this cavern. However, a number of cave-ins and excavation attempts have combined to rearrange the interior passageways and chambers so that it now bears little resemblance to the site the Spaniards chose in the sixteenth century for caching a great fortune in gold and silver ingots.

In recent years a portion of the cave was made available for tourists who would make the short drive to the entrance from nearby Highway 65. The cave differs little from the many other limestone caves in the region, but a hundred years ago it was the center of one of the most intensive treasure hunts ever witnessed in the Ozarks.

The story begins sometime in 1888, though the exact date is uncertain. An old man, most often described as a Spaniard, appeared one day in the settlement of Joplin looking for work. He was hired to mop out one of the local taverns on a nightly basis, but had not been employed long when he came down with a serious illness, probably tuberculosis. Two men, Joplin residents and patrons of the tavern in which the old Spaniard was employed, took pity on the poor sick man, brought him to their room at a nearby hotel, and tended to his ailment. When he got progressively worse, a physician was summoned. After examining the Spaniard the doctor proclaimed he was dying

111

and had very little time left.

After the doctor left the old man summoned his two new friends to his bedside. He weakly waved an arm toward his small pile of modest belongings in the corner of the room and told the two men he wanted them to have his money and possessions in gratitude for their care. The two friends sat up the entire night with the old man, but by dawn he was dead.

Later that day when the men examined the old Spaniard's belongings they found only a few coins, almost enough to provide for a decent burial. The few garments he owned were little more than rags and the men elected to throw them away. As they gathered up the old clothes, a rolled parchment fell from the inside of an old worn coat. Examining it, the two men discovered it to be a map with legends and notations in Spanish. Applying what little Spanish they knew, they interpreted a most amazing story from the old parchment map.

Sometime during the sixteenth century, a group of Spanish soldiers and laborers under the command of one of Hernando De Soto's officers were transporting twenty mule-loads of gold and silver ingots through the Ozarks. The ore had been taken from mines far to the southwest in Texas and was being transported to the Mississippi River, where it was to be loaded onto flatboats, rafted to the Gulf of Mexico, and shipped to Spain. As the Spaniards wound their way through the Ozarks with the pack train in tow, they searched for signs of precious ore.

During an extended encampment in what is now southwestern Missouri, the Spaniards discovered a vein of silver in a cave, and the leader of the group gave orders to begin mining immediately. A crude log fort was constructed as protection against the coming winter and marauding Indians. The mining proceeded smoothly, but Indian attacks occurred with increasing frequency. Eventually the Spaniards decided to hide their gold and quit the area until it seemed safe to return.

After interpreting the old treasure map, the two friends decided that the old Spaniard had come into the Ozarks in search of the long-lost treasure cache and mine but apparently was never able to locate it.

Several weeks after the Spaniard's burial, the two men under-took a search for the cave described on the map. According to the description, the cave was supposed to be in a remote part of Stone County. The map indicated the search was to begin near three large trees arranged in a triangle. Each of the trees had strange crescent-shaped markings blazed onto the trunk. The markings pointed to the site of the fort constructed by the Spanish soldiers, which was supposed to be at the base of an overhanging bluff. Nearby, along the base of the same bluff, was the entrance to the treasure cave.

The map indicated the cave entrance was covered and dis-guised to look exactly like the rest of the bluff. To gain entrance to the cave a barrier had to be removed, exposing a low narrow opening. Once inside, however, the cave was large enough for a tall person to stand. The passageway extended deep into the bluff for over half a mile to where the ingots were stacked. As one explored the passageways, one would pass through thirteen large chambers, each containing impressive cavern formations. At the fourteenth and final chamber, one would find the cache of gold and silver hidden there by the Spaniards in 1522.

The two men searched for the three large trees arranged in a triangle but were never able to locate them. For two years they combed the area when time permitted, always hoping to dis-cover some telltale sign that would lead them to the treasure cave. Finally, after investing two years and a great deal of money in the fruitless search, they gave up and declared the whole episode a hoax. They turned the map over to a Webb City newspaper, which printed it in 1890.

A few months later, one of these newspapers came into the possession of a Stone County resident named J.J. Mease. Mease was no stranger to gold; he had hoped to strike it rich in the California Gold Rush of 1849 but finally came away with noth-ing. Discouraged, he returned to his Ozark Mountain homeland, but his dream of someday discovering gold remained very much alive.

Mease prospected for gold and silver throughout Stone County for a number of years. Following promising leads, he had opened several shafts in the hope of locating silver, but thus far it had eluded him.

Mease was as familiar with the terrain in Stone County as anyone, and when he examined the description of the old Spanish treasure cave in the newspaper, he was convinced he knew the location. He contacted a friend named H.R. Brewer and together they systematically searched for the cave.

One day in the summer of 1894, Mease and Brewer discovered the three large trees with barely discernible crescent-shaped markings on the trunks. Following the signs on the trees, the two men came to a high, overhanging limestone bluff. Near one end of the deeply recessed base of the bluff they found the rotted remains of several large logs and deduced they must have been part of the Spanish fort described on the map. The men observed that the fort had been situated in an ideal site—the overhanging bluff afforded protection from the weather and the position was quite defensible against the potential attack of hostile Indians. Several springs gushing clear cool water were found nearby.

But further examination of the bluff from one end to the other revealed no evidence of a cave! Several times Mease and Brewer searched back and forth along the rock wall, each time coming away perplexed. According to the map and the evidence this had to be the correct site, but they could find nothing.

Mease and Brewer enlisted the help of several neighbors, and soon nearly a dozen men were combing the area in search of some sign of a cavern opening. One afternoon, one of the men, H.O. Bruffet, was idly digging in the soil along the face of the bluff that had been examined at least a dozen times previously. Approximately a foot below the surface Bruffet unearthed a copper bowl. The other searchers were summoned, and together they examined the find. After cleaning most of the dirt from the vessel, Mease pointed to several Spanish symbols engraved into it. On a hunch the men began digging into the ground where the bowl had been discovered. After removing approximately three feet of earth they made an astounding discovery. There, under the layer of dirt that had covered it for centuries, was a large flat stone slab standing vertically against the base of the bluff. On its face were carved several symbols that matched many of the symbols on the old parchment map.

All this time it had never occurred to the men that the cave's entrance lay below the very soil they walked over. The level of the ground at the base of the bluff had been raised to conceal the entrance!

With considerable effort the men hammered the large stone into smaller pieces and removed it. Behind it was a low, narrow opening into a cave. Within the small entrance were several piles of ashes and charcoal suggesting human use or occupation some time in the past.

Just beyond the ashes, the floor of the cave dropped abruptly for a dozen feet before it leveled out again. Three men were lowered by rope to the bottom of the dangerous drop, where they discovered three skeletons. Among the bones were found odd pieces of metal that the men decided were parts of Spanish armor.

Also lying among the bones and artifacts was an ancient mold made of porcelain that was used to form ingots. The mold was six inches deep and approximately two and a half feet long. The inside of the mold was coated with a thin film of silver.

Along one side of the cavern wall at the bottom of the drop were several more inscriptions similar to the ones found on the stone slab that covered the opening.

Convinced that this was indeed the legendary cave that held the long-hidden Spanish treasure, the men agreed to form a company to remove the hoard and split the wealth equally. One of the men, C.C. Bush, volunteered to journey to Galena, the nearest large settlement, to obtain a formal deed to the land on which the cave was located. It turned out that the land was owned by the Frisco Railway, which agreed to sell it to the group for three dollars an acre. The men all contributed equally and purchased several acres of the surrounding land.

Several days later as the group began clearing away the soil and enlarging the opening to the cave, a young man appeared on the scene making inquiries about the digging. He was tall and well-dressed in the manner of an attorney. His skin was olive-colored and he spoke with a distinct Spanish accent. After querying area residents about the excavation in process, he appeared at the scene of the digging.

When introductions had been made, the newcomer came quickly to the point of his visit and made an offer of one thousand dollars for the deed to the land on which the excavation was taking place.

The men refused to sell. They had believed they were indeed on the threshold of finding and retrieving the long-lost Spanish fortune, and the appearance of this young Spaniard offering them a large amount of money convinced them that something of value was to be found inside the cave.

A few days elapsed since the Spaniard first appeared, and during that time Mease and Brewer became good friends with him and learned his reason for wanting to purchase the property.

The Spaniard had in his possession an ancient map similar to the one that had been found many years earlier in the belongings of the dead man at Joplin. This map resembled the one Mease had seen in the Webb City newspaper—it told of the twenty mule-loads of gold and silver, the fourteen chambers to be found inside the cave, and the existence of a thick vein of silver in the fourteenth chamber, a vein of almost pure ore that was mined and smelted by De Soto's men nearly four hundred years before.

The young Spaniard continued to make offers to the men, but all were refused. He left the area quietly and was never seen there again.

Once the opening of the cave had been enlarged and the hazard of the sudden drop overcome, the group entered the cave armed with torches, digging tools, and abundant enthusiasm.

Almost immediately they encountered problems. The floor of the cave was extremely difficult to traverse. Large chunks of rock had fallen from the fractured roof and blocked passage throughout. Water dripped continuously from the ceiling, making the footing slippery. The way through the cave was crooked and replete with sudden drops and rises, and it was only with great difficulty that the men were able to make any progress at all.

The first day of searching the cave took nearly fourteen hours and saw the discovery of only the first three of the large chambers referred to on the maps. One of the men suffered a broken leg and had to be carried out, a task that required almost two days.

On the next attempt to locate the treasure cache, the men carried a large supply of torches and candles as well as provisions to last for forty-eight hours. Their enthusiasm had remained undiminished, but this time they proceeded with greater caution, worrying and wondering what obstacles they might next confront.

On and on they pushed—crawling, walking, climbing, and sliding—for many hours. Finally they passed the thirteenth chamber. Spurred on by the anticipation of finding great wealth at the next turn in the dark passageway, they crawled forward only to encounter their greatest disappointment. When they arrived at what was to have been the fourteenth chamber they discovered it had been effectively sealed by a huge cave-in, with thousands of tons of rock and debris blocking the entrance.

Armed with only picks and shovels, the men began digging into the rubble, but it soon became obvious that they were unequal to the task. The mass of rock that stood between them and the treasure would take months, probably years, to remove by hand.

Discouraged, the men slowly made their way back to the surface to report their disappointment.

After many discussions, the company of men decided that whatever treasure might lie hidden deep within the inaccessible fourteenth chamber inside the mountain was not worth the effort it would take to excavate. The project was abandoned and the company dissolved, and all returned to their businesses, farms, and families.

The dream of finding the hidden wealth did not die in one of the men, however. Frank Mease, the son of J.J. Mease, was only a young boy at the time of the excavation. Frank Mease participated in the digging as enthusiastically as any of the men, doing far more than his fair share of work. He, more than any of the others, was terribly disappointed when it was announced the project was to be abandoned.

Like his father so many years before, Frank Mease nurtured a dream of wealth. As he grew to manhood he continued to nourish his dream—a dream that someday he would be the one to break into that mysterious fourteenth chamber and retrieve the ancient Spanish fortune.

Frank Mease decided to approach the problem of finding the treasure differently. He decided the task of removing the tons of rock debris could be made simpler if lights and power were available to men digging deep below the surface. Heretofore, tallow candles and grass torches had supplied the only light, and Mease believed there was a better way.

He observed that a swiftly flowing stream paralleled the main passageway through the cave. In order to use the energy of the flowing water, he constructed a flume that directed the stream to an area where he constructed a waterwheel turned by the flowing water. The wheel activated a generator that provided electricity for workers in the cave.

Once Mease had strung electric lights throughout most of the passageways and up to the fourteenth chamber, he examined the possibilities of directing some of the flowing water so that it would remove and carry away much of the rock and debris blocking the entrance to the treasure chamber.

As he was making arrangements to begin construction of his labor-saving idea, bad fortune befell the inventive Mease. A huge portion of the cavern roof gave way, and thousands of tons of weakened and crumbling limestone rock crashed to the floor, making passage beyond the third chamber impossible.

With the sudden cave-in, months of planning and labor vanished. After examining the disaster, Mease decided it would be impossible to penetrate the new obstacle.

Being an enterprising man, however, he attempted to make

the best of the unfortunate situation. Advertising the cave as the "Lost Spanish Treasure Cave," he graded a good road from nearby Highway 65 and charged tourists a small admission to visit the cave entrance, where he related the story of the lost treasure. As he profited from this enterprise, he built a gas station and a hotel at the intersection of the dirt road and the highway.

Given the existing research, the available evidence, and the huge investment of time and energy of many men, there seems to be little doubt that a great fortune in Spanish gold and silver does exist deep inside the limestone bluff in Stone County. Several experts on caverns in the Missouri Ozarks claim the Spanish treasure cave is most likely part of an extensive cavern system that runs for several miles deep below the surface. For many years people have searched for a passageway from one of the other caves in this system that might connect with the blocked fourteenth chamber of the Spanish treasure cave. A group of engineers has discussed sinking a vertical shaft from some point on the top of the bluff in an effort to enter the treasure chamber, but the exact below-ground position cannot be determined.

Others have maintained that when the Spaniards hid the treasure deep in the cave they placed a curse on it. The curse provided for disaster to befall any who would attempt to retrieve the great treasure except for the rightful heirs. If one believes in such curses, one must assume this one is still effective.

Buried Gold Coins
on the Missouri

The northern limits of the Ozark Mountains gradually change from the rugged dissected uplands of the interior. Here, near the Missouri River, one does not see the sharp features of the high ridges and deep valleys so often associated with the Ozarks, but rather a series of smoother, undulating hills broken here and there by level patches of prairie and floodplain.

Prosperous farms are found along the level plains adjacent to the Missouri River, with healthy crops growing from the rich dark alluvial soils. In places, ceaseless erosion by the river has exposed bluffs of the more resistant limestone rock of the Ozarks, bluffs that may extend to the river itself. Near one of these bluffs, in 1802, four French traders buried a copper kettle filled with gold coins.

At the beginning of the nineteenth century, St. Louis was the last settlement encountered by trappers, traders, adventurers, and any who would dare to brave the uncharted wilderness that lay to the west. To venture up the relatively unknown Missouri River and its tributaries to the faraway trading posts and beaver streams of Rocky Mountain wilderness was indeed a bold undertaking, for the dangers were many.

Trading posts had been established at the confluences of the Kaw, Republican, Platte, and other rivers, and it was to these sites that the trappers brought their beaver pelts each year to trade for supplies and equipment or to sell for gold.

Several times a year the Missouri River hosted relatively

heavy boat traffic as a result of the loads of furs being floated to St. Louis and the bundles of trade goods and chests of gold being carried to the trading posts upriver.

Some time during the second week of October 1802, a small wooden craft plied up the Missouri, rowed by four Frenchmen employed by a St. Louis-based fur trading company. They were transporting gold coins to trading posts far upriver for use in purchasing prime beaver pelts. In the center of the wooden craft sat a copper kettle filled to the top with gold coins of French origin. In addition to the gold there were several bundles of trade goods, but the primary responsibility of the Frenchmen was to protect the gold shipment—with their lives if necessary.

Rowing upstream on the Missouri River was no easy task, and the party of Frenchmen had not been on their journey long when they began to wish for it to end. They were eager to deliver the gold and the trade goods and be well on their way back to St. Louis before the first winter storms struck the area.

For several days the men rowed, slowly yet unceasingly forging their way against the strong current. Once leaving St. Louis, they were constantly on guard against hostile Indians known to frequent the region. At night they made camp on the riverbanks and posted a lookout. When they ventured inland to hunt for fresh meat, they always divided, one pair hunting while the other remained close to the boat and guarded the gold.

The Frenchmen had not seen a single Indian the entire time they had been on the river. They soon grew complacent and, while previously they constantly scanned the riverbanks with apprehension, they were now content to take turns napping.

Early in the evening of the fifth day of their journey, the men were rowing along and searching the riverbank for a suitable place to camp. They had passed several miles of low bluffs ranging along the south bank, looking for one set slightly back from the water and recessed enough to protect them from the weather.

As they examined the bluffs, dozens of screaming Indians came charging out of the willow break on the opposite shore. As the Frenchmen looked on in horror, the howling mob began

121

firing arrows at them and launching canoes into the river.

Grabbing oars, the four Frenchmen bent their backs to the rowing until the boat fairly skimmed across the surface of the water. In spite of their efforts, however, the small, light canoes of the Indians were gaining on them rapidly.

When it became obvious that the greatly outnumbered Frenchmen would soon be overtaken, they steered their boat to the south bank, deciding it would be easier to defend themselves on solid ground than in a boat on the river.

Landing, the men grabbed their firearms and some belongings and raced about sixty yards to the shelter of a nearby bluff. Two of the Frenchmen quickly returned to the boat, lifted the heavy kettle of coins, and wrestled it to the sanctuary of the bluff.

The sun was beginning to set just as the last two men reached the shelter. Hurriedly, they stacked rocks and tree limbs into an improvised fortress as they prepared for an attack from their pursuers.

The Indians beached their canoes and advanced. As they approached the shelter, a shot rang out from under the bluff and a musket ball penetrated the skull of one of the nearest Indians, dropping him immediately and causing the others to scatter for cover.

During the night the Frenchmen could observe the Indians moving about in the dark, establishing themselves in a semi-circle enclosing the bluff, effectively cutting off any escape route to the boat. The Indians made small camps of two to three men each and built fires to warm them from the chill of the autumn darkness. Throughout the night the four frightened Frenchmen watched the Indian campfires and dreaded the approaching dawn.

Daybreak was accompanied by the sudden arrival of a premature winter storm. A thick, heavy snow fell, reducing visibility to only a few feet, and accumulated to a depth of several inches within two hours. The storm appeared to inhibit the Indians' desire to launch an attack and they remained close to their fires. Once in a while one of them would shoot an arrow into the makeshift fortress under the bluff.

The Frenchmen made themselves as comfortable as possible under the adverse circumstances, but they were gradually running low on firewood and food. One of the men suffered severe frostbite and lay in agony near the small fire.

Another man who ventured forth to get food from the boat was attacked not far from the fortress and was forced to retreat to the shelter.

For four days the Frenchmen remained trapped. During that time the man suffering frostbite died and was buried during the dark of night a short distance from the bluff. The three remaining Frenchmen decided their only chance for survival was to make a break for the boat and try to return to St. Louis.

They realized they would never be able to carry the heavy gold-filled copper kettle while they made their escape, so just after sundown of the fourth day, they carried it some distance from the fortress and buried it, hoping to return for it in the future. After waiting for several hours in the hope that most of the Indians would be sleeping, the three stole quietly into the night toward the river.

Halfway to the boat they were discovered by Indian scouts. The race was on. Firing their single-shot muskets into the group of pursuers, the Frenchmen managed to kill two of the Indians during their flight. Unfortunately, however, only one of the traders made it to the boat.

In pain from severe arrow wounds, the surviving Frenchman launched the boat into the river and, lying in the bottom of the craft, let the current carry him downstream toward St. Louis. For unknown reasons the Indians did not take up pursuit.

Bleeding profusely and lapsing in and out of consciousness, the lone Frenchman floated easily down the river it had taken so much effort to travel only a few days earlier. Somehow he reached St. Louis. Delirious and near death, he was taken from the boat and carried to a physician. The medical man treated the poor trader's arrow wounds and frostbite, but his limbs were so badly frozen that they had to be amputated.

Several days later when the Frenchman regained consciousness, he related the story of the Indian attack, the loss of his

123

comrades, the burying of the gold, and the harrowing escape. He provided a representative of the French fur trading company with a detailed description of the bluff under which the men had taken shelter and told them precisely where the gold was hidden. The fur trading company decided to send a party of men in the spring to retrieve it.

When spring came, however, no such search party was to be sent out because of the recurring news that the Indians of the region were in a hostile mood and had killed several traders trying to pass through the territory.

The following year the trading company organized a group of French trappers to journey to the bluff and retrieve the gold. This group was beset with bad luck, and after several days of travel they all suffered an attack of dysentery and had to return to St. Louis. The fur trading company had other business to attend to, and soon the matter of the buried copper kettle filled with gold coins was forgotten.

In 1835, a large group of French trappers undertook a journey up the Missouri River from St. Louis toward the rich trapping grounds of the Rockies. Five boats in all carried the members of this well-armed party. The sight of these seasoned mountain men must have discouraged Indian attacks, for none of the hostiles was seen.

Several men in this party could recall the story of the buried coins and were determined to search for them. But in the vicinity of the bluff, they encountered a surprise. The ever-shifting channel of the Missouri River had moved. A great flood had caused the river to jump its banks and cut a new channel about a quarter of a mile north of the old one. Still, the men believed that with a little luck they could find the gold. They established a camp along the river and spent several weeks searching the area but were never able to locate the buried wealth.

Years passed, and the once-fertile beaver streams of the Rocky Mountains were being trapped out. The shrinking supply, coupled with the reduced demand for the belly fur of the beaver for hats, signaled the end for trappers and traders in this part of the country. Human traffic up and down the Missouri River diminished to almost nothing. Not until after the Civil War did settlers began swarming westward again, across the Mississippi River and toward the Rocky Mountains and the Pacific coast.

Several newcomers discovered the rich alluvial soils of the Missouri River floodplain at the northern edge of the Ozark Mountains and settled there to try their luck at farming. Soon the entire area was under cultivation. The homesteaders planted crops on every available patch of the fertile river soil, even right up to the bases of several bluffs that fronted the Missouri.

During the 1930s some workmen were preparing a foundation for a new home near the base of one of these bluffs across from the point where the Grand River joins the Missouri. As they were digging into the soft earth they uncovered a skeleton under a low mound. Lying beside the skeleton in this shallow grave was a small copper disc on which was engraved the image of the French flag. Subsequent investigation revealed that a French fur-trading company once based in St. Louis issued discs such as this one to their representatives.

A local medical doctor examined the skeleton and declared it to be that of a white man. It was assumed to be the skeleton of the Frenchman who had frozen to death during the conflict with the Indians in 1802.

The discovery of the skeleton generated renewed excitement about the possibility of a huge fortune in gold coins being cached in the area. Though no organized search had been undertaken since 1835, the tale of the buried treasure was widely known throughout the region and had long since entered the realm of Ozark folklore.

One day an old Indian woman arrived in the area and began making inquiries about the skeleton. Her forefathers had often told her the story of the Indian siege and the great fight waged by the Frenchmen. She possessed a French gold coin of great antiquity and claimed she had some knowledge of the buried gold. For several days she searched many of the local bluffs but came away empty-handed.

125

Around 1940, a farmer plowed up a gold coin while working in his field within thirty yards of a low limestone bluff. The coin bore French inscriptions, and was dated 1796. After showing the coin to several people, the farmer learned it may have been part of the buried treasure he had often heard about as a child. He returned to his field to try to relocate his find but was never successful.

The residents of this part of the Ozarks still firmly believe in the existence of the buried copper kettle filled with gold coins. However, they are quick to point out that there is other wealth to be found here, wealth that to them is far more important than gold: the rich agricultural lands that earn many a livelihood, provide food, and keep the people in tune with the soil and nature. It is not important to them whether the gold is ever found. What is important is the harmony they have achieved with the land, the satisfaction of successfully working a piece of God-given ground and the peace that comes with that effort.

They also talk of the wealth of tales of the early days: tales of adventure, Indian battles, explorers, their ancestors who settled this land, and buried gold. They are proud of their heritage, which includes wonderful stories handed down to them—stories and tales of the region for old folks to relate to their grandchildren. The stories are many and are an enduring part of their culture.

The tales, they readily tell you, can be had for the asking. The gold, buried somewhere in a field near a limestone bluff, is still to be found.

The Lost Cave of Silver

In the year 1800, two friends living in St. Louis undertook an adventure that led them to what may have been one of the richest silver mines on the North American continent. Unfortunately, it also led to their death.

The pair, one a Frenchman and the other a black man, met while working on the docks in St. Louis, where they unloaded freight from the many boats that journeyed up the Mississippi River from New Orleans.

Somehow they acquired an ancient map on which was marked the location of a rich silver deposit in the Ozark Mountains. The silver mine was supposedly very rich and had been worked for many centuries by the local Indians. One version of this tale relates that the friends found the map tucked into the pocket of a coat worn by a dead Indian they discovered near the loading docks. Another claims one of the men won the map in a poker game.

At any rate, the two men persuaded a local businessman to finance an expedition into the remote Ozark Mountains to look for the mine. The businessman agreed in exchange for a share of the wealth. He outfitted the men with good riding horses, a string of pack mules, and supplies to last for several weeks, and they departed for the interior of the Ozarks.

The first two days of the journey were uneventful. The Frenchman maintained a diary and would occasionally scribble notes into it as they rode along.

On the third day of traveling, the men discovered they were being followed by Indians who remained approximately a hundred yards behind, apparently trailing them but obviously in no particular hurry to overtake them. The two friends decided to ride ahead at a faster pace and find a place to hide and let the Indians pass them. They guided their mounts and pack animals into a deep thicket of trees some distance away from the main trail, and when they felt it was safe to proceed they set out once again toward the area indicated on the map. They met Indians a few other times but were neither approached nor threatened by them.

A few days later, following the directions provided on the map, they came to the silver mine. It was not a mine at all, but rather a natural cavern. Sometime in the distant geological past a great earthquake had struck this region, shattering many of the rock strata, severely fracturing the interior of the cave, and exposing a large vein of almost pure silver ore. The vein was described in the Frenchman's diary as being six feet high and about a foot wide.

Evidence of prior mining of the silver lay all about the cave. The men also found a crude smelter in which the ore was apparently melted down and formed into ingots. Several skeletons were also inside the cave.

The two men explored the inside of the cave for several hours and then set about the business of preparing a camp. During the evening meal the Frenchman entered the experiences off the day in his diary.

During the next two weeks, the men dug about twenty-five pounds of pure silver from the rich vein. One evening as they were filling their packs with the ore, they spotted several Indians watching them from the nearby ridges. Fearing hostile action, the men decided they should abandon the area that same night. They returned to the cave and covered the entrance in the hope that others would not discover the silver. At nightfall they quietly broke camp and stole away in the darkness.

During their flight from the Indians, the two friends became lost. Instead of traveling along the trail that would lead them back to St. Louis, they found themselves several miles west of the silver cave. While they debated about the correct route, they noticed that the Indians were still trailing them.

Deciding they would have a better chance if they split up, the two men divided the silver and rode away in different directions.

The Frenchman continued to travel westward for two days and then circled toward the north, eventually coming upon a trail that led to St. Louis. On the afternoon of the third day on this trail, he came upon the body of his friend. The body was lying in the middle of the trail and had over twenty-five arrows protruding from it. The horse and pack mules were nowhere in sight.

The friend had been dead for only a short time and the Frenchman feared the Indians might be close by. Taking a few moments to enter the information in his diary, he mounted up and fled the area at a gallop.

That evening as he set up camp on a ridge several miles away, the Frenchman discovered he was surrounded by Indians who were slowly and deliberately closing in on him. Realizing he would soon meet death in the manner of his friend, he scribbled some final notes in his diary. As the Indians approached, he placed the diary and the map to the silver cave into a pocket in his coat and sat back to await his fate.

Several days later a party of trappers chanced upon his body. As they prepared to bury him they discovered the map and diary stuffed into the coat. Reading his final entry, they learned how he met his death at the hands of the Indians. There was a notation in the diary requesting anyone who ever found it to return it and the map to the businessman in St. Louis who financed the search for the silver cave.

Several days later when the trappers arrived in St. Louis, they turned the Frenchman's belongings over to the businessman. Discouraged by the fate of the two men he had backed, he was unwilling to organize another expedition into the hostile Ozark Mountains in search of the cave. After several months had passed he made the contents of the Frenchman's diary public.

The diary provided directions to the silver cave. It described a fast-flowing creek that gushed out of a limestone cliff and ran for some distance before joining a larger river flowing from the southwest. From the point of this confluence, the two men had traveled northwest for about seven miles to a small valley oriented north-south. From this valley they entered a narrow ravine between two tall bluffs. Deep in this ravine was the fabled cave of silver.

Researchers who have studied the diary and map believe the stream described is the Roaring River. The larger river that flows from the southwest can only be the White River. Thus the lost silver cave would be south of the settlement of White Rock.

Indian hostilities in the deep Ozarks prevented another search for the silver cave for several years and soon the matter was forgotten. Many years later when the diary and map were rediscovered, interest in the mine was renewed and several organized search parties entered the region.

While the directions to the lost cave of silver are clear and precise and should lead a searcher directly to the mouth of the cavern, a significant obstacle has intruded. The location described in the dead Frenchman's diary is now deep under the waters of Table Rock Lake.

Other Tales of
Treasure in Missouri

The Treasure in the Well

John Hankins was a successful farmer who grew corn and feed in one of the broad creek bottoms in the Missouri Ozarks. He and his wife lived modestly in a log cabin he had built. They had no children of their own, but two of Mrs. Hankins's brothers farmed nearby, and the Hankins cabin often was host to nieces and nephews for desserts and storytelling.

Hankins's farm made a decent profit year after year, and he and his wife lived well. He was able to make deposits in the bank at the nearest settlement each year from the sale of his crops and livestock, but he never completely trusted financial institutions to safeguard his money. He made the bank deposits at the insistence of his wife, but unknown to her he occasionally hid money in a secret location on the farm.

Early one morning Farmer Hankins finished breakfast and went to the barn to hitch the mower to his team of mules. Mrs. Hankins was clearing the breakfast dishes when she heard a commotion in the barn. She called out to her husband but received no response. Running to the barn she discovered Hankins lying next to one of the stalls, unconscious and bleeding from the head. Apparently one of the mules had kicked him as he tried to hitch up the mower.

As Mrs. Hankins dragged her husband from the barn he

opened his eyes and tried to speak to her. Though dazed and delirious, he pointed to the well near the house and muttered something about money. When his wife asked him what he meant he again waved an arm toward the well and repeated the word "money." Then he died.

With the help of her brothers, Mrs. Hankins continued to run the farm. One evening as she and her two brothers were seated around the kitchen table, she related her husband's dying words about the well and the money. The next morning the brothers went out to the old well to examine it.

The well had been hand-dug by Hankins many years earlier and the water level could be seen at a depth of about twenty feet. A handmade oak bucket was raised and lowered by means of a sturdy windlass. One of the brothers, seated on the old bucket, was lowered into the well. As he descended he examined the stone sides for hiding places but found the entire wall solidly mortared. When he reached the water line he probed the bottom with a stick and again found nothing. They ultimately decided that Farmer Hankins must have been delirious and didn't know what he was saying.

The following week the well was covered over, the windlass taken down, and a hand pump installed to make the drawing of the water easier for Mrs. Hankins. The old oak bucket was taken to the barn and hung from a nail near the stall where Farmer Hankins was kicked by a mule.

One day about a year later one of the Widow Hankins's brothers arrived at the farm to help with the planting. He brought along his two young sons, who found the old barn a wonderful place to play. The boys entertained themselves in the barn loft playing games in the loose hay stored there.

Eventually tiring of their game, they were climbing down the ladder when one of them accidentally knocked the oak bucket from the nail on which it had hung for the past year. When the bucket hit the floor of the barn, one of the metal bands holding it together slipped off and the bucket came apart. Lying among the pieces were twenty twenty-five-dollar gold coins!

When the brother examined the old bucket he discovered it

had a false bottom in which the gold coins had been concealed.

On being told of the discovery, the Widow Hankins realized that her late husband was attempting to tell her about the hidden gold in the bucket hanging in the well.

The Pot of Gold

The Civil War was responsible for many tragedies. Well over half a million men were killed in battle, and many thousands more returned home shattered and confused as a result of their violent experiences.

One such man was a veteran of the bloody Battle of Wilson's Creek. The atrocities he witnessed during this fight left him so crazed that he was eventually released from his military duties and returned to his home in Cedar County.

The soldier spoke incoherently yet continuously about a buried pot of gold near a church. At first a few people were interested in the story, but they soon became convinced the poor ex-soldier had truly lost his mind and they paid less and less attention to him.

Several years passed and the veteran slowly improved. He was eventually able to hold down a job and provide adequately for his family. His memory of the buried pot of gold also became increasingly clear.

He recalled that he and his two closest friends, on joining the army, agreed to pool their life savings and bury it in an old iron kettle until the war was over. During this time there were no banks in the area, so it was common for people to bury their wealth.

The three of them filled the pot nearly to the top with twenty-dollar gold pieces. With great difficulty, the three men managed to carry the heavy kettle to a church near the small settlement of Church Hollow and bury it in the graveyard. Then they carved a map showing the location of the buried kettle on a nearby flat stone.

The army veteran later learned that the two friends had been killed in the war and left no surviving relatives. He returned to the graveyard at the Church Hollow settlement to dig up the kettle but could not remember the exact place where it was buried. He searched for the flat rock on which the map was carved and discovered it had been moved, thus making the directional notations useless.

Somewhere in the old graveyard, next to a church that has long since fallen down, rests an iron kettle filled with gold coins.

The Lost Jack Fork Copper Mine

Gold and silver are not the only riches to be found in the Ozark Mountains. During the 1850s, a man named John Slater discovered a rich copper deposit and mined over fifty thousand dollars worth of the ore.

John Slater had heard many stories of gold and silver being discovered in the Ozarks and decided to try to find some for himself. He confined his prospecting to an area near the Current River about four miles above the mouth of Jack's Fork Creek. He had no luck finding gold or silver, but he accidentally discovered a rich deposit of copper.

Slater investigated the possibilities of filing a claim on the land where the copper deposit was located but found that it already belonged to someone else. Afraid of relinquishing his discovery, he filed a claim on an adjacent parcel of land and secretly worked the copper mine.

For four years Slater dug copper ore out of the ground and ferried it downriver, where it was eventually sold in New Orleans. Records there indicate he was paid over fifty thousand dollars for his crudely refined copper.

Slater was destined to be foiled, however. During this period the United States government sent representatives into the Ozark Mountains to conduct a formal survey of the land. The survey revealed that Slater's official claim was actually on land that belonged to someone else. An error had been made when Slater filed on the claim, but the U.S. survey was the final word on the matter and Slater was told to relinquish his claim. Fearful that contesting the claim might lead to the discovery of the copper mine, Slater decided to shut down his operation and abandon the area for a time. He covered the entrance to the mine and removed all evidence of mining. He then moved to St. Louis, intending to live there until he could return to the Jack's Fork area and purchase the land on which the mine was located.

Unfortunately, Slater died in St. Louis before he had a chance to carry out his plan. No trace of his copper mine has ever been found.

Fur Trapper's Lost Silver Coins

For many years the trapping of beaver and other fur-bearing animals in the Ozark Mountains provided a good living for the hardy souls who dared risk life and limb in country that was favored by hostile Indians and bandits on the run from the law.

As the nineteenth century drew to a close, however, the demand for furs dropped considerably. As a result, trapping decreased dramatically to the point where only a handful of persistent men entered the mountains each year to harvest pelts.

One of the more successful of these trappers was a Frenchman named Boucher who settled in the area of West Plains, Missouri. Boucher built a sturdy log cabin and moved his wife and daughter into it.

During the winter of 1901-02, Boucher purchased additional traps and supplies and set about laying trap lines in the hope that this would be his most profitable year. The winter was colder than normal and snow fell nearly every day. As a result the coats of the animals were thick and full and Boucher believed they would surely bring a good price come spring.

When spring arrived, Boucher loaded his pelts onto several pack animals and departed for the trading post at nearby Cape Girardeau. As he suspected, his pelts sold for top dollar. With his money, he purchased supplies and returned to his homestead with four hundred silver dollars jangling in his saddlebags.

On the second day of his journey home, Boucher noticed two men following him. He immediately suspected they knew about the money he carried in his saddlebags and were intent on robbing him. He believed the men would wait until he made camp for the night and then try to kill him and take the money. Boucher decided to foil the would-be bandits and, instead of stopping for the night, he pushed on toward his cabin in the hope of reaching it around dawn of the next day.

Just after dawn, Boucher was only three miles from his cabin when he spotted the two men who had been following him. The men were now approaching the trapper at a gallop, quickly narrowing the distance between them and their quarry. Boucher quirted his own mount and pack animals and rode hard toward the cabin.

Riding up to the front door, Boucher called his wife outside and told her he was being pursued and to act as if she didn't know him. He said he was going to ride over to the pond to bury the money and then circle back after the pursuers had left. Boucher then disappeared into the woods, riding toward the pond about a quarter of a mile away.

Within minutes the two men rode up to the cabin and called the inhabitants out. Boucher's wife came out onto the porch, her small daughter clutching at her apron. The men asked her if she had seen anyone ride by and she replied that one man had passed by earlier without stopping. They tipped their hats to her and rode on.

For the rest of the day and all that night Mrs. Boucher awaited her husband's return. When he had not arrived by dawn, she walked all the way to West Plains to get help. After hearing her story, several men volunteered to organize a search party.

The search centered near the pond, but nothing was ever found—no horses, no money, no Boucher. The trapper was never seen again.

What happened to Boucher? Did the pursuers catch him before he had a chance to hide the money? Was he killed? Many people believe the Frenchman buried the money before he was overtaken by the robbers. They suspect that Boucher was killed and his body hidden and his horse and pack animals stolen. They also believe that buried near the pond is an old rotted saddlebag containing four hundred silver dollars.

Hidden Treasure near Springfield

In the early 1930s a prominent Springfield family came into possession of a mysterious letter that described a cave in the region containing a huge Spanish treasure. The letter was written in Delverte, Mexico, and dated May 10, 1858. With great difficulty it was translated into English, and the Springfield *News and Leader* published it in July 1935. Here are the entire contents of that letter:

José Carozzo:
Go to what is now called Springfield,
Greene County, Missouri. It is a village about
twenty miles up the James River above the
old Spanish town of Levarro. Leave the
James River and go to Springfield. It has an
open square in the center. There is an old
road or trail that leaves from the southwest
corner of the square and runs southwest.
Follow this about two and one-half miles.
You will come to a dim road running east and
west. Go west on this road about a half-mile
and you will come to a big spring, some big
timber, and two or three old cabins.
If you look carefully, you will find some
sinks in the ground about four hundred paces
southwest of the big spring, and across the
creek there is a bluff. About three hundred
paces from the center of the bluff and down
the creek, there is another spring, not so
large as the first. Somewhere near the center

of the bluff, and fronting north on the creek, was the main entrance to the cave. It was filled up and covered by a big stone and there are three turkey tracks carved on the stone in a straight line east and west, and two of the same above. Remove this stone and also the filling for twelve or thirteen feet, and you will find a passage that descends for about twelve feet. When you reach the bottom of this descent, you will find a passage bearing nearly south. A little farther on you will find one running southeast, a little farther one running southwest. This is a false passage about thirty feet in length. It was cut to reach a deeper passage coming under the creek from the south side. It was abandoned when the new entrance was made.

This one you follow is the one running nearly south and dips down. You follow this until you enter a large room being used to work as a smelter to make bullion and Spanish money. The tools are there. My father and brother worked there years ago, and they have taken some from there after the Spanish left that country. There is plenty more for a dozen people, and more in sight.

If you cannot find it by these directions, you follow the creek that runs through Springfield and runs southwest. Follow it out to the flat or bottom where you will find a big spring, and just beyond the big spring about three hundred paces there is another creek coming into this creek a little south of east, and it comes together a little north of the east bluff where the cave is, dividing this bluff opposite the big spring and the bluff

138

where the creek runs together. The creek here runs a little south of west.

I think the entrance to the mines was near the center of the bluff, on the north side, fronting the creek and above high water. When you leave the east and west dim road, there are three large oak trees. They are marked: The first tree is marked with a turkey foot; the second tree with two turkey feet; and the third tree has two turkey feet cut on the north side of the tree and pointing south by west. The spring is on the south side of the creek. Four hundred and ninety-six paces from the spring, southwest on the south side of the creek, is the entrance to the mines on the north side of the bluff near the creek.

Be patient and you will find it as the above is described. There are three kegs of gold stored in a niche in the big room, covered with gravel and broken stones.

José, if you succeed in finding this, be on your guard as to Saville.

Interestingly, several years later another letter describing the exact same treasure was discovered. The latest letter, written in the 1890s, had different handwriting but provides essentially the same directions to the cave. The description of the treasure also matches that of the first letter.

Around 1939 yet another letter was found, again providing directions to the cave and the treasure. The letter had fallen into the hands of two men who were using it as a guide to locate the cave. Following the directions in the letter, they found the cave. They removed the stone covering the opening as well as the fill dirt. The interior of the cave closely matched the description in the letter and, though they claimed they conducted a thorough search, the men did not find any treasure.

139

Thirty Bags of Gold

In 1884 a man arrived at the settlement of Lanagan, Missouri, bearing an ancient map purporting to show where thirty bags of gold had been buried over a century earlier. The man was purposely vague about how he had come into possession of the map and provided inquirers only his name, which was Von Wormer.

Tales of buried gold in and around the Lanagan area are common even today. The stories vary according to their teller, but they all involve a group of Mexican miners passing through the area on their way to New Orleans in the early eighteenth century. Exactly where the miners came from was a mystery, but they were leading a pack train bearing thirty bags of gold ore. On approaching the place called Bear Hollow, the miners were attacked by Indians. The frightened Mexicans fought gallantly and succeeded in repelling the attack but suffered severe casualties. Half of the men were killed and most of the pack animals were killed or wounded.

During the night the Indians gathered in preparation for a dawn assault. Meanwhile, the miners were burying their dead comrades. Then they gathered the thirty bags of gold and stuffed them into a nearby deep crevice adjacent to a small stream.

Relieved of their burden, the surviving miners escaped during the night, hoping someday to return for the fortune in gold they had secreted in the rock crevice.

Armed with his map, Von Wormer searched the region around Bear Hollow and claimed to have found the graves of the slain Spaniards. He related that he had dug up several of the graves and discovered mining tools that had been buried with the dead men.

The map was vague about the precise location of the rock crevice in which the thirty bags of gold were cached. It also appeared to Von Wormer that severe erosion during the past century had modified the little valley to the degree that it bore scant resemblance to what was sketched on the map. Unable to

140

locate the gold, Von Wormer left the area, never to be seen again.

In 1928, another man arrived in Lanagan looking for the thirty bags of gold. This man was also in possession of a well-worn map and he spent a great deal of time scouring the Bear Hollow area. After two weeks of searching he returned to Lanagan, where it was learned he was the son of Von Wormer, who had searched for the gold forty-four years earlier!

Buried Jewelry at Neosho Falls

In 1870 a young man moved with his new bride into his family's ancestral home in Toledo, Spain. Over the next few weeks the newlyweds began remodeling the large old home. They had plans to raise a large family and wanted to remake the house according to their perceived needs.

While tearing down a wall in the house the young man discovered an old snuff box concealed within. Inside the box he found a weathered manuscript that gave a detailed account of his grandfather's search for El Dorado.

When the young man showed the manuscript to his mother she told him the story of his adventurous grandfather.

The grandfather had been a soldier and had traveled around the world. When he resigned his commission in the Spanish army he was not content to remain home doing nothing. Always intrigued by the Spanish search for El Dorado nearly two centuries earlier, he organized a party of adventurers to journey to the New World to take up where Coronado left off. He located a financial backer who provided the men with a fortune in jewels to be sold or traded along the way for supplies.

The men sailed to the New World but were never successful in discovering the fabled lost city of gold. Instead of digging up treasure, however, the party of adventurers was responsible for burying some. During one point of the journey, they decided to bury the container of jewelry and retrieve it at a later time. For reasons never explained the box of jewels was never recovered and the old manuscript provided a detailed description of its location:

> Proceed up the river called the Mississippi
> beyond where it is joined by the Red River,
> thence up the Arkansas River to the
> promontory known as Dardanelle Rocks.
> Passing this point proceed another one
> hundred miles upriver. From here, travel
> overland due north for fifteen days to an area
> wherein is located a waterfall, the only one
> to be found in the area. At a point halfway
> between the falls and a small creek to the
> north will be found a large flat rock with an
> arrow carved upon the surface. From this
> rock walk ninety paces east, the direction in
> which the arrow is pointed. Then walk ten
> paces south. The box of jewelry is buried
> here.

The young man who discovered the old manuscript in the snuff box journeyed to America in 1880 to search for the treasure. His trip up the Mississippi and Arkansas rivers was uneventful, but when he reached the Ozark Mountains he became lost and wandered around for many days. He nearly died from starvation and exposure, but somehow, after several weeks of searching, found the flat stone on which the arrow was carved—though he failed to locate the buried jewelry.

Following the directions given in the old manuscript, one will arrive at a waterfall near Neosho, Missouri. A short distance to the north of the waterfall is Turkey Creek. In between these two landmarks supposedly lies the large flat stone with an arrow carved into it.

It is suspected that the grandson who searched for the box of jewelry had become disoriented as a result of the hardships he endured and had difficulty identifying the exact location at which the treasure was buried.

Given the many years that have elapsed since the box of jewelry was buried, it is likely that the image of the arrow has long since eroded away, or that the tangles of briars and brush in the little valley have covered the stone. The box of jewelry most likely still lies buried, approximately one hundred steps east of a point midway between Neosho Falls and Turkey Creek.

OKLAHOMA

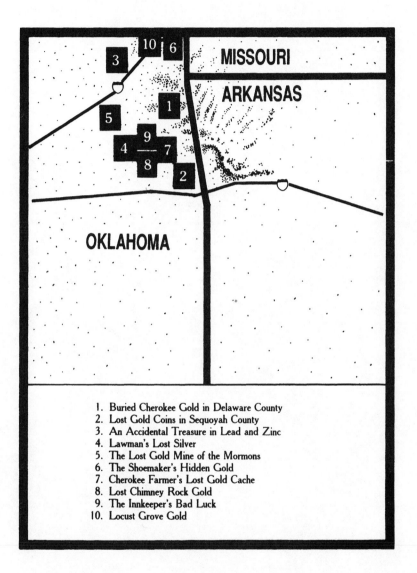

1. Buried Cherokee Gold in Delaware County
2. Lost Gold Coins in Sequoyah County
3. An Accidental Treasure in Lead and Zinc
4. Lawman's Lost Silver
5. The Lost Gold Mine of the Mormons
6. The Shoemaker's Hidden Gold
7. Cherokee Farmer's Lost Gold Cache
8. Lost Chimney Rock Gold
9. The Innkeeper's Bad Luck
10. Locust Grove Gold

Buried Cherokee Gold
in Delaware County

In 1830, the United States forcibly removed thousands of Indians from their homelands in the southeastern part of the country, including Florida, Georgia, and the Carolinas. Affected were what came to be known as the Five Civilized Tribes: Cherokee, Choctaw, Chickasaw, Creek, and Seminole. Most of the Indians transplanted to Indian Territory (now Oklahoma) were provided with plots of land for farming. Many of them went willingly, but some were not anxious to vacate age-old homelands, the lands that had been settled and occupied by their ancestors for countless generations.

Many of the Indians who were not inclined to move had large farmsteads, some of them equal to the largest plantations that were to evolve in the South over the next few years. Some of the more prominent and powerful Indians owned slaves, sometimes numbering into the hundreds.

One such successful farmer was named Lacey Mouse. Mouse owned one of the largest Indian plantations in the Carolinas and was not enthusiastic about abandoning it for the journey to Oklahoma. He tried to bribe government officials to let him remain, but to no avail. Loading his possessions on several wagons and taking about thirty of his slaves, he left for Indian Territory.

Along the way, Mouse's slaves heard many stories about fiercely cold winters awaiting them in Oklahoma, and they feared they would freeze to death if they moved there. During the trip several of them escaped. By the time Mouse reached the Mississippi River he decided to sell the dozen that remained.

Lacey Mouse always prided himself in having the strongest, hardest-working slaves in the land of the Cherokees. This "prime stock" brought top dollar and Lacey Mouse was paid off with a large bag of gold. He added this to the already large purse of wealth he had accumulated from years of farming in the Carolinas.

A few weeks later, he arrived at his parcel of land in the western part of Delaware County in the low rolling foothills of the Ozarks.

The story soon spread that Lacey Mouse was a wealthy man, but he always refused to discuss the amount of gold he possessed. Fearful that someone might try to take his gold from him, Mouse buried his fortune somewhere on his land one night.

Mouse operated a successful farm in Delaware County for many years and became one of the more prosperous Indians in the territory. He was respected by all who knew him and was eventually elected to some minor governmental position.

One evening in 1864, Lacey Mouse and a visiting relative had just completed their evening meal when they heard riders approach. Fearing trouble, Mouse sent the cook and housekeeper out the back door and encouraged his relative to hide under the bed. Mouse took a seat, lit his pipe, and waited to see what would happen. Within moments, three men stormed into the cabin and demanded Mouse's gold. Calmly, the Cherokee farmer refused. At this point one of the men bound him while the others searched the cabin for the gold. Remarkably, the outlaws never discovered the relative hiding under the bed.

When they couldn't find the gold, one of the men pulled a pistol from his belt and held the tip of the barrel to Mouse's head, telling him he would die if he didn't reveal the location of his wealth. Again Mouse refused, and was instantly shot through the head. After searching the cabin for a few more minutes, the outlaws fled, leaving the fearful relative cowering under the bed on which lay the dead Cherokee.

With the first light of morning, the relative came out from his hiding place, ran to the cabin of the nearest neighbor, and told the story of the murder. A group of men made an attempt to track the killers of Lacey Mouse, but lost the trail just a few miles from the farm. The men were never found.

The next morning, Lacey Mouse was laid to rest in a small plot on his farm.

Speculation immediately turned to the whereabouts of Lacey Mouse's wealth. Within days after the burial, local residents searched all over his farm to see if they could discover the Cherokee farmer's gold, but with no success.

Over the years the story of Lacey Mouse and his great wealth took on legendary proportions in the Indian Nations. Several organized attempts were made to locate the hiding place of Mouse's gold, but all ended in failure.

One day in 1943, according to a story told by an aged area resident, a hired hand was preparing some ground on what was once the Lacey Mouse farm. Using a two-horse team, the farm hand was plowing rows and breaking up an area of long dormant soil, readying it for a crop of corn.

The hand worked for most of the day, unhitched the animals, fed them, and put them up for the night. Just before sundown and just after supper, he walked out to the field to admire his work. Out near the middle of the field he saw the glimmer of the setting sun reflecting off several small objects. Curious, he walked into the field until he reached the spot. There, lying in the freshly turned rows, were several gold coins and the remnants of an aged leather sack.

The farm hand gathered up as many of the coins as he could find and returned to his cabin. At sunrise on the following day, he carried a shovel out to the spot where he found the gold coins. For the entire day he neglected the plowing and concentrated on digging up the ground where the coins were discovered. Though he dug two to three feet into the ground in a wide area, he was unable to locate more coins.

Did the hired hand accidentally stumble onto the location of Lacey Mouse's buried fortune in gold? Could his plow have snagged the leather sack just below the surface and carried it for several yards before eventually spilling its contents out onto the freshly plowed rows?

Several more attempts were made to locate the lost treasure of Lacey Mouse, but there is no evidence that his cache of gold coins was ever found.

Today, what was once the impressive farm of Lacey Mouse, prominent Cherokee landowner and farmer, is a brush- and briar-covered patch of land in the foothills of the Oklahoma Ozarks known as the Spavinaw Hills. Beneath the scrubby growth, perhaps by now entangled in the roots, may lie several more rotting leather sacks, stuffed with gold.

Lost Gold Coins in Sequoyah County

During the Civil War, soldiers from both the Union and Confederate armies sometimes occupied parts of Indian Territory. While no major battles were fought in this region, some aspects of the war did inflict some element of tragedy upon many of the area residents.

The Indians who lived in the region were, for the most part, neutral during the conflict—they had no interest in the philosophical differences between northern and southern white men. One advantage to having troops stationed in the Indian Territory, however, was that the region was made safer from the outlaw swarms that habitually sought refuge here. But once the troops withdrew, many desperadoes saw an opportunity to enter the area and renew depredations.

Usray was an Indian who lived with his son, daughter-in-law, and their one young child in the wooded foothills of the Ozark Mountains just east of Sallisaw. He had been granted a parcel of land on which he raised a few crops and some hogs and cattle. But Usray was best known for his fine horses. Anyone in the area who had need of a good work animal, a decent riding horse, or even a blooded racing horse would visit the Usray farm.

When the northern soldiers occupied this region, they occasionally found it necessary to replenish their supply of mounts. They soon learned that the best horseflesh to be obtained in these hills belonged to Usray. Several times they visited the Usray farm to buy mounts and pack animals, always paying in gold coin.

A frugal man, Usray had little need of the money and worldly goods, so he deposited the gold in a tin box that he kept hidden in his cabin, intending someday to give it all to his son.

As the war began to wind down, the Union soldiers gradually pulled out. At first Usray regretted the departure of the soldiers and the loss of the opportunity to do more business with them, but all things considered, he was happy to see them leave—happy, at least, until outlaws began moving back into the area.

Concerned that bandits might visit his farm now that he was without military protection, Usray pastured his best stock in a concealed meadow several hundred yards from the cabin, hoping the animals would escape the eye of roving horse thieves.

He was also concerned about the cache of gold under the floor of his cabin. He removed the tin box with the gold and added to it his wife's jewelry and a gold watch he had owned for many years. He wrapped the box in an old sheepskin rug and told his grandson he was going to bury it in the woods where it would be safe from marauders.

The little boy walked with Usray as far as the spring from which the family drew water. Telling the child to wait there, the old Indian disappeared into the hills. After about a half hour Usray returned to the spring and told the boy he had buried the box of gold and jewels where no one would ever find it.

That evening, as the Usray family sat down to their evening meal, they heard riders approach and call for whoever was in the cabin to come out. Fearing the newcomers might be outlaws, Usray hid his family under the floor of the cabin and walked outside to meet them.

Four men sat on horseback just beyond the small porch. They were a dirty lot and could be mistaken for nothing other than outlaws. The leader, who had a scarred face and unkempt hair spilling out from a wide-brimmed felt hat, spurred his horse a few steps toward the old man. He said he knew of the recent gold payment for the horses and demanded it be turned over immediately. He wore several pistols in his belt, and as he spoke with the old Indian, he gestured sharply with a rifle he carried in his right hand.

152

Calmly, Usray answered that he had earned that money and needed it for his family. He said he was not about to turn it over to worthless men too lazy to work for a living.

Angered, the leader asked once again for the money, warning Usray that if he did not turn it over he would pay with his life.

In response, Usray stood squarely on the porch and folded his arms across his chest in a gesture of defiance. Unafraid, he held the gaze of the outlaw.

At a signal from the leader, another of the group rode forward, threw a lasso over the old man, and yanked him off the porch and into the dirt. Tying the other end of the rope around his saddle horn, the outlaw dragged the Indian across the clearing to the edge of the woods near the spring. There the bandits pulled the old man to his feet and asked him once again for the gold, telling him he would hang if he didn't hand it over. Again Usray refused.

One member of the outlaw band adjusted the loop around Usray's neck while another tossed the opposite end over a low-hanging branch of a nearby oak tree. Together, they pulled the old man into the air and let him hang there for several seconds before releasing the rope and letting him drop to the ground. Dazed, Usray gagged and choked, trying to force air into his lungs.

By this time, Usray's grandson had crawled from his hiding place under the floor of the cabin and watched in horror as the bandits tortured his grandfather.

Several more times they hoisted the Indian, letting him feel the rope choking the life out of him. Just when it seemed he would surely die, they would drop him once again to the ground and repeat their demand. Still the old man refused to reveal the location of the gold.

One of the bandits removed Usray's moccasins and threatened to pull out his toenails. In response, the Indian spit on his tormentor. When they proceeded to remove his toenails, the old man did not give them the satisfaction of crying out, but stoically bore the pain.

Frustrated, the outlaw leader stabbed the Indian and had his compatriots hang his body from the limb.

The outlaws then turned their attention to the cabin. Ignoring the sobbing grandson, they turned over furniture and ransacked the small home until they were certain the gold was not there. The outlaws never discovered the frightened family members hidden under the wooden floor. Finding nothing of value in the cabin, they rode away.

When the outlaws were gone, the grandson informed the others and all came out from hiding. The boy told them what he had seen them do to his grandfather. They all went to the spring, cut the old man down, and cried over his body.

After the burial the next day, the grandson told the other members of the family about Usray's taking the tin box full of gold and jewels out into the wooded hills and burying it where "no one would be able to find it."

While Usray had no need for gold or money, he died protecting his wealth presumably so that his descendants would inherit it. But before he had the opportunity to tell his son where he had buried the gold and jewels, he lost his life. Several attempts were made to locate the hiding place of the Union gold payments to the old Indian, but history does not record that it was ever found.

An Accidental Fortune in Lead and Zinc

Patrick McNaughton was born and raised in the Tennessee hills in a family that was accustomed to poverty and hardship. He was one of seven children, and it soon became clear that he would have to strike out on his own so he would not be a burden to his mother and invalid father.

Since no work was available in the area, McNaughton walked all the way to Fort Smith, Arkansas, with no money in his pocket and only the clothes on his back. He was thirteen years old.

In Fort Smith he immediately found work as a laborer. By day he toiled at the loading docks on the Arkansas River and by night he slept in alleys and under porches. Frugal by nature, he refused to spend any more money than was necessary to survive.

In time the young McNaughton took a job with a freighter who hauled goods from Fort Smith to Springfield, Missouri. While thus employed, he learned to handle a wagon and team and was soon given the responsibility of hauling freight through the rugged Ozark Mountains. He continued to save his money with the intention of starting his own freighting business.

McNaughton's travels took him to new and exciting parts of the frontier West. He found work as a teamster and freighter in Arizona, Utah, and Texas and often delivered goods to mining camps. While visiting these settlements he learned to recognize gold and silver and eventually acquired the rudiments of prospecting from the miners he came to know.

The lure of the potential wealth to be found in precious ores in the western ranges appealed to the young man's sense of adventure, but his conservative nature and frugal approach to life kept him occupied with the security of hauling freight.

By the fall of 1877, Patrick McNaughton had grown to be a tall, rangy man. He was sturdy of build, known throughout many parts of the West as a competent freighter, and was typical of the tough and persevering individual the rugged frontier was known to spawn. Like many others of his day he sported a long handlebar moustache. He seldom wore anything but overalls, and a well-worn bowler covered his balding head.

Late October in 1877 found McNaughton carrying a load of freight from Sherman, Texas, to Kansas City, Missouri. After crossing the Red River into Oklahoma, he picked up an aged Indian he found walking along the road. The Indian explained to McNaughton that he was an elder in the Shawnee tribe and was trying to return to their lands near Vinita in northeastern Oklahoma.

Since the old man looked half-starved, McNaughton shared his rations with him and saw that he rested comfortably in the back of the wagon.

Eventually they arrived at the Shawnee reservation near Vinita, where they were greeted by members of the tribe. They welcomed the return of the elder and made plans to celebrate the event with a feast that evening. McNaughton was invited to attend. Itching to be on his way, the freighter nevertheless remained at the encampment and helped the Indians celebrate the return of one of their own.

The next morning, as McNaughton was readying his team, he was approached by the old Indian who invited the young man to walk with him for a while. The Indian expressed his gratitude to McNaughton for caring for him and transporting him back to his family. In appreciation, he said he wanted to share a secret of the Shawnees that would lead his new friend to great wealth and happiness.

The Indian told the freighter of the existence of a long-lost Spanish silver mine about a two-day wagon ride from the village. Occasionally, he said, several Shawnees at a time would journey to the mine and retrieve some of the bright metal from which they fashioned ornaments. He showed several of these ornaments to McNaughton, who judged them to be made from pure silver ore of the highest quality.

The Indian scratched the directions to the mine in the dirt, bade farewell to his new friend, and returned to the village.

As McNaughton continued on his journey to Kansas City, he pondered the tale related by the Indian. He was convinced the old man was telling the truth about the Spanish silver mine, but he was reluctant to give up the secure income of the freighting business to go chasing after silver. He thought about the times he visited the mining camps of the West, where he was often tempted to sell everything in order to search the mountains and streams for gold. The excitement of the lure of wealth and adventure fought with his conservative and frugal side. As he whipped his team along the trail he became more and more confused about what he should do.

By the time McNaughton had reached Seneca on the Oklahoma-Missouri line, he had made up his mind. After dinner at a small inn, he located a man who would haul the freight the rest of the way for him. Then he rented a buckboard and two strong horses to carry him and a wagonload of supplies to a remote part of the Oklahoma Ozark hills described by the old Shawnee Indian.

From Seneca, his trail took him westward into the unsettled regions along the Spring River in the land of the Peoria Indians. The trail was little used and the country was rugged, thus making passage difficult. To add to the problem, the autumn rains caused the rivers and creeks to swell, and several times McNaughton was forced to wait until the rains subsided and the streams were safe to cross. At the end of the fourth day, he arrived at the site described by the Indian. Remarkably, he said in later years, he was able to step from his buckboard and walk right up to an ancient shaft in a matter of a few moments.

As McNaughton walked throughout the area he came upon more shafts, eventually locating a total of twenty-three over a forty-acre area.

Knowing a little bit about mining, McNaughton noted that all of the shafts were round, dug in the manner of traditional Spanish mining. Several of them penetrated well over three hundred feet into the ground.

That evening as McNaughton set up camp in the dark, he pondered the fortune that awaited him on the morrow.

The next morning McNaughton began a systematic exploration of the mines. He fashioned several torches out of the tough grass that grew in profusion. He entered each of the shafts over the next few days seeking indications of silver.

In most of the tunnels he found great quantities of lead. He knew this was not unusual, for his experiences told him that silver was often found in association with lead deposits. McNaughton found evidence of silver mining in nearly all of the shafts, and he recovered several small nuggets of silver from the mining debris on the ground.

While McNaughton found abundant evidence that silver was indeed mined from these shafts, he was unable to locate a vein of the ore that appeared productive. For several days he continued to explore the ancient Spanish mines but found little to reward his efforts. Finally, he decided that whatever silver might have existed there had been long since mined out and further efforts would be fruitless.

McNaughton cursed his bad luck and began to regret the time lost from his freighting business. As he guided the buckboard along the return trail, his keen eyes scanned the surrounding hills, searching for some sign of silver. Now and then he would stop at a promising site and examine the rock more closely. He continued to find a lot of lead, but no silver.

As McNaughton rode along he realized he was doing what he always wanted to do. He became fired with the excitement of the search for wealth; it had taken hold of him and would not let go. While he worried about his freighting business, his heart was in the search for silver. It was obvious that a great amount of silver had been taken from the area. He knew there was still more silver in these hills and felt certain he could find it. Acting on a hunch, he stopped at the Peoria Indian agent headquarters and requested permission to do some prospecting on the Indian lands. The agent informed McNaughton of a law expressly prohibiting such activity in Indian country and turned him down.

Frustrated, McNaughton returned the buckboard and team to Seneca. As soon as he could arrange for transportation, he left for his home in Sherman, Texas.

Once in Sherman, McNaughton enlisted the help of an influential rancher who in turn asked the Interior Department about gaining permission to prospect on Indian lands. Encouraged by the response, McNaughton journeyed to Washington, D.C., to meet with Interior Secretary Carl Schurz. Schurz was sympathetic to McNaughton's plea and granted permission to prospect, but specifically forbade the extraction of minerals from the Peoria land.

Encouraged, McNaughton arranged to purchase leases from the Peoria Indians and made preparations to begin his work. He invested the last of his savings in equipment and supplies in the hope of locating the wealth he believed lay beneath the limestone crust of the Ozark hills.

For weeks he searched, often doubling back to make certain he had not missed anything important, but the results were always the same. He continued to find plenty of lead but no silver. When his supplies finally ran out, McNaughton was discouraged and disheartened. As he was a man not accustomed to failure, this was a heavy blow to his self-esteem.

That night as he sipped coffee in front of his campfire, he pondered his luck. His thoughts kept returning to the great quantities of lead he had discovered during his search for silver. Suddenly he was struck with an idea. He would mine the lead!

The next morning McNaughton made another sweep of the area to inventory the amount of lead he might be able to extract when he made a fascinating discovery. Along with the lead he found great quantities of zinc. It wasn't silver, to be sure, but it could still earn him a fortune.

He returned once again to Texas to formulate plans to extract the lead and zinc from the Ozark hills. His main obstacle was the

Interior Department order banning all mining in the Peoria lands.

Not to be denied, McNaughton entered into several weeks of negotiations with Indian leaders and the federal government and was finally granted permission to dig. He borrowed money and purchased mining equipment. In a short time, he was realizing his dream as lead and zinc were being mined.

McNaughton called his organization the Peoria Mining Company after the local Indian tribe, and he soon had over three hundred men working for him. Eventually a town, named Peoria, sprang up complete with hotel, post office, and school. Within weeks several other mining concerns moved into the area, obtained rights, and began extracting lead and zinc. The year was 1891 and the northeastern Oklahoma Ozarks were experiencing a lead and zinc mining boom.

But with so many shafts penetrating the crust of the hills and so much of the mineral being extracted, it was inevitable that the boom was not to last for long. The huge deposits were soon exhausted, and eventually one company after another packed up and left. By 1896, five years after McNaughton sank his first shaft, Peoria, Oklahoma, was on its way to becoming a ghost town.

Patrick McNaughton never realized the wealth he originally anticipated from his mining adventure, but he earned enough to live comfortably for the rest of his life. He never located the silver he originally set out to find, but rather by accident reaped a fortune in lead and zinc. As a result of McNaughton's efforts, several other sites in northeastern Oklahoma, southeastern Kansas, and southwestern Missouri were prospected for lead and zinc and, over the years, billions of dollars worth of these minerals were mined.

Lawman's Lost Silver

During the last half of the nineteenth century, the re-motely settled area known as Indian Territory was rapidly becoming a haven for outlaws and renegades. For many years, organized law enforcement stopped at the western border of Arkansas and the outlaw element was relatively safe from pursuit. Hundreds of the lawbreakers found refuge in the vast and lawless spaces of what eventually became the state of Oklahoma.

The rugged Ozark hills and valleys where Indian Territory, Arkansas, and Missouri came together afforded some of the best hiding places, and criminals were densely concentrated in these western reaches of the Ozarks.

Occasionally groups of outlaws would leave this refuge to make raids on farms and travelers in Arkansas and Missouri, killing, robbing, and raping in the process. They would retreat to the sanctuary of the Oklahoma Ozarks before lawmen could arrive at the scene.

The situation became so critical that federal marshals were eventually ordered into these remote parts of Indian Territory to capture known outlaws and return them to stand trial at Judge Isaac Parker's court in Fort Smith.

Dozens of United States marshals and deputies operated throughout much of the eastern part of the territory until Oklahoma achieved statehood in 1907. Given the wild and somewhat primitive conditions under which these men were forced to work, and given the inherent dangers associated with their task, they compiled an impressive record during the years they were active.

Among the more efficient and effective of these heroic lawmen was Deputy United States Marshal Joseph Payne. Payne was assigned to Judge Parker, who in turn assigned him to cover the wild and hazardous Ozark region of Indian Territory. In the first few months Payne gained a reputation as a competent lawman. Because of his outstanding record of bringing criminals to justice, Parker gave him the most difficult assignments.

In the spring of 1881, Payne was sent into the hills a few miles south of Tahlequah, some twenty miles west of the Arkansas border, to track and apprehend perpetrators of a raid on a farm near the state line. The outlaw group numbered five, and it was a testimony to Judge Parker's confidence in Payne that he sent him out alone.

Payne tracked the outlaws for several days through the hills and valleys of this western fringe of the Ozarks until the trail led him to a narrow valley sheltered by steep bluffs. He decided not to enter the valley alone, believing the sensible thing to do would be to return to Fort Smith for reinforcements.

During the several days of tracking, he had exhausted most of his rations. As the area through which he was traveling was full of deer, he decided to do some hunting and smoke some meat. Staking out his horse in a narrow meadow, he took his rifle and followed fresh deer tracks into a promising-looking stand of trees in a nearby valley. The little valley had been carved out by a small, fast-flowing stream that ran into the Illinois River about a mile to the west.

Payne spotted several deer but none presented a clear shot. After hunting for two hours and not having anything to show for his efforts, he was frustrated and tired. He paused by the stream to rest for a while.

Payne removed one of his boots to check for wear on the sole when a glint of color from the stream attracted his attention. Replacing the boot, Payne walked over to the shallow creek and observed a vein of color three feet wide bisecting the limestone rock of the stream bed. The vein disappeared under the banks on each side.

Payne entered the creek and, using his knife, probed at the vein. It had a soft texture and he was able to gouge out several small pieces.

Returning to the bank, Payne examined his find and was surprised to discover it was pure silver. He returned to the creek, dug into the banks on both sides, and found that the vein continued for several yards in each direction.

The apparent high quality of the ore, the thickness of the vein, and the fact that it extended a considerable distance just below the shallow soil layer gave Payne reason to believe he had discovered a very rich lode of silver.

Payne immediately abandoned the deer hunt and returned to Fort Smith as fast as he could ride. He requested and received leave from his duties as deputy marshal and returned to his find.

On this trip Payne brought along a hand drill that he used to probe the depth of the vein. The drill was four feet long, and he found silver at that depth just as pure as that dug from the surface. Payne estimated he had several tons of the rich ore under his feet.

Payne was aware of the federal restrictions on prospecting and mining on Indian lands, so he decided to proceed cautiously.

In Fort Smith, he made discreet inquiries about the possibility of obtaining permission to mine in Indian Territory, but he was discouraged at every turn. He knew it would not be possible to do any kind of large-scale mining without being detected and he was unwilling to risk the penalties to which he would be subjected should he be discovered.

When he could find the time, Payne returned to his secret location and dug enough silver to fill a saddle bag. He never carried much of the ore at any one time for fear of arousing suspicion.

His law enforcement duties often took him far from his silver, and sometimes several months would pass before he could return and dig some of the ore. On one of the rare occasions he was able to visit the site he accidentally rode into an outlaw camp. Gunfire was exchanged, and Payne was lucky to escape with his life. The incident discouraged him from returning for

163

nearly two years, and when he did he remained nervous and frightened the entire time.

During one of his infrequent trips to the creek, Payne decided to conceal the vein of silver so it could not be discovered by others who might pass this way. He felled several large trees across the creek and constructed a makeshift dam to divert the path of the flowing water. Then he covered the vein with several smaller limbs and forest debris. As many times as he had been to this site, he believed he would have no trouble relocating it.

With increasing frequency, Payne's law enforcement assignments took him far from his silver for long periods of time. The Indian Territory continued to fill with outlaws, and marshals were working longer and harder trying to bring criminals to justice.

Years passed before Payne found an opportunity to return to the vein of silver, but when that opportunity finally arrived, he became ill and unable to travel.

His illness grew progressively worse and, as he lay close to death, he told a close friend of the existence of the silver in the remote valley of the Oklahoma Ozarks. He described the area near the creek, noting certain landmarks. He also drew a map showing how to reach the site.

Joseph Payne never recovered from his illness and died in 1904. Several weeks later the friend tried to locate the silver. Using Payne's map, he ventured into the Ozarks in search of a particular narrow valley with a fast-flowing stream.

For weeks the friend searched the hills south of Tahlequah but found the map useless. While Payne had been able to ride straight to the creek, he was unable to communicate the directions adequately on his map. Eventually the friend gave up and burned the map.

If Joseph Payne was correct, then somewhere in the low hills in the western part of the Ozarks just south of Tahlequah lies a fortune in pure silver. Payne claimed discovery of this supposedly rich deposit but was unable to mine it. Others may have searched for it but if they discovered it they kept it a secret. Some searchers believe that Payne's improvised dam across the creek might have rearranged the channel so that all evidence of the silver is now hidden under several inches of soil.

Today this area is popular with deer hunters and it is likely that some of them enter the little valley in search of game, just as Joseph Payne did over one hundred years ago. They may be tracking game across the very layer of soil that covers the lawman's lost silver.

The Lost Gold Mine
of the Mormons

During the first two decades of the twentieth century,
Pryor, Oklahoma, was the setting for both good times and bad.
Residents of this small town in the northeastern part of the state
just west of the foothills of the Ozarks, boasted that it was one of
the most progressive cities in Oklahoma. At the same time,
however, outlaws of one stripe or another called it home. Shoot-
ings, knifings, and robberies were common, and the comings
and goings of the lawless element were an unfortunate fact of
life in Pryor. While the local Chamber of Commerce extolled the
wonders of the Oklahoma hills, the town itself retained the
atmosphere of wilder days when it was Indian Territory.

There was one aspect of the town, however, that nearly
everyone pointed out with pride: the Pryor Orphans' Home.
Even though economic times were hard and many were without
work, the home stayed open as a result of donations from
citizens and various churches.

The Reverend W.T. Whittaker had founded and operated the
orphanage, and it was largely due to his persuasive manner that
the institution was able to pay its bills on a regular basis. When
not on the premises, the Reverend Whittaker rode a carriage
throughout the county pleading for contributions. He worked
seven days a week at keeping the doors of the home open.

One morning in the spring of 1921, Reverend Whittaker was
running errands in town and stopped at the post office. He found
among the mail an envelope with an Ohio postmark. Curious, he

tore it open and read the letter.

The writer, an Ohio resident, told Whittaker that he had been provided his name and address by one who attested to his honesty and dependability. The writer also stated that his source of information claimed that Whittaker was familiar with the Spavinaw Hills region of the Ozarks several miles east of Pryor. Following this introduction, the letter continued with an interesting story.

The letter writer had recently learned of a very rich gold mine in the Spavinaw Hills. He also claimed he had maps of the area and would pay Whittaker a large sum of money if he would guide the Ohioan into the region and provide him with men to help excavate the gold should they locate it.

Whittaker, foreseeing the opportunity to acquire funds for the orphans' home, decided it might be worthwhile to participate in the gold-hunting venture. He returned home and wrote a letter to the Ohioan tentatively agreeing to the proposition and requesting more details.

The return mail brought the story. The Ohioan had recently come into possession of the diary of a man who had worked in the gold mine many years earlier. The man was one of twelve Mormons who were exploring the Spavinaw Hills in search of a suitable location for a settlement when they accidentally discovered a rich vein of gold in an outcrop of the weathered limestone that forms these hills. Believing they were sent by God to discover this gold, the Mormons immediately established a tiny settlement and set to the task of mining and smelting the ore. The gold was to be shipped to Salt Lake City, to help fund the construction of the temple.

Day after day, from dawn until late in the evening the men worked in the mine, stopping only to eat, rest, and conduct worship services. They removed tons of rock from the shaft, separated the ore from the matrix, and fashioned eighteen-inch ingots in a crude homemade smelting operation.

After several months of hard work, the Mormons had accumulated several hundred bars of the gold ore, which they stacked along one side of the mine shaft. They planned to purchase mules and carry the gold to Salt Lake City once the vein of ore was exhausted.

The operation was not without trouble. Repeated encounters with outlaws and ruffians as well as occasional gunfights forced the Mormons to abandon their mining temporarily. Because of the increased harassment, the men decided it would be best to cover and conceal the mine shaft, sealing the gold ingots within. Having done so they departed, intending to return when the outlaw menace was eliminated.

For reasons unknown, the Mormon miners never returned to the valley to reclaim their gold. Years passed, and the story of the lost Mormon mine came into the possession of the letter writer from Ohio by way of the diary of one of the miners.

Convinced of the authenticity of the tale, Whittaker spent the next few days lining up men to accompany him and the Ohioan on an expedition into the Spavinaw Hills. Once this was accomplished, Whittaker decided it was time to write to the man and tell him everything was ready to proceed and to come at once.

Bad luck befell the good reverend, however, for on his way home to write the letter he was stricken with a heart attack. Whittaker lay in a coma for several days, unable to speak. Finally, in the presence of family and friends, he died.

Several weeks later, members of his family discovered the correspondence from the Ohio writer. Unaware that the man was awaiting a return letter from Reverend Whittaker, the family ignored the matter. It is presumed that the Ohioan believed Whittaker was not interested in the project and so he apparently never wrote again.

Over the next few years the story of the Lost Mine of the Mormons surfaced from time to time, and men would enter the Spavinaw Hills with the hope of locating the lost cache. Searchers for the mine discovered evidence of a small abandoned settlement in one of the valleys. Not far from this discovery they found the remains of a primitive smelter. The searchers spent several days in the area but could not find the mine.

More time passed and the city of Tulsa developed plans to create a reservoir on the Neosho River to be used as a water supply. Once the dam was constructed, water backed into several of the secluded valleys in the Spavinaw Hills.

Many who have searched for the lost gold mine of the Mormons believe that the actual site of the diggings was covered when the valley was filled to form Spavinaw Lake, forever covering the hundreds of golden ingots stacked against the walls of the old mine shaft.

The Shoemaker's Hidden Gold

In the summer of 1870, an elderly German arrived in Indian Territory leading two mules. His ragged and dirty appearance suggested he had obviously been traveling for a long time, and the mules appeared weary from the burden of the heavy loads they carried.

The old fellow stopped at several of the farmhouses in the area and offered to work in return for some food and a place to sleep. He made it known that he was a cobbler and soon found plenty of work mending the boots and shoes of nearly everyone in the region. The old man was friendly and got along well with the locals, but most of the time he preferred to be alone. At times he appeared somewhat secretive, and when anyone approached his mules he would chase them away. Once, as he was repacking a load on one of the animals, someone reported seeing several leather sacks filled with gold coins.

The old shoemaker had been in the area for several weeks when he finally set up residence on a parcel of land fronting the Spring River just a few miles northeast of present-day Miami, Oklahoma. No other white residents were nearby, and his closest neighbors were members of the Piankashaw Indian tribe, a small group of Indians that had been moved to the territory from Kansas only three years earlier.

The shoemaker constructed a rude cabin from native material. Those who chanced near his residence were greeted in a friendly manner by the German, but he remained secretive and never allowed anyone in his house.

One day a traveler arrived at a nearby settlement and spotted the old German purchasing a few items at the trading post. The traveler related to several of the citizens that he had known the shoemaker many years earlier in the old country. He said the German came from a wealthy and influential family but, for reasons unknown to anyone, had became a cobbler, traveling from village to village repairing boots and shoes. After working thus for many years, the German journeyed to the United States. He landed somewhere on the East Coast and immediately set out for the West. He worked his way across the country performing odd jobs and cobbling. Most of those who encountered him found him somewhat eccentric but harmless.

The traveler also said that the shoemaker was rumored to have carried much of his family's wealth with him when he came to America.

Aside from his infrequent visits to the nearest settlement, hardly anyone encountered the old shoemaker save for a few of the Piankashaws living nearby. The German became close friends with one particular young member of the tribe and occasionally invited him to share a meal. One day, as the two sat on the ground in front of the cabin, the shoemaker confided in the Indian that he had great wealth in gold coins. He showed the young Piankashaw a large tin box in which he claimed his fortune was kept and confessed to him that he was unable to sleep at night for fear that someone would steal his treasure. The Indian suggested to the shoemaker that he hide his gold someplace where no one could find it.

The German considered this idea for several days and finally decided to follow the advice of the Indian. For several days, the shoemaker explored the area around his cabin until he finally located a suitable hiding place.

Near the point where Rock Creek flows into the Spring River is a high limestone bluff containing several deep crevices. Entering one of these narrow cracks in the rock, the shoemaker followed it until it became too dark to see. Fashioning a torch from grasses that grew along the creek, he re-entered the crevice and, inching forward on his stomach for several dozen yards, followed it until he came to a large room in which he was able to stand to his full height.

The next day, with the help of his mules, the shoemaker carried his fortune to the crevice. After several trips, he finally succeeded in sliding the tin box and his many sacks of gold coins through the narrow crevice and into the room. Using the light from a torch, he arranged the tin box in one corner of the room and filled it with the sacks of gold. Then he crawled back through the narrow opening and returned to his cabin. Several days later he told his young Indian friend what he had done and related that he had slept peacefully for the first time in weeks.

A year passed and the old shoemaker grew weak from a sickness that caused great fits of coughing. The sickness ravaged his body and left him unable to rise from his bed without difficulty. His Piankashaw friend tended to him as best he could, but it was clear the old man was dying.

One day when the Indian brought some food to the old shoemaker he found him nearly dead. The old German pulled the Indian close to him and whispered the secret location of his hidden gold. He told the young Piankashaw that he wanted him to have his wealth for being his friend and for caring for him during his sickness. He told the Indian the money was to be used to benefit his tribe.

A few days later the old man died. The Piankashaws buried him next to his cabin and conducted a simple service in the manner of the Indians.

One morning a few days following the burial, the Indian set out in search of the shoemaker's hidden gold. He easily located the confluence of Rock Creek and the Spring River and immediately spotted the limestone bluff described by the old man.

In searching the bluff, the young Indian found many crevices in the rocky face, but none that yielded a fortune in gold coins.

Many times the Indian searched the area now known as Devil's Promenade, but the crevice through which the old shoemaker moved his fortune eluded him. After several weeks of searching with no success, the Indian gave up, and the story of the old shoemaker's lost gold persisted as legend among his tribe for over a century.

In 1979, Weldon Bobcat, a Kiowa Indian who has spent a lot of time around the Spring River, related an interesting story. Several boys had been playing near Devil's Promenade a few summers before when one of them entered a narrow crevice he found in the face of the bluff. Crawling flat on his stomach, the youth discovered the crevice extended far into the cliff for several yards. When he exited, he told his companions that it appeared the crevice opened into a room large enough to accommodate several people, but he confessed to being afraid of the numerous nests of spiders through which he would have had to crawl in order to reach the chamber.

It is possible that the boy had accidentally discovered the hiding place of the old shoemaker's gold, but being unaware of the legend, he saw no need to enter the chamber where the old tin box filled with gold coins has rested quietly for over a century.

Cherokee Farmer's Lost Gold Cache

Jim Bobb was one of several children of a Cherokee family that farmed a small patch of land near Baumgarner Hollow in the Ozark hills, several miles east of Tahlequah, Oklahoma. The small farm was granted to the elder Bobb during the settlement of the Cherokee Indians into this area, and he made a decent living raising hogs and growing corn in the good river bottom soil. Life was generally good for the Bobb family.

Jim Bobb, unlike his siblings, possessed a wanderlust and often spoke of wanting to visit faraway places. When news about the California gold fields reached this isolated area of Indian Territory, Jim Bobb packed his few meager belongings and left, heading westward to seek the wealth he dreamed of.

He toiled for two years in the California Rockies, panning gold from hundreds of the small glacially fed streams that pour down out of the mountains. He experienced some successes and was careful to save as much as was practical. By the time he returned home to the farm in Oklahoma, he brought with him a large pack filled with gold dust and nuggets.

Jim Bobb moved in with his family and resumed working on the farm. With some of his newfound wealth, he gradually added to the family holdings by purchasing adjacent acreage, putting together a large and efficient farm. In time he married, built a stout cabin on the property, and was soon the father of a fine son he named Robin.

As time passed, Jim Bobb, with Robin's able assistance, developed a fine herd of cattle, expanded the corn fields, and turned the family farm into a very profitable enterprise. Income from the Bobb farm was more than adequate, and the profits were added to the already large pile of gold dust and nuggets kept hidden under a floor board inside the cabin.

Robin Bobb grew to manhood and maintained a deep interest in the farm. As his father grew feeble with age, Robin took on more of the responsibility for the operation and proved capable of carrying on the family tradition. By the time Jim died, the wealth that had accumulated under the cabin floor was so great that the son decided it was necessary to find a new location for it.

Having no experience with banks and bankers, Robin Bobb simply elected to find a suitable hiding place some distance from the farm, a place to which he could easily return and extract some of the gold when necessary. He removed the cache of wealth from under the floor of the cabin and stuffed it into a large old cooking pot, which he wrapped in heavy canvas. Securing the heavy load onto a pack horse, Robin Bobb rode into some low rocky hills of the Ozark Mountains just east of the Illinois River. Locating what he believed to be a secure spot, he concealed the cooking pot full of gold and returned to his farm.

More years passed and, as Robin Bobb told the story, there was no need to retrieve any of the hidden gold, for the farm prospered and provided well for him and his family. Neighbors had heard stories of the fortune Jim Bobb brought back from the California gold fields in his youth, but the farmer always refused to discuss it with anyone. In fact, Robin Bobb never revealed the location of the hidden gold to anyone in his own family.

One autumn, Robin Bobb suddenly became ill and died within a few weeks. Though he left no directions to the hidden gold cache, several family members undertook a search for it in the general area they believed it to be. But somewhere in the hills east of Tahlequah, the great wealth of Robin Bobb remains unclaimed to this day.

Lost Chimney Rock Gold

Chimney Rock, a tall spire of sedimentary rock and well-known Oklahoma Ozark landmark, was once the site of an extended gun battle between outlaws and a pursuing posse. This prominent landform, some five miles southeast of Tahlequah, casts a shadow over two mule loads of gold buried somewhere near its base.

The gold that was supposed to have been buried near the base of Chimney Rock came from Louisiana. Six desperadoes rode into a northern Louisiana town, robbed a storehouse in which the gold had been kept, and fled north and east toward Indian Territory, then a well-known haven for outlaws.

Within moments of the robbery, a dozen citizens of the town saddled up, secured provisions, and rode out in pursuit of the outlaws. For several days and nights the chase continued, with the pursuers occasionally getting close enough to the bandits to fire shots. The outlaws, leading two pack mules loaded down with the gold, would somehow manage to elude the persistent Louisianans and the chase was on again.

One evening, at a point between the Illinois and Wauhillau rivers in what is now Cherokee County, the outlaws were overtaken by the pursuers. A brief gunfight ensued with two of the robbers being killed. The remaining four jumped back onto their horses, grabbed the reins to the pack mules, and forded the Illinois River, about two miles from Chimney Rock. From this point they fled toward the forested hills in the distance.

The heavily laden mules were slowing the harried outlaws and the men decided it would be best to take cover and defend themselves against the persistent pursuers. As they rode toward Chimney Rock, now looming in the distance, a third outlaw was shot out of his saddle. Without pausing to ascertain whether or not the man was dead, the others spurred their mounts toward the safety of the woods, finally entering a thick stand of trees near the base of Chimney Rock. Here they dismounted and sought cover from which to defend themselves against the Louisianans.

The ensuing gunfight lasted well into the night with no casualties to either side. Fearing they would be overtaken if they fled with the heavily laden and now very tired mules, the outlaws, using the cover of darkness, decided to hide the gold in the many rock crevices they found near the base of Chimney Rock. Dividing the loot into several small portions, they wedged the gold into nearby crevices which they then covered over with dirt and forest debris.

Running low on ammunition, the outlaws decided to make a break from their position and ride deeper into Indian Territory where they believed they would be safe from further pursuit. They intended to return at a later date to retrieve the gold they had hidden in the cracks of the weathered limestone rock.

Just before dawn broke over an adjacent ridge, the remaining three outlaws dashed from the woods on horseback. The pursuers, anticipating such a maneuver, intercepted them between Tahlequah and Fourteen Mile Creek. All three outlaws were killed during the subsequent gun battle.

The Louisianans were convinced the gold was cached somewhere in the woods near the base of Chimney Rock where the outlaws hid during the night. The bandits were observed carrying the gold into the woods but they obviously did not have it in their possession when they fled from their hiding place. Returning to the site, the Louisianans searched a wide area for the rest of the day, but were unable to locate any of the gold. Dejected, they returned home.

Many who have searched for the gold near the base of Chimney Rock believe that the outlaws disguised the hiding places to look exactly like the surrounding forest. As the search continues, Chimney Rock, like a lone sentinel, stands above the surrounding forest, mutely guarding the fortune in gold hidden near its base.

The Innkeeper's Bad Luck

The old Indian had traveled many days on foot before arriving at the inn just outside the Tahlequah settlement. He stood at the bottom of the wooden steps leading up to the wide front doors and kicked the road dust from his moccasins. Adjusting the pack on his back, the Indian climbed the steps and entered the inn.

The innkeeper looked warily upon the old man as he came through the door. He had seen this type before—travelers with no money who would occasionally check into the inn, stay for a few days, and disappear in the middle of the night without paying the bill. The year was 1895, a recent drought made times hard, and few travelers carried much money.

The Indian approached the desk and inquired about a room. Eyeing the traveler suspiciously, the innkeeper noted the ragged and filthy clothes. He was about to have the Indian ejected from the premises when the traveler pulled out a roll of currency and asked the price of a room for a week. Seeing the large wad of money changed the innkeeper's attitude, and he forthwith assigned a room to the old man, collecting for a week in advance.

During the next few days, the innkeeper observed that the visitor would rise early in the morning and leave without eating breakfast. Somewhere he had obtained a horse and would ride out into the Ozark hills east of town. The Indian would stay gone all day, returning after sundown and immediately retiring to his room. The innkeeper was curious about the business of the

Indian and was inclined to inquire, but the old man always managed to avoid any conversation.

At the end of the week, the Indian approached the innkeeper and asked for an audience with him. Taking the Indian into his office, the innkeeper motioned him to a chair and poured him some coffee. The Indian came immediately to the point of his visit and related to the innkeeper a remarkable story of a buried fortune in gold somewhere in the hills to the east.

The Indian explained that he was a member of the Cherokee tribe and recited a long and impressive lineage that suggested he was related to chieftains and important elders of the tribe. Growing impatient with the old man's genealogy, the innkeeper encouraged him to get on with the story.

The Cherokee unfolded a tale about Chief Blackface, so called because of his mixed Seminole and African ancestry. Blackface and his followers made their camp in the densely wooded Ozark hills of the Cherokee and Choctaw nations in northeastern Oklahoma during the early part of the 1830s. Never one to take to the sedentary life of farming and raising a family, Blackface and his cutthroats resorted to attacking, robbing, and often killing travelers, prospectors, traders, and even other Indians who chanced near their hiding place.

One day one of Blackface's scouts reported the approach of a large Mexican pack train winding its way through the rugged hills nearby, apparently bound for St. Louis. With no warning, the renegade Indians charged out of the hills and attacked the pack train. The battle was brief and by the time the dust had cleared, all of the Mexicans lay dead on the trail. The Indians rounded up one hundred mules, most of which were carrying packs filled with gold bars.

With his small Indian army, Blackface herded the mules into the hills toward a secluded cave. There he unloaded the gold from the animals and carried it deep into the cave.

Several weeks later, Blackface and his followers attempted a raid on another pack train, but this time the muleteers were well-prepared. No sooner had the Indians charged out from hiding than the Mexicans circled their animals and began to fire away at the raiders. The battle raged for several hours, but Blackface's small and ill-armed force was no match for the Mexicans. Most of the Indians, including Blackface, were killed.

The old Cherokee told the innkeeper that as a child, he often heard this story from his grandfather who also professed to have knowledge of the location of the secret cave in the Ozarks that contained Blackface's cache of gold. The Cherokee told the innkeeper that he believed he was close to locating the cave but he was running low on money. If the innkeeper would allow him to remain at the inn for a few more days, he said, he would share the wealth with him when it was discovered.

The innkeeper was intrigued by the tale. Although suspicious, he agreed to allow the Indian to remain as a guest at the inn for a month while he searched for the treasure.

One evening, about two weeks later, the Indian rushed into the inn and gestured to the innkeeper that he needed to speak with him. Expecting an excuse, the innkeeper reluctantly waved the old man back into the office. There, visibly excited, the Indian related how he had finally located the lost cave of gold.

The innkeeper, excited by the Indian's discovery, suggested they leave immediately and retrieve the riches. The old man held up a hand and told the innkeeper that this must be done according to the Indian way. The Cherokee insisted the innkeeper be blindfolded on the journey to the cave and would be allowed to remove the cover only when in sight of the treasure. The innkeeper argued, but the Indian was adamant. Finally he agreed to be blindfolded.

The next morning the two rode to the edge of the clearing in which the inn was located and into the woods. Once they were out of sight, the Cherokee covered the innkeeper's head with a sack made of a dark coarse material. The sack was secured around his neck, making it impossible for him to see. For several hours the Indian led the innkeeper on horseback along a twisting route. Finally they halted, dismounted, and walked to a rock ledge. At that point, the innkeeper, still blindfolded, heard the Indian moving some heavy rocks, presumably ones that were blocking the entrance to the cave. The Indian then told the innkeeper they would have to crawl some distance into the cave. The two men crawled on their hands and knees for nearly a half-hour before they were able to stop and rise to their full height. By this time the innkeeper's pants were torn and his knees were bleeding.

Once inside the large chamber, the Cherokee removed the blindfold and held his torch high to illuminate the cavern. When his eyes adjusted to the light, the innkeeper gasped as he looked upon the great fortune of which the Indian spoke. Against the far wall of the chamber stood six large containers that reminded him of huge butter churns. They were filled to the top with bars of gold, each one about twelve inches long. The innkeeper inspected one of the bars, scratching into it with a knife, and determined that it was fashioned from the purest gold he had ever seen.

Overtaken with excitement at witnessing this vast wealth, the innkeeper told the Cherokee he wanted to take the gold to the inn immediately. The Indian said that was not possible until certain Cherokee rituals were completed. The innkeeper objected, but the Indian was persistent and the innkeeper finally agreed to wait. The Indian said they would be able to remove the gold within one week.

Once again the innkeeper was blindfolded and led from the cave. They stopped at the entrance where he heard the Indian replace several stones. The two men then retraced the trail back to the inn, and when they reached the clearing the blindfold was removed. As it was late and he was weary, the innkeeper went immediately to bed.

The next morning the innkeeper went to check on the Cherokee only to discover he had apparently not spent the night in his room. Making inquiries, he learned that the Indian had gone into town the night before, had gotten into a fight, and stabbed a man to death. The police were summoned and the Cherokee took flight into the woods east of town with the law officers in pursuit.

The next evening the police returned, having been unable to capture the fleeing killer.

For many years following the experience, the innkeeper recalled to others his vision of the immense wealth that lay within a secret cave in the Ozarks. His dreams were filled with images of the large containers filled to the top with bars of gold. He cursed himself often for listening to the old Cherokee.

As time passed, the story of Chief Blackface's lost cache of gold became part of the legend and lore of the Seminole-Negroes who inhabit this part of the Indian Territory. Several members of the tribe searched for the lost treasure but apparently with no success. In 1905, an Oklahoma newspaper reported that several members of the tribe had finally located the lost cache, but it was later determined to be a hoax.

During the early 1930s, reports surfaced that the old Cherokee had been seen in the area. As recently as 1936, several Tahlequah residents were organizing to try to find the Indian, who by that time would have been quite old. They were never successful.

Locust Grove Gold

Somewhere in Ottawa County a few miles west of Miami, Oklahoma, stands an old grove of locust trees. The grove is adjacent to the low hills that mark the westernmost limit of the Oklahoma Ozarks. Beneath the stand of locust trees may rest a fortune in gold that has lain there undisturbed for nearly 150 years.

In April 1842, according to legend, a small band of Mexicans was leading a pack train from Texas to St. Louis, skirting the western fringes of the Ozark Mountains and trying to avoid the unfamiliar terrain of deep and narrow canyons within the range. They were miners transporting three mule-loads of gold, the fruits of several years of hard labor in a long-forgotten gold mine in Texas.

One of the members of the party observed a group of riders approaching along the trail from the south at a rapid pace. Fearing bandits, the Mexicans decided to hide their gold before the group arrived, intending to return for it when it seemed safe.

On the other side of a low rise, out of sight of the pursuers and just off the trail, the Mexicans hastily dug a shallow trench. From the mules they unloaded the deerskin sacks heavy with gold and deposited them in the excavation.

After covering the hole, one of the Mexicans pulled from his pocket a small leather sack of locust seeds and sprinkled several handfuls atop the freshly turned earth. He explained to his comrades that, should they find it necessary to vacate the area for an extended period of time before returning for the gold, the locust seedlings that would soon sprout would serve as a marker for the buried fortune in gold.

The Mexicans mounted their horses and continued to ride northeastward, hoping to give their pursuers the impression that they were merely a group of poor men on a journey and not worth the trouble to rob.

The riders eventually caught up with the Mexicans several miles farther along the trail and killed all but one. The survivor was picked up two days later by a migrating band of Peoria Indians. The Peorias cared for the wounded Mexican for several weeks, but his wounds were serious and it was apparent he would not live much longer. Just before he died, he called the chief of the tribe to his side and told him of the three mule-loads of gold he and his companions buried along the trail near the Ozark hills. He expressed gratitude to the chief for trying to save him and explained he wished for him to have the gold for his tribe. He provided directions to the site and told about planting the locust seeds.

The Peoria Indians were not a people concerned with great wealth, and the story of the buried gold meant little to them.

Twenty years later, the Peorias were relocated to Ottawa County, where they settled into a routine of farming and raising horses on the good land near the low rolling hills of the Ozarks. Baptiste Peoria, chief of the tribe, recalled the tale of the dying Mexican and noted that the new home of the Peorias was near the area he described. In 1868, Baptiste Peoria discovered a locust grove just off the main road leading to Missouri and declared it to be the one described by the Mexican.

The Peoria Indians no longer exist as a tribe, but those who claim to know say that the locust grove is still there. After nearly 150 years, the stand of trees has grown full and thick, covering nearly a quarter of an acre. There are many living in Ottawa County who still believe that the three mule-loads of gold hidden by the Mexican miners still lie just beneath the tree-shaded ground.

References

Allsopp, Fred W. *Folklore of Romantic Arkansas,* vol. 1. The Grolier Society, 1931.

Anderson, LaVere Schoenfelt. "When There Was Gold In Them Thar Hills." *Tulsa Daily World,* Mar. 22, 1931.

_____. "Buried Treasure in the Devil's Promenade." *Tulsa Daily World,* June 14, 1931.

_____. "Death Haunts the Trail of Buried Slave Gold." *Tulsa Daily World,* June 21, 1931.

Bowers, Rodney. "Looking for Lost Spanish Mine." *Arkansas Gazette,* Sept. 25, 1988.

"Buried Treasures Were Never Found." *Wilburton (Oklahoma) News,* Nov. 24, 1905.

Collins, Earl A. *Legends and Lore of Missouri.* San Antonio, Texas: The Naylor Company, 1951.

Curlee, Mabel. "Hidden Treasure." *Baxter County History* 3.3, 1977.

Garland, Russell L. *Immigrants in the Ozarks.* Columbia: University of Missouri Press, 1939.

Hutchinson, H.B. "Daddy of Lead-Zinc Mines Tells His Story." *Daily Oklahoman,* May 11, 1930.

Jameson, W.C. "Tobe Inmon's Lost Silver Bullets." *True West* 33.3

(March 1986): 60-61.

_____. *Buried Treasures of the American Southwest.* Little Rock, Arkansas: August House, 1989.

Lambrecht, Gordon. "Gold." *Baxter County History* 1.4 (1975).

Leet, L. Don, and Judson, Sheldon. *Physical Geology.* Englewood Cliffs, New Jersey: Prentice-Hall, Inc., 1965.

McCall, Edith. "Lost Mines Discounted by Historian." *Branson Beacon,* December 16, 1982.

McCulloch, James A. "Another Piece in the Yoachum Puzzle." *Treasure Search* 16.6 (Nov.-Dec. 1988): 6-10, 26.

Morrow, Lynn, and Saults, Dan. "The Yoachum Silver Dollar: Sorting Out the Strands of an Ozarks Frontier Legend." *Gateway Heritage* (Winter, 1984-85): 8-15.

Pipes, Gerald H. *Lost Treasures of Table Rock Lake.* Reeds Spring, Missouri: Ozark Books, 1959.

Rafferty, Milton D. *The Ozarks: Land and Life.* Norman: University of Oklahoma Press, 1980.

Rascoe, Jesse. *Oklahoma Treasures Lost and Found.* Fort Davis, Texas: Frontier Book Company, 1974.

Ross, S.W. "Tales of Hidden Treasure along the Illinois." *Tulsa Daily World,* June 28, 1931.

_____. "Old Nation Indians Seek Lucky Cherokee." *Tulsa Daily World,* February 23, 1936.

Steele, Phillip. *Lost Treasures of the Ozarks.* Springdale, Arkansas: published by author.

Tatham, Robert L. *Missouri Treasures and Civil War Sites.* Boulder, Colorado: H. Glenn Carson Enterprises, 1974.

_____. *Ozark Treasure Tales.* Ragtown, Missouri: R.L. Tatham Co., 1979.

Wilson, Steve. *Oklahoma Treasure and Treasure Tales.* Norman: University of Oklahoma Press, 1984.

Buried Treasures of the Appalachians

Legends of Homestead Caches,
Indian Mines and Loot from
Civil War Raids

For my son
Luke

Contents

Prologue

For many years I have searched for, researched, and collected tales of buried treasures and lost mines associated with the Appalachian Mountains. The Appalachians have always been one of my favorite places, and when the time came to put some stories together in a book, I decided to go there again for a while to get reacquainted with the land and the people I have come to respect and admire.

On this trip, I wanted to avoid the big cities and concentrate on the rural areas and the remote settlements where a way of life common to several generations past is still led by many of the residents.

As I drove through isolated valleys and hollows and across lonesome ridgetops, I found it hard to believe the gentle rolling landscape of the Appalachian Mountains was the product of violent upheaval of the earth's crust accompanied by massive folding, faulting, and volcanic activity millions of years ago. As I inhaled the sweet aroma of the green fields and watched dazzling displays of butterflies coloring the landscape, I was struck again with the odd truth that this range of mountains, once higher than the Rockies, that had been a place of bloodshed in the French and Indian War and the War Between The States, that had seen poverty and suffering, prosperity and progress, contains some of the most serene, tranquil, and placid environments on the continent. During their life of well over two hundred million years, the Appalachian Mountains have mellowed into a comfortable, peaceful haven that is a balm for the spirit, an elixir for the soul.

Reminders of the eons-old processes that created this range were apparent along many of the roads I traveled: layered outcrops of highly fractured and weathered limestone; seams of coal, which have sometimes supported the area's economy; occasional outcrops of granite, suggestive of the igneous forces deep below the crust that formed rich veins of gold and silver.

The people I encountered here were as much a part of the landscape as the rocks and trees. Salt-of-the-earth types they were, and their creased features reminded me of the worn limestone on which they walked. I saw few young people in these remote settings; most of those I met were old-timers, and they were often wary of strangers—retiring, almost secretive, and very territorial.

The few I managed to coax into conversation spoke a dialect I have been told can be traced to Elizabethan England, and many had decidedly old English surnames like Yadkin, Cabot, Calloway, and Williams. Here and there, one could detect the presence of Indian blood among them, an element that lent further mystery to their mien.

Many were reluctant to talk to me at first, but when my intentions became clear, they opened up. At first they were cautious, but before long, they were open and free in conversations as if they craved the opportunity to tell newcomers of the wonders of their valleys and mountains. They told of living off the land, of poaching game and gathering ginseng, of whiskey stills. They told me about folk treatments for ailments such as cancer and arthritis, and how they seldom visited physicians and hospitals. And they told many stories of lost mines and buried treasures.

I had heard a number of the stories before, but the native versions were always a little different, perhaps a bit more personal. Many others were completely new to me. The captivating tales were about the rich mines and buried ingots of gold and silver of the Spanish explorers who came there centuries ago, about Indian silver in abundance, about the mining activities of the first settlers, about Civil

War loot—about fortunes made and cached and forgotten and lost. They told of the ongoing search for many of these treasures and of clinging to the belief that the tales are true and that it is only a matter time until someone chances upon a lost fortune.

These stories are a strong and important component of the culture of these mountain folk. Long tucked away in the isolated recesses of the mountains, their ways of life and their folktales remained elusive, almost unknown, for generations. Now the people and their stories are the object of study and analysis at major universities throughout the country—folklorists from as far away as Europe are arriving in the Appalachians regularly to record the ways of these mountain people.

Returning to my home and manuscript, I reread many of the stories I intended to include in this book. It occurred to me that some of them lacked two essential ingredients— the flavor of the Appalachian people and the strong sense of place one feels when in these mountains. Using what I learned from the folk, I rewrote many of the stories and added bits of color and information gleaned from my visit with the mountain people.

These stories belong to them.

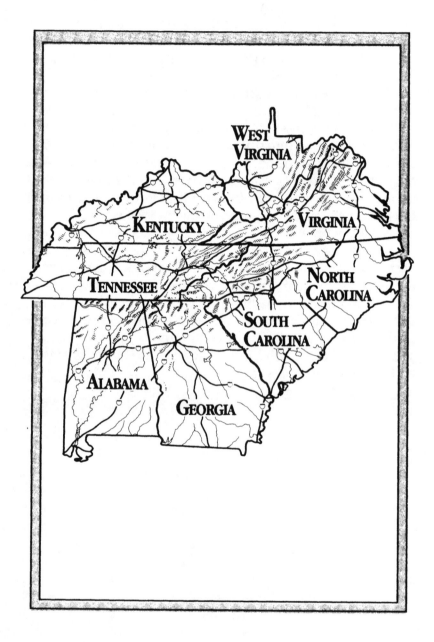

Introduction

Of all the major mountain ranges in North America, none possesses more enduring images than the Appalachians. Our sterotypes are strong: many of us see the Appalachian Mountains as rugged and remote, a setting for feuding and moonshining, populated by religious fundamentalists and backward hillbillies resisting every encroachment of civilization. We also think of the Appalachians as rich in the tradition of oral history and folklore, and rife with wonderful tales of long ago. Prominent among them are colorful legends of lost and buried treasures.

Because modern Appalachia is much like any other settled portion of the United States, perceptions of backwardness are largely unfair and inaccurate, though, to be sure, there are people living in remote sections of these mountains whose activities, priorities, and social structures differ little from those of a hundred years ago. Today, however, the Appalachian range has been transected by interstates and railroads, accommodates several major universities, medical centers, and industrial and corporate complexes, and claims among its cities some of the most progressive urban areas in the country.

The Appalachian Mountains have fascinated Americans, and the range played a significant role in the early settlement of the United States. Within the geographic realm of the Appalachian Mountains wars have been fought, fortunes made and lost, some unique cultures spawned and others forced into extinction.

The Appalachian Mountains are a complex region, both environmentally and culturally. They are home to a great diversity of natural settings and people, and within their borders can be found a variety and abundance of natural resources, recreational opportunities, wildlife habitats, and climates.

Origins

The Appalachian Mountains spread across fourteen states and comprise a major physiographic component of the nation east of the Mississippi River. The range is considerably older than the Rocky Mountains in the west, having matured over the past 225,000,000 years into a stable, tectonically inactive range manifesting comparatively little faulting and no active folding or volcanism, although these processes were very common early in the evolution of the mountains.

The Appalachian Mountains separate the coastal plain of the eastern seaboard from the extensive plains bordering the valleys of the Ohio and Mississippi Rivers to the west. The Appalachians are physiographically characterized as a combination of highly folded regions and extensive plateaus that separate the central part of the range from the Atlantic coastal plain to the east and the interior lowlands to the west. Millions of years of erosion, primarily from rivers and streams, have reduced the once towering Appalachians to a series of gently rounded and smoothly sculpted low-lying mountains. The relatively soft sedimentary rocks which make up much of the plateau provinces have been worn into deep valleys creating significant relief between the uplands and lowlands.

The Appalachians had their origins well over two hundred twenty-five million years ago. Around this time, called the Paleozoic Era, the region of North America that was to become the Appalachian Mountains was a Mediterranean-type sea. For millions of years, sediments from the adjacent lands washed into this sea, building to a thickness of thousands of feet, and above these sediments lay the weight of the shallow sea. As the sediments accumulated and increased in thickness and weight, they caused the underlying crust to sink, thus creating a huge trough called a geosyncline which deepened at a rate of about one foot every ten thousand years.

Near the end of the Paleozoic Era, the sinking and resulting trough-development movements were reversed— the now lithified sediments in the huge geosyncline were folded and uplifted as a result of compressional stresses from repeated long-term collision of two great continental plates. As the plates collided, one overrode the other, resulting in intense fracturing and folding accompanied by occasional volcanism. This occurred at least three times during the period, and the result was the gradual elevation of a vast area that became the Appalachian Mountains.

During the folding and fracturing of this part of the earth's surface, molten material from deep below the crust intruded into zones of fracture and weakness. As the pressurized magma worked its way up through the crust, it traveled far from its heat source and, lacking sufficient pressure to break through to the surface, cooled underground over successive centuries, eventually producing vast formations of granite threaded with rich seams of gold and silver.

Once the Appalachians were uplifted to significant altitudes, the mountains were exposed to highly efficient erosion by flowing water, glaciation, and wind. As a result, much of the granite and other igneous rocks with their veins of gold and silver were exposed at the surface. The weathered rock debris resulting from erosion was carried downslope toward the Atlantic Ocean, burying the volcanic and metamorphic roots of these Paleozoic mountains in sediments reaching hundreds of feet thick.

The varying intensities of the folding and faulting processes caused such significant differences in topography throughout this vast and unique geographic area that scientists have classified the range into four distinct subdivisions, or provinces: the Piedmont Plateau, the Blue Ridge, the Valley and Ridge, and the Appalachian Plateau.

The Piedmont Plateau, which provides a transition from the higher elevations of the range to the Atlantic Coastal Plains of Maryland, Virginia, the Carolinas, and Georgia, is composed primarily of gneiss, schist, marble, quartzite, and slate, all metamorphic rocks formed from the intense heat and pressures of earlier geologic eras.

The Blue Ridge province, following the general direction of the Appalachians, runs approximately southwest-to-northeast and varies in width from five to fifty miles. The mountains here generally rise from one to five thousand feet above the Appalachian Plateau, reaching 6,684 feet at Mount Mitchell in North Carolina. The Blue Ridge is composed primarily of granite and gneiss, with some sedimentary formations, mostly sandstone, siltstone, and conglomerate. The Blue Ridge, while exhibiting some folding, was subjected to intensive faulting and fracturing during the Paleozoic Era.

The Valley and Ridge Province of the Appalachians varies from twenty-five to seventy-five miles wide, is highly faulted, and also displays some impressive folding. Sandstone, shale, and limestone are the most common sedimentary rocks in the region, with the limestone providing ideal conditions for the formation of the numerous impressive and extensive cavern systems found throughout the province.

The Appalachian Plateau, separating the higher elevations of the interior from the riverine lowlands to the immediate west, range from one to three thousand feet in altitude and are composed primarily of highly dissected sedimentary rock. The dissections have created impressively deep valleys throughout much of the region.

As these once lofty mountains eroded, the weathered products of the igneous, metamorphic, and sedimentary rocks contributed to the wide variety of soils found throughout the region. On the sloping hillsides, the soil layers remained somewhat thin but sufficient to support stands of hardwoods and softwoods. In the bottomlands between the ridges, thicker, richer soils accumulated that would later attract farmers and other settlers.

Cultural Environment
The history and culture of Appalachia are at least as significant as its physical setting is beautiful.

Though there are some major urban centers, much of the Appalachian Mountains today remains a world apart, its inhabitants leading lives distant from some of the standards and concepts familiar to other North Americans. This relative isolation, though commonly believed to be widespread, occurs in remote and often widely separated pockets throughout the region. Within these pockets of remnant cultures, a few people live much as their forbears did a hundred or more years ago.

The Appalachians were long avoided by whites. They were seen as a significant barrier to settlement and westward migration—travel into, across, and through the rugged wilderness was often difficult, fraught with hazards such as hostile Indians, rough passage, and flooded rivers. Even so, people continued to come—in search of land, of freedom, of wealth.

The first Appalachian settlers were, of course, the native Americans. These early inhabitants were primarily hunters, gatherers, and fishermen, but some also practiced comparatively sophisticated agriculture, cultivating corn, tobacco, squash, and beans.

Little is known about the Indian occupation of much of the northern Appalachians, but the historical record of Cherokee habitation in the south is quite thorough. In addition to being efficient hunters and farmers, the Cherokee knew how to extract precious-metal ores from the stone matrix of the surrounding hills, and probably learned some new techniques from the early Spanish explorers. With the refining of gold and silver, the Cherokee and neighboring tribes became noted for their skill in fashioning fine jewelry and ornaments. The Indians were also known to store large quantities of the valuable ore.

In the early sixteenth century, the Spanish arrived in the Appalachian Mountains. Soldiers, miners, priests, and explorers under the leadership of Hernando de Soto journeyed to the New World under orders of the Spanish king to secure lands and search for wealth, wealth that was to be taken by whatever means and returned to the motherland to fill the depleted treasury.

The Spaniards came to Appalachia and on several occasions located gold and silver in the rocks of the great mountains. More often than not, de Soto's men merely took over mines that had been worked by the area Indians, but history records that the Spanish experienced amazing success at extracting the ore, smelting it into easily transportable ingots, and shipping it back to Spain.

Generations later, other whites entered the area. Lured by abundant game, a few hardy trappers and hunters journeyed to the Appalachians and returned to the eastern colonies with tales of natural bounty. In their wake came a few of the more adventurous eastern colonists. Initially, the plateau provinces on the edge of the range attracted the newcomers—the best soils were located there, and agriclture was most promising.

As whites gradually moved into the area in pursuit of hunting, trapping, and agricultural opportunities, the Indians were initially very friendly and often served as benefactors to the newcomers, bringing them offerings of their harvests from the fields and forests. Many of the early settlers married into the tribes and acquired Indian land.

After the French and Indian War of the 1750s and 1760s, the British government moved to consolidate control over the Appalachian region. Once the Indian threat was reduced, more and more whites were encouraged to settle in the region. Revolutionary War and French and Indian War veterans were given land grants, the size of the allocation depending on rank and length of service. In addition to veterans with land grants, many squatters found their way onto the rapidly growing plantations and farms.

With the increase in white population, the relationship between the newcomers and the Indian residents grew antagonistic as hunting pressure and competition for land developed. The Indians, regarded until then as friends and allies, were portrayed as ruthless savages bent on destroying white settlers. Tensions grew, conflicts resulted, and the situation grew more strained year by year.

As if all these pressures were not bad enough, about the same time, in the 1760s, gold was discovered in the southern Appalachians, and many intent on getting rich off the newly opened ore fields migrated into the range. As the numbers of white settlers, miners, and soldiers increased, the few Indians that remained were eventually forced off their tribal homelands.

Meanwhile, European newcomers to the colonies were finding conditions considerably more crowded than they had anticipated. The abundant lands and opportunities they believed awaited them in the New World didn't seem to be where they were, so they sought them in the Appalachians, just a few days travel to the west.

The population of whites in the Appalachians continued to grow. Early settlers in the region were primarily English, and these were followed by large numbers of Germans and Scotch-Irish. In lesser numbers came French Huguenots, the Swiss, and other northern Europeans.

The Germans and Scotch–Irish quickly established some of the more extensive farmsteads on the rich alluvial bottomlands, and around these growing and prospering farms, settlements evolved, churches were constructed, and towns began to grow.

Blacks were brought from the deep South to the southern Piedmont to work on cotton and tobacco plantations. Though some blacks worked in the coal mines, only a few ventured into the interior of the Blue Ridge and the Valley and Ridge provinces, and many abandoned the

Appalachian region altogether during and after World War II for job opportunies in the industrial north.

During the 1860s, the Appalachians, as well as other parts of the country, were torn by the War Between The States. Life was disrupted, settlements and farms abandoned, mines closed down, and businesses left in ruins. During the War, millions of dollars in gold and silver payrolls and money for arms, ammunition, and equipment moved through the area. Much of it was stolen, hidden, hoarded, or lost.

The post–War period saw the Appalachian countryside filled with desperate men and outlaws. Banditry was common, and travelers moved through the area at great risk to their lives. After this relatively brief period of outlawry, the area evolved into relative peace and renewed growth and prosperity.

Today the Appalachian Mountains are home to an eclectic cultural mix of various races and ethnic groups, each bringing its part over the years to the diversity, uniqueness, and progress of the region. Every one of the cultures has influenced the region's "personality," contributing to its economy, its educational system, its cultural heritage, and its folklore.

Buried Treasure in the Appalachians

There is much Appalachian folklore that concerns lost and buried treasures, some tales derived from the legacies of the native Americans, others from those of Spanish conquistadors, early white settlers, and the War Between The States. The folklore is distinctly Appalachian, and the tales are replete with colorful narratives of the place, the people, the times, and the age-old quest for wealth and buried treasures.

The lure of lost treasure is a powerful one, and hundreds of Appalachian residents as well as travelers to the area have succumbed to it during past generations. Hard times in the Appalachians caused many mines to close, farms to be abandoned, and people to leave, but the search for buried treasure went on unabated, perhaps even stronger. Some communities in Appalachia did not survive, but the stories did, and like the ancient mountains themselves, they endured.

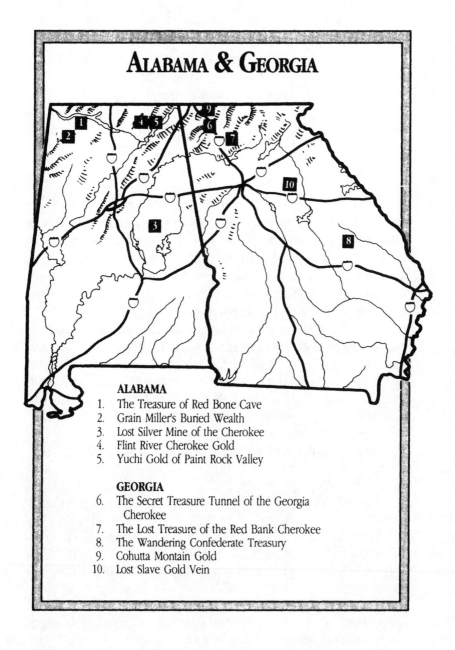

Alabama & Georgia

ALABAMA

1. The Treasure of Red Bone Cave
2. Grain Miller's Buried Wealth
3. Lost Silver Mine of the Cherokee
4. Flint River Cherokee Gold
5. Yuchi Gold of Paint Rock Valley

GEORGIA

6. The Secret Treasure Tunnel of the Georgia
   Cherokee
7. The Lost Treasure of the Red Bank Cherokee
8. The Wandering Confederate Treasury
9. Cohutta Montain Gold
10. Lost Slave Gold Vein

The Treasure of
Red Bone Cave

Somewhere on the north side of the Tennessee River
near Muscle Shoals is an elusive limestone cavern which
may contain several million dollars' worth of gold ingots
and jewelry. This treasure cave has been known of for
centuries, but efforts to locate it during the past two
hundred fifty years have not succeeded.

Legend attributes the origin of the gold to Spanish
explorers who came to this region under the leadership of
Hernando de Soto. In 1538, Charles V of Spain gave de Soto
ample funding and a company of more than six hundred
men to travel to the New World to search for silver and
gold. The ore was to be smelted, cast into ingots, and
shipped to the motherland, Spain.

Arriving in Florida after months crossing the Atlantic
Ocean, de Soto and his company of soldiers, miners, and
priests traveled, explored, and prospected vast portions of
the southern United States from the east coast to the Ozark
Mountains. According to ancient records and documents
found in Spanish monasteries, the explorers were successful, for they eventually shipped hundreds of millions of
dollars' worth of gold and silver back to the Iberian peninsula.

As well as mining for it, de Soto's men took great
quantities of gold from several of the Cherokee villages
they encountered in their explorations. Though the

Cherokee did not measure wealth with gold, they used the metal to fashion bracelets and other jewelry. When the Spanish saw the abundance of gold the Indians possessed, they took it by force, often killing hundreds of the red men in the process. The jewelry was melted down and formed into brick-sized ingots.

A Spanish detachment that had just raided several Cherokee villages was leading a gold-laden pack train of some forty horses when it chanced upon a friendly Chickasaw encampment in what is now northeastern Alabama. The settlement was a few miles south of the Tennessee River along a tributary that provided good water for drinking and crops.

As winter was coming, the Chickasaw invited the newcomers to remain in their village until the cold weather passed. The Spaniards accepted the invitation and lived for a time with the Indians, joining in their hunts for game.

When spring finally came, the Spaniards began preparing to travel to the southwest to rendezvous with de Soto at a location designated earlier. Before their departure, however, the leader of the party demanded of the Chickasaw chief some one hundred of the tribe's young women to accompany the soldiers on their journey. When the chief refused, the Spaniards became belligerent and threatening.

While they were loading their gold on the pack horses, the Spaniards were surprised by a sudden attack from the enraged Chickasaw. Panicked, the soldiers hastily mounted their horses and fled from the village, leaving behind the great treasure in gold ingots.

The Chickasaw pursued the Spaniards northward to the bank of the Tennessee River. With their retreat cut off, the soldiers turned and fought. The battle lasted nearly an hour, and when it was over, most of the Spaniards had been killed.

After returning to the village, the Chickasaw chief ordered all the treasure carried to a cave across the wide river to the north and concealed within it.

This done, the Indians ignored the great fortune in gold cached in the limestone cavern except when some small amount was needed to make jewelry and ornaments.

The Chickasaw village thrived over the ensuing years, and it was a large and happy community that greeted a young white trapper who entered the region in 1720 in search of beaver. The trapper wanted to try his luck along some of the small streams found in the area. He came to the Chickasaw village and requested permission from the chief to set his traps in the nearby streams.

The Chickasaw chief, impressed by the young man, granted permission and invited him to live in the village. He did so, and during the following weeks, the chief became very fond of the trapper.

The chief had only one child, a daughter, and as he was very old, he was concerned that she find a husband and provide him with a grandson who would eventually lead the tribe. The daughter had spurned the courtship of the many Chickasaw braves, and the chief was beginning to wonder if she would ever wed. The daughter did, however, find the young trapper to her liking, and soon the two of them were spending time together.

One night, about two months after he first entered the Chickasaw village, the trapper was awakened by two Indians. Without a word, they tied his hands behind his back and placed a blindfold over his eyes before he could identify them. He fought as hard as he could, but their combined strength was too much for him. Once he realized he was helpless, he ceased to struggle, and the Indians whispered that no harm would come to him if he followed their instruction.

All the rest of that night and the morning of the following day, the trapper was led through the woods. Once while the group was stopped to rest, the blindfold slipped slightly from the captive's eyes, and he momentarily saw before him the wide expanse of the Tennessee River and the high limestone bluffs that rose in the distance beyond.

A few moments later, he was placed in a canoe and rowed across the river. After a brief hike, the three men came to a place where the air was cold and the ground was damp. The trapper could hear the squeaks of bats and realized he was inside a large cave.

Fifteen minutes further into the cave, the Indians called a halt, untied the trapper, and removed the blindfold.

The three men stood in a large chamber illuminated by torches. As the light flickered on the walls of the cave, the trapper looked around and recognized the chief of the Chickasaw village and one of his braves. The chief directed the trapper's eyes to one of the walls of the cave.

Stacked like cordwood against the far wall of the chamber were hundreds of ingots of pure gold, reaching nearly to the ceiling. At the foot of the stack were several chests filled with golden jewels and other valuables.

The chief told the trapper the tale of the long-ago Spaniards' visit. The chief also told him that the gold he saw in this room was only a part of the total amount hidden in the cave.

Taking the trapper to another chamber in the cave, the chief pointed to several skeletons propped against one wall. He said they were the bones of the warriors that had died in the battle with the fleeing Spaniards. The bodies were placed in the cave so their spirits could guard it against intruders.

The chief came forward and laid a hand on the trapper's shoulder. He told the young man that if he married his daughter, all the treasure in the other room would be his to keep. If he chose not to marry the daughter, he would be allowed to leave the village unharmed but was not to know the location of the treasure cave.

The trapper considered his options. If he married the chief's daughter and remained in the remote Indian village, the wealth would do him little good, as he would have no opportunity to spend it. Remembering his view of the river and the limestone bluff when the blindfold slipped from his eyes earlier that day, he believed he would be able to return and locate the cave on his own.

The trapper told the Chickasaw chief he wanted a few days alone to consider the offer. The chief agreed, reattached the bindings and the blindfold, and led the trapper from the cave.

Darkness fell long before the party could reach the village, and as they were all tired, the chief decided to camp for the night near the bank of the river. Late that night, the trapper killed the two Indians while they slept and threw their bodies into the river. He then fled on foot to Fort Rosalie in the Natchez Territory, reaching it after a harrowing journey of several days.

At the fort, the trapper invited an old friend to join him in his search for the great treasure of what he called Red Bone Cave, naming it after the skeletons of the red men he saw within it.

Hiding by day and searching by night, the two men spent the next several weeks trying to find the cave. The trapper's friend grew weary of the fruitless search and soon returned to Fort Rosalie.

Now alone, the trapper decided to return to the Chickasaw village. Wary at first, he was surprised when he was warmly welcomed by the Indians. He learned later that no one had ever known that the chief and his accomplice had kidnapped him and taken him from the village that night a few months earlier. The disappearance of the chief and the brave remained a mystery to the Indians.

Using the excuse of trapping for furs, the young man continued his search for Red Bone Cave. He eventually married the daughter of the dead chief and settled in the village, and though he searched for many years, he was never able to find the cave again.

In 1723, the trapper's wife died from malaria, and he eventually returned to Fort Rosalie. The settlement, however, had long since been abandoned. It lay in ruins, its people massacred years earlier by the Natchez Indians.

The trapper took up residence in the abandoned fort and remained there for the rest of his life. He made several more forays into the Chickasaw wilderness to find Red Bone Cave, but never succeeded.

In his later years, the old trapper often visited with the boatmen who plied the Tennessee River. He told them his strange tale of gold bars stacked like cordwood against the back wall of the elusive cavern.

Many thought the old trapper was crazy, but his tale has endured to the present and has inspired hundreds to search for the gold lying deep within Red Bone Cave.

The Miller's Buried Wealth

C. E. Sharps was a well-known trader, landowner,
and businessman who operated in and around Florence,
Alabama during the 1890s. Sharps not only had a penchant
for making money, he had a passion for hoarding it. As a
result of his many successful business enterprises and his
miserly ways, C.E. Sharps became one of the wealthiest
men in northwestern Alabama.

It was not unexpected, then, when Sharps purchased
White's Mill. The old mill, which served most of the farmers
and residents in the area of Florence, had flourished for many
years, and Sharps intended to make it even more profitable.
In addition to charging the patrons of the mill a small fee
for grinding their corn, Sharps began to make large purchases of the crop, which he ground into flour and sold to
the Florence citizens. Sharps also bought about a hundred
acres of forest land nearby which he planned to clear and
plant with corn and other crops. Though intent on reaping
large profits, Sharps also provided important jobs for community residents with his mill and related farming activities.

An quirk of Sharps's was that he always insisted payment for flour or grinding be made with gold coins. Thus
the businessman accumulated a substantial fortune in gold
over the years.

Always distrustful of banks, Sharps buried his wealth
in several locations around Florence. The gold from the

operation of the mill was buried somewhere in the forest nearby. Every two weeks or so, Sharps counted the gold he had taken in from the mill, put it in a feed sack, and carried it to a secret location in the forest where he buried it.

Sharps employed his young nephew, Grady Sharps, as an accountant and bookkeeper at the mill. Many times, Grady watched his uncle carry the gold-filled sack out into the nearby woods. The old man always returned without the sack some thirty minutes later.

Grady knew his uncle was burying his wealth somewhere out in the forest, and he longed to know where. Several times, he considered following his uncle, but timidity overcame his greed.

Grady Sharps was a competent bookkeeper and a clear asset to his uncle's business. A family man, Grady often dreamed of the life of luxury a great fortune would provide, but he lacked his uncle's aggressive business orientation. A thin, sallow fellow who looked a bit rodentlike, Grady always seemed content with his life but secretly dreamed of wielding power and possessing wealth.

Once when Sharps left the mill office with a sack of gold coins, Grady followed him to the limits of the mill property. Because C.E. Sharps was known for his violent temper, Grady was terrified to think what might happen if he were discovered. He quickly returned to his desk inside the mill as his uncle, toting the gold-filled burlap sack, disappeared into the dense woods.

Later, Grady actually followed his uncle into the forest. On that day, the young nephew watched as Sharps filled the feed sack with the precious gold coins, tied a knot in it, and left the mill. Replacing his pen in the ink well and closing the account books, Grady waited for a few minutes, then rose from his seat and went to the front door of the mill office. In the distance, he could see his uncle disappearing into the forest. Grady hurried to the place where he had last seen the old man and silently followed his tracks. He stayed close enough to keep his uncle in sight but far enough away so he would not hear him.

Once in the woods and out of sight of the mill, Sharps paused every few steps and looked around to make certain he was not being followed. When he believed it safe, he went on a little way, only to stop and repeat the process again and again.

Each time his uncle paused, Grady was sure he would be discovered. With each step his fear grew, but he knew he was close to discovering his uncle's cache of gold. Finally, though, Grady grew so terrified his uncle would see him that he turned and fled back to the mill. The nephew never found where the uncle buried his wealth, and he never tried to follow the old man again.

By June of 1899, the mill had been in operation under Sharps's ownership and management for several years and had prospered nicely. Sharps decided it was time to make some repairs to the old structure, and he hired several men to do the work.

Sharps was supervising the reshingling of the mill roof one morning, shouting instructions to several of the laborers. While directing a worker, he lost his footing, slid down the steeply angled roof, and plunged into the mill pond some seventy feet below.

Sharps could not swim, and drowned before anyone could reach him. With him went the knowledge of the location of the huge cache of gold in the nearby forest.

For several months thereafter, Grady Sharps retraced his uncle's trail into the forest. Dozens of times he arrived at the spot where he had turned and fled in fear of discovery, but from that point, he could never decide which direction to take. Finally, the nephew gave up in frustration.

The historic White's Mill still stands, a relatively quiet tourist attraction in a picturesque part of Appalachian Alabama. Somewhere, a short distance from the old mill, lies a fortune in buried gold coins, undisturbed for nearly a century.

Lost Silver Mine of the Cherokee

About twenty-five miles east of Birmingham, Alabama, lies a portion of the ancient homeland of the Cherokee Indians. The Cherokee were a relatively peaceful tribe that tolerated the settlement of whites in the area with dignity, forbearance, and friendliness. They often traded with the newcomers.

The Cherokee were distinct from many of the region's other tribes because of the finely crafted silver necklaces and armbands with which they adorned themselves. The ornaments were fashioned from the purest silver ore, and the craftsmanship was the finest ever seen. The origin of the Cherokee silver was often a topic of discussion among whites, but the Indians refused to reveal the secret.

When coal was discovered in the area in 1832 and large-scale mining began, the influx of whites to the region caused concern among the Cherokee, but the Indians stayed friendly and continued to welcome the newcomers.

The new coal mining community was called Ironton. Because of the opportunities available in this booming settlement, it grew rapidly.

Arriving shortly after Ironton's boom was one Dr. Isaac Stone. Though it is doubtful Stone ever attended a medical college, he opened an office, called himself a physician, and proceeded to treat the ills and infections of the community. Stone was quickly successful and was generally regarded as an important citizen of the town.

In 1834, an epidemic of measles broke out among the Cherokee, and the entire village near Ironton was infected. Dozens died and hundreds more were sick and immobilized from the disease. Stone, hearing of the Cherokee's plight, volunteered to travel to the village and treat the Indians. For several days, he stayed with the tribe, ministering to the stricken, until the dread disease finally ran its course, and the tribe was restored to its collective health.

In gratitude, the Cherokee invited Stone to remain in the village for a few days as they prepared a feast and celebration in his honor. The physician agreed and moved into one of the huts.

While tending the sick, Stone could not help but notice the many fine armbands, necklaces, and other jewelry made from silver. He was intrigued by the great wealth to which the Cherokee seemed to have access.

During his stay in the Indian camp, Stone met an elderly Indian named Chief George. Stone and the old man enjoyed each other's company and often engaged in animated talk.

One afternoon, Chief George told him that he held an important position within the tribe—he procured silver from a secret mine northwest of the village. Twice a year, said the Indian, he would select three or four young braves to help him lead a pack train into the mountains to the mine, dig the precious silver, load it onto the horses, and carry it back to the village. There the tribe artisans would fashion the ore into the fine ornaments worn by both men and women.

During a conversation with the old man, Stone tried to learn the location of the mine, but Chief George quickly changed the topic and would not answer the physician's questions. He did, however, make Stone the gift of a silver bracelet.

Several times, Stone purchased cheap whiskey in Ironton and offered it to the Indians in an attempt to loosen their tongues about the silver. His efforts failed.

Finally, the feast and celebration ended, and Stone went back to Ironton. He carried with him, though, an impelling desire to find the rich silver lode of the Cherokee and mine it for himself.

Several months later, Stone told some friends of the secret Cherokee mine. At first they were skeptical of the tale of a rich silver mine, but they were soon won over when Stone showed them the fine bracelet he'd been given.

Stone told his friends that the time was approaching when the old Indian would lead one of the trips to the secret mine to get ore. He suggested hiding nearby and trailing the pack train to the source of the wealth. After the Indians had gotten what they needed and left, Stone told his friends, the men could enter the mine and take what silver they could carry. Stone's friends agreed to join him in locating the mine.

On pretense of checking on the Indians' health, Stone went to the Cherokee village and learned when Chief George would leave for the mine.

Several days later, as the morning sun broke over an adjacent ridge, the old Indian, accompanied by three young braves, led several pack horses from the village as Stone and his companions lay watching, concealed in the nearby woods. When the Indians had a long enough lead, the poachers mounted and followed, staying far enough behind to avoid being seen.

They followed for about three hours and finally arrived at Wolf Creek. There they lost the trail. The tracks of the ponies entered the creek but didn't reappear on the other side, and the gravelly bottom of the fast-flowing stream yielded no clues to the direction the Indians had taken.

Frustrated, Stone and his men separated into two groups and searched both sides of the creek for several miles in each direction. They could find no place where the Indian's ponies had left it.

After several hours of searching, one of the men noticed a curious-looking rock on the creek bank, a rock that seemed out of place. Thinking it had been kicked up by one of the Indian ponies, he dismounted, picked it up, and examined it. Deducing nothing from the four-pound chunk of rock, he casually placed it in his saddlebag and went on with the search.

Late that evening, as Stone and his party convened in the woods at the point where they had first begun tracking the Indians, they saw Chief George and his braves leading the heavily laden pack horses into the Cherokee village! Discouraged, the men returned to Ironton, and Stone never again tried to find the silver.

Several months passed, and the story of the Cherokee silver mine was told throughout the area. Soon, prospectors and treasure hunters were combing the hills near the Indian village in search of the ore. It was never found.

Some time later, the tracker who had found the curious rock retrieved it from his saddlebag. On a hunch, he had it assayed and was surprised to learn it was a freshly mined piece of high-grade silver ore. The discovery spurred a renewed search for the mine, but once again, nothing was found.

When the Cherokee were removed from the region and relocated to Arkansas and Oklahoma, it was said they gathered up much of their fine silver jewelry and ornaments and buried them inside the mine. They sealed the mine entrance and covered it so it would look like the surrounding forest. The leaders of the tribe vowed they would return one day and retrieve the jewelry, but they never did.

Ironton is a ghost town now, and save for the scars of coal mining in the area, there is little evidence that it was once a thriving community. Few people can remember the exact location of the old Cherokee village, but somewhere about a half day's ride from the site may lie one of the richest silver mines east of the Mississippi River.

Flint River Cherokee Gold

Near the southern end of the Appalachian Mountains, in northeastern Alabama not far from present-day Huntsville, a group of Cherokee once settled and farmed a fertile valley adjacent to the Flint River. For centuries, the Indians lived in peace and harmony, raising crops and hunting the abundant game in the nearby forest. The Cherokee, like most Indians, had little use for money and material wealth, so precious metals like gold and silver were useless to them as units of exchange. The Indians did, though, fashion handsome jewelry and ornaments from the valuable metals when they were available.

Legend says that the Flint River Cherokee occasionally traded for gold with other tribes far to the east. The specific source of the gold is unknown, but it is a fact that gold was often found and mined in parts of the Appalachians. Travelers and traders who chanced upon the Indian settlement near the Flint River often remarked on the abundance of gold ornaments and jewelry the Cherokee wore.

As the relentless tide of Anglo settlement flowed into the southern Appalachians during the 1830s, many newcomers coveted the fertile bottomland of the Flint River Cherokee settlement. The earlier friendliness of trappers and traders in the region was soon replaced by the greed and hostility of settlers. When the whites tried to force the Cherokee from their rich farmland, violence erupted, and the Indians repelled the aggressors.

The Cherokee were helpless, though, against the clandestine political maneuvering that eventually forced them off their homeland at bayonet point. Higher powers decreed that the Flint River lands should be opened to white settlement, and the Indians were forcibly removed by the U. S. Army to reservation lands in what was eventually to become Oklahoma.

The journey from the Flint River settlement to the unfamiliar environment of "Indian Territory" was traumatic for the Cherokee. They were soon followed by hundreds of people from other southern tribes also evicted from the ancient homelands and forced to follow what came to be called the Trail of Tears.

Powerless to resist the hundreds of armed soldiers commanded to escort them to the Territory, the Flint River Cherokee made preparations for the long journey.

Because few of the Indians had horses, they would travel on foot, and whatever belongings they took would have to be carried on their backs. Much had to be left behind. Because gold was heavy and of no immediate use to them, the Flint River Cherokee collected all their fine ornaments and jewelry and placed them in a large clay pot. The tribe elders then transported the heavy pot to the edge of the cultivated bottomland and into the nearby woods. In a large clearing, they chose an appropriate place to bury this fortune in gold jewelry.

After the large pot of gold was cached, one of the Indians made cryptic slash marks on several nearby white oak trees.

When they returned to the village, another of the elders made a map on a tanned deer skin. The map showed the location of the village, several important landmarks, and the buried pot of gold. When the map was completed, the maker rolled it up and placed it in a leather bag. The elders agreed that when the tribe was settled into the new lands in the west, they would return for the gold.

The journey along the Trail of Tears was one of terrible deprivation and hardship. Many of the Flint River Indians died of exposure, sickness, and starvation, and it was a decimated tribe that finally reached the assigned lands in the Territory.

Life for the Cherokee was hard in their new home. The men toiled in the fields trying to coax crops from grudging soil, and the women did the best they could to provide decent homes for their families. In time, the Indians, burdened with the fight for survival, gradually lost their enthusiasm for retrieving the pot of buried gold near the old Flint River settlement.

The treasure map prepared by the tribal elder was passed from relative to relative until it finally came into the hands of a Cherokee known only as John. John's grandmother had cared for the map for many years and passed it on to his mother. When she died in 1912, it fell into John's possession.

John grew up in Indian Territory hearing the tale of the buried pot of gold jewelry somewhere near the old Flint River settlement. When he got the map to the treasure, he decided that as soon as he could, he would go to the ancient homeland of his people and try to find the fortune. John had notions of using the wealth to build a reservation hospital for his tribe.

In 1914, when John was fifty, he boarded a train in Indian Territory and made the long journey to northeastern Alabama. He carried only a small pack containing a change of clothes and the treasure map.

Arriving at the little settlement of Ryland, John asked for directions to the old Flint River settlement. He learned the place was now a large farm called Bellfaun and was owned by a man named Shelby Collum. John hoisted his pack over his shoulder and undertook the twenty-mile hike to Bellfaun.

It was early evening when John arrived at the Collum farm and was directed to the main house by one of the farm hands. The Cherokee introduced himself to Collum and told him his reason for coming. He politely asked permission to search the farm for the buried pot of gold jewelry.

Collum, who did not like the looks of the Indian, refused him and told him he didn't want him on the farm.

At this point, John pulled the ancient treasure map from his pack and showed it to Collum. The apparent authenticity of the map softened Collum's attitude, and he asked John to tell him more about the treasure.

John explained the history of the Cherokee gold and told Collum he would share a portion of it with him if he would only relent and let him conduct a search on the farm.

Collum was a shrewd man and not one to pass up such an opportunity. He knew it would cost him nothing to allow the Indian to search the farm, and if the buried wealth were found, it might mean that Collum would share in a magnificent fortune. He agreed to John's proposition. He told John he could spend the night in the barn, and they would begin the search early the next day.

The next morning after breakfast, John and Collum embarked on a search for the gold. John walked in the lead, and from time to time halted and consulted the map for a specific landmark.

At one point, John stopped at a tree and pointed to a very old slash mark low on the trunk. The tree was an ancient white oak, and the cut was partially overgrown— but it was clearly a man-made mark. John pointed to the map, which showed a similar mark.

They found several more trees with similar markings as they walked around the farm. In one particularly thick part of the woods near the edge of Collum's tilled acreage, John found a large tree with the image of a human foot carved into it. John turned in the direction the foot indicated, and after several more paces found himself in a wide clearing ringed by huge white oak trees.

John walked over to one of the trees and found several carved symbols on the trunk, beginning at knee level and extending up as high as John could reach.

The Cherokee regarded the markings in silence for several minutes. Finally, without a word, he turned and walked away, never to be seen again.

Because the Indian left with no explanation, Collum assumed the carvings on the tree indicated someone had returned earlier and recovered the treasure. The farmer gave the matter no further thought until three years later.

While searching for a stray calf in the spring of 1917, Collum came to the clearing he and John had visited three years earlier. The clearing looked much the same—except for an excavation near the center. On closer investigation, Collum discovered a large round hole approximately four feet deep. Weeds growing in the excavated dirt suggested to the farmer the hole had been dug at least a year earlier.

What had been removed from the hole? Farmer Collum pondered that question all his life. Did the Cherokee John return under cover of night and dig up the treasure so he would not have to share it with Collum? Was a treasure found at all? Does it, in fact, still lie somewhere in the clearing in the woods adjacent to Bellfaun Farm?

The mystery has never been solved.

Yuchi Gold of Paint Rock Valley

It was the last year of the seventeenth century, and the small company of Spanish soldiers was about to undertake a most perilous journey, a journey to transport millions of dollars' worth of gold bars across the frontier to a distant point on the east coast of Florida.

For six long years, the Spaniards had labored in a rich gold mine deep in the heart of the Sierra Madres of northern Mexico. The original company of some two hundred officers, soldiers, miners, and priests had been assigned by the Spanish government to extract the precious metal from the grudging rock of the Sierra Madre. The original force had been depleted to sixty by Indian attacks, disease, and starvation, but with the help of Indian slaves, they stayed and continued the mining operation.

At the end of each month, the raw gold was melted down and poured into molds to make brick-sized ingots which were stacked along one wall of the mine awaiting transport to Spain. Sometimes as many as several hundred gold bars would accumulate before an escort from the government leaders arrived.

About three times a year, a big pack train—about sixty mules—would come from Mexico City with supplies. Slaves would then load the bars onto the mules, and the wealth would be taken to the Mexican gulf coast, transferred to a ship, and sailed to the Iberian peninsula.

The officers in charge of the mine began to cast greedy eyes on the gold. After the first year of operation, they agreed among themselves to cache every fifth ingot in a secret hiding place, intending to ship the gold clandestinely to Europe and set themselves up in business. When enough gold had been stockpiled to satisfy the officers, they planned to pack it north, cross the Rio Grande, and make their way to a designated point somewhere on the northeast coast of Florida. Arrangements had been made with a renegade ship captain to haul the riches back to Europe, where the officers intended to live out their lives in splendor.

Sometime during the winter of 1699, the officers decided they had put aside enough gold to make them wealthy men. They were ready to undertake the journey to Florida. The gold was loaded onto pack mules, and the unsuspecting enlisted men were commanded to escort the vast wealth across the continent. Before abandoning the area, the Spaniards executed all the Indian slaves, stacked their bodies in the mine, and sealed and disguised the entrance.

Several days later, the party crossed the Rio Grande near what is now Del Rio, Texas, and proceeded eastward. There were many rivers to cross in the Texas country, and the spring rains had swollen most of them to flood stage, making travel difficult and often delaying the march for days at a time. The Spaniards also had to deal with hostile Indians along the way, and by the time they reached Louisiana, their numbers had decreased significantly. With fewer men, the pack train of some twenty mule-loads of gold ingots was becoming increasingly difficult to maintain.

As the Spaniards neared the Louisiana gulf coast, they learned the Indians in the area were preying on travelers and trappers. Visitors to the region were often tortured, killed, and mutilated. The heads of victims were put on pikes and set in the middle of the trail as a warning to outsiders.

Because of the Indian depredations, the Spaniards made a wide swing northeast and passed through what is now central Mississippi and Alabama. Here they were attacked several times by still other tribes, forcing them to veer even further northeast. Eventually they reached a point just north of present-day Tuscaloosa where the officers ordered a halt so that men and livestock might rest up from the arduous journey.

One evening while the Spaniards were dining around the campfire, a war party of some seventy Indians poured out of the forest and attacked and killed every one of them in minutes.

The Indians were of the Yuchi tribe, closely related to the Cherokee. Ordinarily, they were not warlike, but like most of the other tribes in the region, they resented the encroachment of outsiders on their land.

The Indians, who used gold to make jewelry, led the ingot-laden pack mules back to their village in Paint Rock Valley, about twenty miles east of present-day Huntsville. There, the Yuchi chief ordered the gold stashed in a nearby cave. He did not want any evidence of the intruders' wealth around should his village be visited by friends of the Spaniards.

Over the next several generations, Indians occasionally visited the cave to remove some of the gold for making jewelry, but other than the loss of those small amounts from time to time, the cache remained virtually undisturbed.

During the Indian removal of the early 1830s, the Yuchi tribe was ordered to vacate Paint Rock Valley. Before leaving, many of the Indians went to the cavern and divided some of the gold within. Several families tried to carry some of the heavy ingots on their journey along the Trail of Tears, but they were forced to bury them along the way. Some members of the tribe escaped the military escort and fled eastward to Tennessee with their share of the gold, settling eventually at Henderson Ridge.

The greatest portion of the Spanish ingots remained in the cave.

Sometime in the mid–1920s, an aged Indian appeared at Paint Rock Valley leading two fine mules. He claimed he came from Henderson Ridge and was descended from the Yuchi Indians who had originally settled the valley. The old Indian was impressed with the bountiful farming area that was once the site of the village of his forefathers, and he was friendly to all he met.

The Indian said he was looking for two able-bodied young men to help him load some heavy objects onto the mules, and soon acquired the services of two strapping youths, each about sixteen years old.

The old Indian, the boys, and the two mules left early the next morning and began a long trek out of the valley and into the limestone hills. From time to time, the Indian would call a brief halt while he checked notations on a very old map he carried. About an hour into the journey, the Indian told the youths they would have to be blindfolded the rest of the way. At first they demurred, but the old man said it was the Indian way of doing things, so they humored him and let their eyes be covered. With each of the boys holding onto the tail of a mule, the Indian led the way deeper into the hills.

The men had walked and climbed for another hour when the youths suddenly noticed the air had turned cooler and they could hear the echo of their own footsteps. The Indian removed their blindfolds, and they found themselves inside a great cavern with water dripping from ceiling and walls. The Indian lit a torch, handed each of the youths two burlap sacks, and led them deeper into the cave.

After another twenty minutes of negotiating several big boulders and narrow passageways, they came to a large chamber. Against one wall of the chamber were piled dozens of good-sized rocks, which the Indian asked the boys to remove. They did so and found an irregular jumble of hundreds of brick-sized bars of some kind of metal. One of the boys picked up a bar, hefted it, and suggested it might be lead because of the weight. The Indian merely nodded and asked them to fill the burlap sacks with as many of the bars as they could carry.

The three men made a total of four trips back into the chamber, carrying out burlap sacks containing three or four of the heavy ingots each time. With difficulty, the Indian loaded the bars into several stout leather packs which were tied to wooden pack frames on the two mules. When all the packs were full, the Indian had the boys cover the rest of the ingots with the large rocks they had removed earlier. Though they had carried out several dozen, hundreds still remained in the chamber deep within the cave.

When they were ready to leave, the Indian again blindfolded his two helpers. Assured they could not see anything, he led them back to the valley. The next day, the old Indian was seen leaving the valley leading the two heavily laden mules toward Tennessee. It was the last time he was seen.

Several years later, the two boys—now grown men with families—heard the tale of the rich store of Spanish gold ingots cached in a limestone cavern somewhere back in the mountains surrounding Paint Rock Valley. It was then they realized they had carried gold, not lead, out of the cave for the old Indian.

For many years afterward, the two men tried to find the cave again, but they never did.

The Secret Treasure Tunnel
of the Georgia Cherokee

In 1835, the Indian Removal Treaty was signed by the leading Cherokee chiefs, and the long wait for the order to leave their homelands and make the journey to the far west had begun. Before the great migration to what would eventually become Oklahoma, the leaders of the northeastern Georgia Cherokee plotted to conceal their vast wealth from the greedy white settlers who were moving into the region.

The northern Georgia Cherokee were wealthy even by the white man's standards. For many generations, these Indians had traded with tribes as far away as Virginia. Gold from the rich mines of the Virginia Appalachians was particularly prized by the Georgia Cherokee, and with it they crafted the ornate jewelry they wore.

Shortly before the removal treaty was to be signed, Rising Fawn, the district chief of the northeastern Georgia Cherokee, called a meeting of all the area subchiefs at his home in Settendown Creek. Rising Fawn proposed to construct a tunnel in the nearby mountains and hide all of the Cherokee wealth in it. When the time was right, a delegation of Indians would be sent from the newly assigned lands in the Territory to retrieve it.

All of the subchiefs present at the meeting agreed except for the leader of the Red Bank tribe. For reasons of their own, the Red Bank Indians decided to cache their wealth independently of the other Indians.

Attending this meeting was one Jacob Scudder, a white man who had married into the tribe and eventually became a blood brother and subchief. Scudder, who was not required to leave the area, was appointed caretaker of the Cherokee wealth in the absence of the Indians, an honor which Scudder accepted willingly and with great humility.

Construction of the tunnel began immediately, and each of the subchiefs sent teams of laborers who worked day and night burrowing into the hard rock of the southern Appalachians.

The excavation of the tunnel was to remain a secret from any and all white men (except for Scudder), and when trappers and soldiers visited the area, the digging halted immediately and did not resume until the newcomers had left.

The tunnel was sited in an area completely unsuitable for living, grazing, or growing crops. The ground was rocky, the soil thin, the water scarce, and the timber puny and scattered. In short, it was an area unappealing to the white settlers.

The tunnel itself, when completed, was just over two hundred feet long, and extended deep into a steep rocky outcrop. Along the sides of the long tunnel, the diggers excavated square, room-sized chambers to be used as vaults. Each tribal division was assigned a vault in which to store treasure and other important belongings. The entrance to each vault was a low doorway about three to four feet high.

Soon the announcement came that the Indians were to be removed from their homelands. When word reached the northeastern Cherokee, they had only forty-eight hours to prepare for the long journey. During that time, families carried their gold and other valuable possessions to the secret tunnel. Many walked, with their gold and jewels in packs strapped to their backs; a few came on horseback, leading ponies laden with the accumulated wealth of several generations. Others canoed up the Etowah River to the secret tunnel. Family by family, they deposited their wealth in the tunnel, all intending to return someday to retrieve it.

While the tunnel was being dug, the Cherokee carved and scratched many cryptic symbols on the exposed rocks and outcrops around the region, symbols that allegedly pointed to the location of the hidden treasure.

Coinciding with the removal announcement was a proclamation that in January of 1838, a new federal mint would be opened at Dahlonega, about twenty miles to the north. A gold deposition center had been ordered by the federal government to accommodate the miners, settlers, and soldiers in the area. The new mint required gold bullion for the minting of coins. Most transactions in the region had until then been conducted with gold nuggets and gold dust. All other forms of money were virtually useless there.

According to information gleaned from old Cherokee documents, the Indians robbed an important shipment of gold bound for the new mint. An unescorted wagon carrying the gold was traveling toward Dahlonega from the United States Treasury Department along the old Federal road. Where the road wound through a particularly dense section of forest, five masked Indians halted the coach and relieved it of seven fifty-pound gold bars. It is believed that the robbery was planned by Chief Rising Fawn and executed by five of his most trusted braves. The seven bars were presumably taken to the tunnel and added to an already large fortune.

Not far from Settendown Creek lived two white families. They had settled in the region several years earlier and were friends with the Cherokee. On the evening before the Indians were to leave, while the two families were visiting at one of the homes, the men walked down to Rising Fawn's village to bid the Indians a safe journey and help them load their belongings. The Indians were surprised by the sudden visit of the two white men as they were loading gold for transport to the secret tunnel.

In the center of the village, a large horse-drawn sled with wooden runners stood, piled with jewelry, gold nuggets, bags of gold dust, and other precious artifacts. Several large clay pots were being filled with gold nuggets. Wide-eyed at the sight of such fantastic wealth, the men could only stand and watch.

Rising Fawn spotted the two and led them to a part of the village where they could not see the loading of the treasure. As they talked, the men spotted the sled being pulled away by a team of four horses and disappearing into the forest on the other side of the village. Presently, Rising Fawn and the two men bid each other goodbye, and the farmers left.

Later that evening, the two men decided that after the Indians left the area the following morning, they would go back to the abandoned village and follow the skid marks of the sled, seeking the treasure's hiding place.

The next morning, the two men tracked the sled. For half a mile, the trail was easily followed, but then the tracks entered a shallow creek and vanished. For the rest of the day, the two farmers searched up and down the creek for some sign of the tracks. They never found any.

Just before dawn that day, the last of the Cherokee treasure had been deposited in the vault. Inside the tunnel were several deadfalls. Should anyone but a Cherokee familiar with the tunnel somehow have gained entrance, they would likely have been killed within minutes by one of the traps.

When the wealth was secured and the deadfalls arranged, the opening was filled with large rocks and covered with dirt to make it look like the surrounding landscape.

Jacob Scudder and his family watched with sadness as the last of his Cherokee friends and relatives abandoned their homeland and departed on the infamous Trail of Tears. For many years, Scudder lived in and farmed the fertile valley, all that time watching over the secret treasure tunnel.

Scudder never saw any of his Indian friends return to recover the buried treasure. Occasionally he heard from one of the chiefs, but their messages dwelt mostly on the hard life in the Territory and the continuous fight for survival.

Scudder grew old and finally died at his farm on Settendown Creek. When he passed away, he apparently took with him the secret of the Cherokee treasure tunnel in the nearby mountains.

Searchers since have found many of the carved symbols on the rock outcrops throughout the area, but thus far the cache of gold in the secret tunnel has eluded them.

The Lost Treasure of the Red Bank Cherokee

While most of the northern tribes of the Georgia Cherokee, under the leadership of Chief Rising Fawn, agreed to relocate peaceably to Indian Territory in the west, the Red Bank tribe resisted every effort of the United States government to remove it from its ancient homelands along Bannister and Bruton Creeks in what is now Forsyth County.

The Red Bank Cherokee numbered about one hundred twenty. Fiercely independent, they seldom went along with the dictates of the district chief. Like most Indians in the region, they possessed stores of gold accumulated over the years in trade with tribes far to the east. The Cherokee prized gold solely for its natural beauty and used it only to make jewelry, but when settlers moving into the area showed a preference for the yellow metal, the Indians began to see the ore as an item of barter. After many generations of trade with the gold-rich eastern tribes, a number of Cherokee families had built huge fortunes of gold nuggets and dust.

The Red Bank Cherokee were among the richest of the northern Georgia tribes. When Chief Rising Fawn proposed that all Cherokee conceal their wealth in a secret tunnel and return for it later, the Red Bank tribe alone refused to go along with the plan. *(See the preceding story, "The Secret Treasure Tunnel of the Georgia Cherokee.")*

Always independent, the Red Bank Indians distrusted Rising Fawn and thought him easily intimidated by U. S. Government officials. Likewise, they distrusted Scudder, the white subchief whom Rising Fawn appointed as guardian of the hidden gold. Several of the Red Bank Cherokee accused Scudder of plotting with the whites for the removal of the Indians so that he could secure their abandoned land as well as their abandoned wealth.

As the time for removal approached, the Red Bank Cherokee finally realized resisting the soldiers would be futile, and they relented. The night before they left, the tribe met and decided to bury their gold along the banks of Bannister and Bruton Creeks, mark the spots, and return later for the treasure.

All through the night, the Indians placed their gold in clay pots, chose locations, dug holes, and buried their fortunes. They then carved and scratched locational markers on granite outcrops and stones in the area. One particular stone, an oblong granite boulder weighing more than two hundred pounds, was inscribed with the key to the locations of all the gold caches, believed to number between eight and twenty-five. The total value of the buried gold of the Red Bank Indians is estimated at $2.6 million at today's exchange rates.

Forced to vacate their lands at bayonet point the next day, the Indians put up some mild resistance. After two members of the tribe were executed by the army soldiers, they finally turned and began the long trek to Indian Territory.

Almost a hundred years later, in November of 1932, three boys were playing along the bank of Bannister Creek where it ran through the farm of one F. R. Groover. One of the boys noticed a large, whale-shaped granite rock carved with many curious figures and symbols. The boys had heard the tale of the buried Cherokee treasure many times and decided the rock must mark such a cache.

Suddenly seized by an uncommon sense of propriety for boys that young, the three of them approached farmer Groover and asked permission to dig for gold on his farm. Groover, an intolerant and cranky sort, refused permission and ordered the trio off his land.

That night, the three boys returned to the Groover farm with shovels and picks. With considerable difficulty, they rolled the huge rock aside and began digging. About two feet below the surface, one of their shovels struck a clay pot. Excited, the boys removed the dirt from around the pot, and with an effort, they lifted it to the grassy surface.

The youthful treasure hunters could scarcely contain themselves when they held a lantern above the pot and peered into it. Inside the vessel they found golden jewelry, gold nuggets, and pouches of gold dust. The value of their find was later estimated at $15,540 in 1932 dollars.

Word of the discovery eventually reached Groover, and he soon found the fresh excavation on his farm. He promptly filed suit against the three boys for the return of the gold, which he claimed rightfully belonged to him. Unfortunately for the young treasure hunters, the court found in favor of Groover.

Sometime during the early 1960s, the large stone that marked the disputed cache was obtained by researchers at the University of Georgia and taken to that campus, where it still is. According to the archaeologists who have examined the stone, the carvings of double circles, stick men, and other odd figures describe locations of buried treasure. Unfortunately, finding the locations of the caches of gold depends on the original position of the large stone, and that exact site remains a mystery.

Interviews with many elderly Red Bank Cherokee in the early part of the twentieth century substantiated that the treasure caches could be found by deciphering the markings on the large stone and using its location as a starting point.

Several old-timers who lived near the Groover farm claimed to know the exact location of the stone before it was removed by University of Georgia officials. However, when directions interpreted from the stone were followed, nothing was ever found.

In 1951, before the stone was removed, several Cherokee men traveled from Oklahoma to the Bannister Creek area in search of the stone. They found it, took several photographs of the markings, and spent a week searching for the gold caches. Like previous searchers, they were unsuccessful.

Sam Cranford, an aged part–Cherokee whose grandfather once owned the land on which the Groover farm lay, explained why the searches failed. Cranford told investigators that the point from which the rock was removed was not the original location. He claimed the stone was inadvertently pushed several dozen feet from its original place by a road grader as a road was being widened.

Anyone who knew the original location of the great stone has long since passed away. While the mysterious markings of the stone have been translated, the information is useless as long as its original position remains unknown.

Until then, millions of dollars of Red Bank Cherokee treasure will probably remain hidden not far below ground near Bannister Creek.

The Wandering Confederate Treasury

The spring of 1865 saw the end of the Confederate
States of America: it had suffered terrible defeats, its leaders
were leaving, and its treasury was rapidly running out of
money. Jefferson Davis and his cabinet held their last
official meetings in April at Abbeville, South Carolina, and
Washington, Georgia, as the group fled encroaching Union
forces.

The Confederate treasury, a still-significant store of
gold and silver coinage, likewise was moved from the
depository at Richmond, Virginia to some undetermined
southern location. Some researchers believe the treasure
was ordered removed by the departing leaders to protect it.
Others of a more cynical nature suggest the deposed leaders
wanted the wealth somewhere they might quickly get their
hands on it should the nation crumble at the hands of the
conquering Yankees.

When General Robert E. Lee told President Jefferson
Davis that Grant's forces had penetrated the Confederate
lines at Petersburg and Richmond was about to be taken,
Davis ordered an evacuation of the region. He assigned
William H. Parker to move the treasure.

Parker was a captain in the Confederate navy and took
his new assignment quite seriously. On the afternoon of
April 2, 1865, with the help of some sixty midshipmen
from a training vessel anchored on the James River, Parker

loaded the entire wealth of the Confederate treasury into a boxcar. It was to be the first of many transfers. Around midnight, the train departed Richmond bearing an estimated one million dollars. (Some estimates have ranged as high as thirty million dollars, but little evidence has been offered to support those claims.)

When the train reached Danville, Parker received additional orders to move the treasure on to Charlotte, North Carolina, and store it in the abandoned United States mint there. No sooner was this done than Parker learned Stoneman's cavalry was headed in his direction and might be interested in the treasure.

Parker had the treasure removed from the mint, packed in barrels and sacks of coffee, flour, and sugar, and reloaded onto the train. Then, to Parker's dismay, he discovered that the railroads were out of service beyond Charlotte. He hastily transferred the containers onto wagons.

While loading the treasure, Parker learned that Varina Davis, the wife of the Confederate president, was living in Charlotte with her children. Parker found her and persuaded her to travel south with him under military escort before the Union soldiers arrived.

On April 16, the Parker detachment arrived at Newberry, South Carolina. The trains were running, so Parker had the treasure-filled barrels and sacks loaded into another boxcar and continued to Abbeville.

When the detachment reached Abbeville, Mrs. Davis decided to leave the train and stay with some friends who lived in the quiet South Carolina town. Parker was less at ease than Mrs. Davis. Convinced the Union cavalry was hot on his heels in pursuit of the treasure, he wished to abandon the area immediately. He decided to travel on to Washington, Georgia, a few miles across the Savannah River to the southwest. As the train didn't go that way, Parker once again ordered the gold and silver loaded onto wagons. He bid farewell to Mrs. Davis and crossed the river into Georgia.

That part of Georgia had not suffered much from the northern raids, and Parker felt certain he could find a sizeable Confederate military unit that could take over the gold and silver he was transporting in the wagons. The captain was anxious to be rid of the responsibility of the entire wealth of the Confederate nation.

On arriving at Washington, Parker heard that a command of some two hundred Confederate soldiers was holding Augusta, about fifty miles to the southeast. After trading flour and coffee to Washington residents for eggs, milk, and chickens, Parker had his men load the treasure once more in a railroad car, and he ordered the train to Augusta.

At Augusta, the frustrated Parker discovered it was not as easy to reassign the treasure as he had hoped. The officers there informed him the war was over and that they were merely awaiting the arrival of the Union troops to arrange for an orderly surrender of the town, get their pay, and go home. Possession of the Confederate treasury would seriously complicate matters, they informed Parker, and they wanted nothing to do with it. One of the leaders advised Parker to return the treasure to the civilian leaders of the Confederate government, who at that very moment were fleeing Union soldiers across the Savannah River into Georgia. Among those in flight was President Jefferson Davis himself.

Mistakenly, Parker decided Abbeville would be the likeliest place to find Davis to ask him what to do with the treasure. He believed Davis knew his wife was there and would try to find her. The fastest route to Abbeville was back through Washington, so the captain ordered the train to return. There, the monotonous task of loading the gold and silver onto wagons was once again undertaken, and the journey to Abbeville was underway.

Less than an hour out of Washington, Parker, much to his surprise and chagrin, encountered Mrs. Davis and her children fleeing Abbeville with a small cavalry escort. She told Parker that she had not seen her husband and had no idea where he was.

On April 28, Parker and his command finally arrived at Abbeville, unloaded the wealth from the wagons, stored it in an empty warehouse just outside town, and placed a heavy guard around it.

That evening as he was dining, Parker received word from one of his scouts that a large contingent of Union forces was a few miles north of the town and would arrive soon. Panicked, Parker ordered his men to reload the treasure into a railroad car. He ordered the engineer to prepare to depart, but before the train could be started, several hundred soldiers appeared at the north end of the town, riding straight for the train.

Fortunately for the harried Parker, the soldiers turned out to be a Confederate company escorting President Davis and what was left of his cabinet. Parker greeted Davis and related his misadventures with the Confederate treasury. To his great relief, Davis ordered the responsibility for the gold and silver transferred to the acting secretary of the treasury, John H. Reagan. Almost as quickly, Reagan transferred the responsibility to John C. Breckinridge, the secretary of war. Breckinridge, not excited about the burden of responsibility for the wealth of the Confederate nation, passed it to General Basil Duke. Duke had no one to pass it on to, so he assumed the assignment with his customary rigid military bearing and dignity.

Duke was one of the few remaining Confederate generals, and his command was a motley assortment of nearly a thousand poorly armed and equipped volunteers who were deserting in droves. When the soldiers learned the war was over, several at a time would simply slip away and return to their farms throughout the devastated south.

Around midnight of May 2, Duke urgently ordered the wealth transferred once again from the boxcar to several wagons. Duke had learned earlier in the evening that Union patrols were thick in the area, and he would be lucky to transport the gold and silver farther south and away from the advancing Yankees. Duke believed Union officials were aware the treasure was in the area and were determined to seize it. With a force of about a thousand Confederate troops, Duke moved the treasure out of Abbeville in the dark of night. Jefferson Davis and his remaining cabinet, grateful for the escort, rode along. Several of the troops stayed far to the rear of the column keeping an eye out for pursuit, and dozens more rode along the flanks prepared to ward off an attack by the Yankees.

During the rest stop around midmorning of the next day, May 3, Duke promised his soldiers that when they reached Washington they would be paid in gold from the treasury they were escorting. Knowing the war was over and anxious to be on their way, the troops clamored for payment on the spot. The soldiers were also concerned that Union troops might suddenly appear and seize the money before they could get what they were due. For the rest of the day, Duke and a paymaster counted out thirty-two dollars to each soldier in the command.

This done, the wagons were escorted across the Savannah River toward Washington, Georgia. Every few minutes, Duke got word that Yankee soldiers were only minutes away from attacking his column. At the first opportunity, he ordered his command to leave the trail and take refuge in a large farmhouse belonging to a man named Moss. The barrels and sacks of gold and silver were unloaded from the wagons and stacked in the farmhouse kitchen. Duke then stationed his men at strategic points around the farmhouse, ready to hold off a Yankee attack on the traveling treasury. The attack never materialized.

The Confederates spent the night at the farm, very few of them sleeping since they anticipated trouble at any moment. When scouts reported the next morning that no Yankees were in sight, Duke ordered the treasure reloaded onto the wagons, and it was carried into Washington without incident. At Washington, Duke turned the wealth over to Captain Micajah Clark, whom Jefferson had earlier that day, in his last official act as president of the Confederacy, appointed treasurer of the Confederate States of America. Then Davis, along with his wife and children, fled deeper into the south. They were captured six days later.

Captain Micajah Clark decided that his first obligation as Treasurer was to count the money. According to the Treasury record, the exact amount was $288,022.90. It was considerably less than what Parker had left Richmond carrying, and through the succeeding years, there has been much speculation as to what happened to the rest of the money.

Parker, writing some thirty years later, suggested that Clark may have submitted a false accounting of what was turned over to him and kept the difference.

Many believe that Jefferson Davis, before turning the treasury over to Clark, appropriated much of the wealth and fled with it, burying portions of it in several locations before he was captured.

In any event, Clark paid off a few more soldiers out of the funds and had the rest repacked in kegs and wooden boxes.

On May 14, two officials representing a Virginia bank arrived in Washington with a federal order for the total amount of the treasury. The bank apparently held a claim on the wealth, and the two men were commissioned to secure it and return it to Richmond.

Following the military order to the letter, Clark turned the entire treasury over to the two bank representatives who in turn had it loaded onto wagons and, under protection of a military escort of some forty soldiers, left for Richmond.

Most of the soldiers in the escort were young, and very few had seen any action during the war. For that reason, the two bank representatives were nervous throughout the trip. Soon after the column left Washington, a scout reported they were being followed by a gang of outlaws made up of discharged Confederate soldiers and local hooligans. The soldiers were ordered to take extra precautions as the small wagon train lumbered toward the Savannah River.

Travel was slow, and on the afternoon of May 24, the party pulled into the front yard of the home of the Reverend Dionysius Chenault, only twelve miles out of Washington. The wagons were pulled into a large horse corral and drawn into a tight defensive circle. The guard was doubled and posted about the corral that night while the rest of the command tried to sleep.

Around midnight the outlaws struck. Firing only a few shots, they surprised the inexperienced federal guards, who quickly surrendered. The guards were tied up, and the remaining soldiers, who awakened at the first sound of gunfire, were held at gunpoint by several of the outlaws. The leaders of the gang smashed open the kegs and boxes containing the gold and silver coins and stuffed their saddlebags full of the booty. Thousands of dollars' worth of Confederate wealth was spilled onto the ground as the greedy outlaws filled their pockets. Finally, carrying all they could hold, they mounted and rode away on horses barely able to carry both treasure and rider.

One of Reverend Chenault's daughters estimated that well over a hundred thousand dollars' worth of gold and silver coins was recovered from the ground the next day.

The outlaws rode northwest to the bank of the Savannah River. Learning they were being pursued by both Confederate soldiers and local law enforcement officials, they hastily dug a pit and buried their wealth in a common cache, intending to return for it when the pursuit was abandoned. A company of soldiers reportedly encountered the bandits the next day and killed all of them. The incredible wealth of gold and silver coins is believed still to lie buried on the south bank of the Savannah River.

Members of the Chenault family hurriedly gathered up the fortune in coins that had spilled onto the ground during the robbery. Placing the gold and silver into kitchen pots and wooden crates, they buried it adjacent to a nearby tributary to the Savannah River. No representatives of either the Confederate or Union government ever returned to the Chenault farm to claim that treasure.

The Reverend Chenault cautioned his family against digging up the treasure until such time as the passions of the war died down and it would be safe, but it is believed the treasure was never recovered.

Searchers for the treasure buried on the Chenault farm are routinely disappointed to learn that the small tributary near where it was cached has been inundated by the waters of Clarks Hill Lake. According to the U.S. Army Corps of Engineers, the Chenault portion of the Confederate treasure lies beneath some thirty feet of water.

Cohutta Mountain Gold

There is gold in the Georgia Appalachians, and lots of it. Eons ago, when the great mountain range was taking shape, tectonic forces deep beneath the crust were activated. Molten rock under tremendous pressure fought to break through the crust and spread out over the landscape, but the crust held, keeping the magma trapped beneath thousands of feet of rock, where it began to cool. The suppressed volcanic material eventually hardened to form granite and related rock. Scattered here and there within the vast underground bodies of igneous intrusive stone, impressive veins of gold-filled quartz formed.

As centuries turned into millennia, and millennia into several-million-year geological epochs, pressures within the earth forced some of the granite masses closer to the surface. Ages of erosion by wind and water removed hundreds of feet of sedimentary deposits, eventually exposing the ancient granite.

As streams flowed across the exposed granite, eroding the coarse surface particle by particle, entrapped minerals were exposed. Early Indians who settled in this region often found gold in these mountains, sometimes in great quantities. They mined it, stored vast amounts of it, and used it primarily for ornaments and jewelry.

When white trappers and traders arrived in the Georgia Appalachians, they saw the fine gold of the jewelry with which the Indians adorned themselves, and they craved its ore.

Soon prospectors and miners came, rediscovered some of the gold, and established mining enterprises. When most of the Indians were removed from the region in the 1830s, greedy and enterprising whites moved into the lands formerly held by the Indians and began extracting the riches from the rock.

Several tales of vast gold deposits have come from the area around Cohutta Mountain, about two-and-a-half miles east of Chatsworth, Georgia, near the Tennessee border.

Prior to the Indian Removal of the 1930s, a man named William Hassler built a grist mill on the creek that still bears his name. Hassler had settled in the region several years earlier and made friends with the Indians living nearby.

The largest of the Indian villages was spread out over the flood plain of Hassler Creek just east of the mill. Hassler ground corn for the Indians and also traded items he shipped in from Virginia. When he first began dealing with the Indians, he saw that they had a lot of gold, and he asked them to pay with that metal.

Whenever the Indians ran low on gold, Hassler noticed, three or four of the elders would leave the village and travel along the creek upstream toward Cohutta Mountain. They were usually gone for three or four days, and when they returned, they carried leather ore sacks filled with gold nuggets that looked to be cut from a rich vein.

Hassler suspected that the Indians had a rich gold mine back in the mountains, and he was determined to discover its location. One day when he saw four tribal elders departing for Cohutta Mountain, he called for one of his slaves. The miller told the slave, a mere boy, to follow the Indians at a discreet distance and try to find their gold mine.

All day long the young slave followed the trail, staying well behind the elders and just out of sight. When he reached the base of Cohutta Mountain, he lost sight of the Indians and could not locate the trail. As he searched the ground for some sign of passage, the four Indians appeared out of the surrounding forest and encircled the tracker. They told him if he ever followed them again, they would kill him and all of his family. The Indians then marched the young slave back to the mill and presented him to Hassler with the same warning. With that, the elders departed, trotting back toward the mountain. Several days later, they were seen returning with more sacks full of gold nuggets. The Indians carried on trade with the miller as if nothing had happened.

With the death threat hanging over him, Hassler never again tried to find the secret gold mine on Cohutta Mountain.

Many years later, during a lull in the War Between the States, two soldiers named Pence and Wells were granted a short leave to return to their homes near Cohutta Mountain to round up hogs. As best the story can be reconstructed, the men were hiking along a small stream on the mountain when they discovered the old Indian gold mine. Each man dug several ounces out of a large gold-laced vein deep inside the mine and then, pockets full, continued their search for the stray hogs.

Once all the hogs were found, the two men had to return to their military unit. They put the gold in a shot pouch and hid it in the hollow of a chestnut tree on the mountain. They planned also to return to the mine for more gold after they had served their time in the Confederate army.

In the ensuing months, Wells was killed in action and Pence was wounded badly enough to merit a discharge. The trauma of the war apparently affected Pence's mind to the degree that he had difficulty sleeping and remembering things. His neighbors claimed he had simply gone crazy from his experiences in the war.

After several months, Pence had marginally recovered from his wound, and decided to make the long hike to the chestnut tree of Cohutta Mountain and retrieve the pouch of gold. He planned to cash in the ore, buy mining equipment, and extract more gold ore from the old Indian mine.

Pence searched for several days but couldn't find the chestnut tree. He claimed that the tree was no longer there, but it is likely that he simply couldn't find it again.

For the rest of his life, Pence tried to find the ancient Indian gold mine. Years of fruitless searching made him completely lose his mind, and he was eventually sent to an institution. To the last, Pence never wavered from his tale of the rich gold mine he and his friend Wells had discovered that day.

Around the turn of the century, an old Cherokee Indian showed up in the town of Chatsworth. The old man was little more than a derelict, clothed in tattered rags and obviously hungry. He tried to get work at several places but was chased away. On his second day in town, he struck up a conversation with a group of men and told them that if they would give him six hundred dollars, he would lead them to the ancient Indian gold mine on Cohutta Mountain.

Two men, James Mullins and Jim Sellers, knew the story of the mine, and they agreed to take the risk.

The next morning, the Indian led Mullins and Sellers to Cohutta Mountain on horseback. For a day and a half, they traveled up ravine and narrow valley, into regions the two men had never seen. As they rode, Mullins and Sellers carefully noted landmarks so they could return to the mine, should it be found, without the help of the Indian.

Midway through the second day, the three men rode right up to the gold mine. In two hours, Mullins and Sellers dug enough gold from the exposed vein to fill their saddlebags. The old Indian tended the horses and watched as the men carried their new-found wealth from the mine.

When their packs were filled, they followed the Indian out of the mountains and back to Chatsworth. Pleased with their investment, Mullins and Sellers paid off the old

Indian, who immediately left town and was never seen again.

Mullins and Sellers got rich from selling the gold they had brought back from the old Indian mine, but nine months later, their money was gone. They organized a second trip to Cohutta Mountain and the gold mine.

On the morning of the second day out from Chatsworth, Mullins and Sellers got lost. They recognized none of the landmarks on trails, were hopelessly confused, and eventually returned to Chatsworth without finding the mine. The two men tried several more times, but always failed.

During the 1930s, a man named Fletcher prospected on and around Cohutta Mountain. Fletcher was originally from England and had come to the United States to seek his fortune in the gold fields of Georgia. By the time he arrived, however, most of the mining operations had closed down. Undaunted, the Englishman decided to try his own luck at prospecting and mining and settled in the Cohutta Mountain region, believing that the exposed granite hills still held the promise of gold.

After many trips into the mountain, Fletcher returned from one with a sackful of gold he claimed to have dug out of an old abandoned mine. The gold was very pure, and the sale of it made Fletcher rich.

Later, Fletcher fell ill and was given only days to live. Just before he died, he asked that his bed be taken outside where he could gaze upon the mountain. He gave the remainder of his fortune and a description of the mine to a friend who had ministered to him during his illness. Fletcher told him that inside the mine was a thick vein of quartz woven with one-eighth-inch thick strands of pure gold. Fletcher gave directions to the mine, but the friend could not remember them.

A few days later, Fletcher passed away, and the secret of the last gold mine of Cohutta Mountain apparently died with him.

The Lost Slave Gold Vein

Jacob Scudder, longtime friend and ally of the Cherokee Indians, was a prosperous Cherokee County farmer. He owned hundreds of acres of rich Georgia bottomland, raising on it bountiful crops of corn and fine herds of cattle and horses.

Slaves worked Scudder's farm. The farmer was reputedly kind and fair to his workers, fed them well, and saw to it that they were never overworked in the fields. When gold was discovered in the county during the 1840s, Scudder even allowed his slaves to pan for gold after their day's work was done. The only restriction he placed on them was that they had to give him the first option to purchase their gold. In this way, Scudder gained a great deal of gold, and many of his slaves bought their freedom.

One of Scudder's most valued workers was a slave named Black Dan Riley. Black Dan was in his forties, soft-spoken, and a competent and valued field hand. The other slaves looked to Black Dan as their leader, and he was often their spokesman when important issues arose.

Scudder and Black Dan got along very well, and when the slave approached the farmer about purchasing freedom for himself and his wife, Lucinda, Scudder readily agreed. Scudder offered to set Black Dan up as a sharecropper, providing him with a piece of land on which he could build a cabin and raise livestock of his own. Black Dan and Lucinda agreed to stay.

Gold fever was running through America then. Gold had been discovered in Virginia several years earlier, prompting a rush of people into the area and creating several boom towns in the rugged Appalachians to the northeast. Just two years earlier, gold had been discovered about two miles southwest of the Scudder farm, and miners and opportunists from as far away as New York and Pennsylvania were flocking to the northern Georgia Appalachians to pan independently or work for the newly created Franklin Gold Mining Company or establish businesses.

In 1849, gold was discovered in California. The promise of instant wealth was so great that easterners flocked to the Golden State in droves. Many of the men working for Georgia's Franklin Mines pulled up stakes and joined the great westward migration.

While Black Dan Riley had had some success in panning for gold in the small streams of Cherokee County, he longed to try his luck in the California gold fields. The fever burned hotter as he watched several of his friends pack up and undertake the long journey to California.

While farming his sharecropper plot and dreaming of California gold, Black Dan kept panning in the small streams near the Scudder farm. One day, he crossed one of Scudder's wide cornfields to reach a narrow creek that marked the eastern boundary of the property. Black Dan had not worked the little stream before and was anxious to see if it had any potential.

As he panned likely spots, Black Dan could see slaves working Scudder's cornfield on the other side of the stream. Once in a while, one would wave at him, and he would wave back. Black Dan kept panning, gradually moving upstream.

At a gentle bend in the stream about fifty yards up, Black Dan found some color in his pan. Fifteen minutes of working the site rewarded him with some tiny nuggets. Feeling lucky, he moved a little farther up the stream and began panning another site. He found several more nuggets, and this time they were larger, coarser, and more numerous.

He moved upstream and excitedly panned another spot. Again he found even larger, coarser nuggets—so large and plentiful, in fact, that he could actually see them lying in the bottom of the stream bed.

Black Dan knew enough about gold to know he was getting close to the source, most likely an exposed vein higher up. For most of the day, he panned his way carefully up the stream, feeling sure he was closing in on the source of the gold.

Finally, he reached a spot where his efforts yielded no gold. Deducing that the vein was somewhere between where he then stood and the last place he had panned, some thirty yards downstream, he began his search.

Black Dan walked up and down both sides of the stream several times and found nothing, so he decided to pan the stream every ten feet or so until he isolated the source. Eventually, he narrowed his search to a length of about twenty feet.

On one side of the stream, the land sloped upward, and patches of exposed rock could be seen along the bank. Black Dan focused his attention on these outcrops. Digging near the bottom of one, he found the top of a thick vein of quartz. Carefully brushing the dirt away, he discovered pure gold densely laced throughout. Here, at last, was the source of the gold in the stream.

As Black Dan dug several chunks of the ore from the rich vein, he pondered his future. The desire to go to California still burned in his heart, but he also believed he had stumbled onto a small fortune in gold right at his fingertips. He decided to go home and speak to Lucinda about the matter, and together they would decide.

Before leaving the site, Black Dan carefully covered over the exposed quartz vein and pocketed the day's yield. He walked home.

That evening over supper, Black Dan and Lucinda agreed to travel to California to try their luck in a new place. If they were not happy there, they would return to their northern Georgia farm and dig the gold there.

The next day, Black Dan sold his gold to Scudder for seventy dollars, bid the farmer farewell, and took off for California, Lucinda with him. Scudder wished his friend luck and invited him to come back if the California adventure proved unsuccessful.

But Black Dan did well in the California gold fields. He filed on several claims, all of which richly returned gold ore. After three years of panning in the California mountains, Black Dan and Lucinda had an impressive sum of money. Tired of living in primitive conditions in the mountains, they moved to a big city on the California coast where they lived comfortably for the next twenty years.

When they were in their sixties, Black Dan and Lucinda began to miss their old home in Georgia. They spoke often of the simple life and the slower pace they remembered in the Appalachian hills. By this time, they had spent most of what had been earned in the gold fields, but they still had enough money left to be considered wealthy by anyone's standards.

They returned to Georgia and settled onto a piece of land not far from where Black Dan once sharecropped for Scudder. Scudder had passed away years earlier, and others had taken over his farm.

One day, Black Dan gathered up his gold pan and a shovel and set out for the small stream and the gold-filled quartz vein he had discovered more than twenty years earlier. He found the stream with no trouble, got his bearings, and walked to where he remembered the vein to be. As he climbed the slight incline to the upper reaches of the stream, he noted that during the twenty years he was away, the landscape had changed considerably. Much of the woodland he remembered had been cut down and turned into pastures. The little stream had shifted its course in several places and looked much different. And where before there had always been a strong flow of water, the creek now only held a trickle.

Black Dan panned parts of the little stream as he searched for the quartz vein. He was rewarded with some fine dust in the bottom of his pan, but nothing like he had found twenty years earlier. He tried to remember where he was standing when he waved at the slaves working in Scudder's field so long ago, but everything seemed so different now. Black Dan was confused.

When Black Dan reached the place where he thought the rich quartz vein was, he dug into the sloping hillside under one of the rock outcrops. He found nothing. He dug in several more places, but still no quartz. Discouraged and tired, the old gentleman went home, planning to try again the next morning.

The next day was no more fruitful. Panning in the stream sometimes yielded small amounts of gold, but Black Dan was not satisfied. He longed to find the rich vein.

Months passed. At least twice a week, Black Dan could be seen exploring the little stream in search of the elusive vein. When he grew too old to dig, he hired a boy named Carnes to accompany him. He told young Carnes the story of his lost gold and promised to share it with the lad if they found it.

Black Dan showed Carnes how to pan the gold out of the stream and taught the boy much of what he knew about the gold mining business. For months they searched the low hills around the little stream, but the quartz vein eluded them.

Black Dan Riley died without ever finding his vein. For several years, Carnes continued to search for the gold he firmly believed must exist near the stream at the base of one of the outcrops, but he never found it.

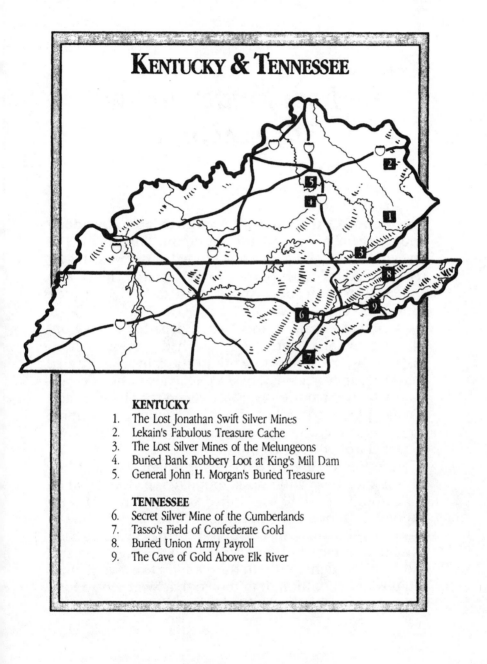

KENTUCKY & TENNESSEE

KENTUCKY
1. The Lost Jonathan Swift Silver Mines
2. Lekain's Fabulous Treasure Cache
3. The Lost Silver Mines of the Melungeons
4. Buried Bank Robbery Loot at King's Mill Dam
5. General John H. Morgan's Buried Treasure

TENNESSEE
6. Secret Silver Mine of the Cumberlands
7. Tasso's Field of Confederate Gold
8. Buried Union Army Payroll
9. The Cave of Gold Above Elk River

The Lost Jonathan Swift Silver Mines

Throughout the Kentucky Appalachians, abundant evidence can be found of ancient mining and smelting of silver ore. Some of the long-abandoned mines were dug by Spanish soldiers under Hernando de Soto. The French also mined silver from these Appalachian rocks during their occupation of the new world.

When the Spanish and French departed the region, Shawnee Indians, many of whom had previously been enslaved by the whites to work in the mines, continued extracting the precious ore. Occasionally, Cherokee Indians who wanted the silver would raid the Shawnee and take temporary control of one or more mines. For almost three hundred years, millions of dollars' worth of silver was extracted from these rich mines.

Into this setting arrived one Jonathan Swift in 1760. Little is known of Swift's background. It is believed that he came from England to the United States around 1750. He claimed a sailor's background but bore himself like an educated gentleman. Speculation arose that Swift had been wanted for piracy and other crimes on the high seas and that he had sought refuge in the colonies to evade capture and possible execution. It is known that Swift served for a time with General Braddock during the French and Indian War in 1755.

After mustering out of the British army, Swift wandered to the bustling cities of Washington and Alexandria on the Potomac River. It was in Washington that Swift met George Mundy and learned of the rich silver mines of the eastern Kentucky Appalachians that would forever be linked to his name.

For one so young, George Mundy (whose name is given in some accounts as "Alfred Mundy") had already experienced a lifetime of hardship and a heartstopping array of adventures. Mundy had been a mere boy in 1752 when he accompanied a party of trappers into the eastern Kentucky wilderness. The men were trapping and trading for hides and pelts which they planned to sell in the larger cities in the east. While camped in what is now Wolfe County, one of the trappers shot and wounded a bear, which sought refuge in a nearby hole in the rock wall of a mountainside. The trapper ordered young Mundy to enter the cave and tie a rope around the bear's legs so it could be dragged out. As Mundy, grass torch in hand, crawled on hands and knees through the narrow opening, he discovered it was actually the entrance to a long-abandoned mine. Curious, he moved deeper into the shaft. At one point, the light from his torch reflected off a thick vein of glistening silver along one wall. Noticing his torch was nearly burned out, Mundy returned to the entrance and told the others what he had found.

The trappers, excited about getting rich off their discovery, immediately began enlarging the tunnel and mining the ore. Their skills were primitive and their efforts clumsy, but they soon dug out a large quantity of silver. As work progressed in the mine, the men occasionally noted Indians watching them from the nearby ridgetops. Since the Indians never approached or threatened, the trappers saw no need to post a guard.

One morning, as several woodsmen were loading sacks of silver ore onto their horses in preparation for departure, they were suddenly attacked by the Indians. After a brief and futile defense, all the woodsmen were killed except for young Mundy. During the fighting, the boy hid in the mine, where he was discovered by the raiders. Because of his youth, Mundy was taken captive to be raised by an Indian family and used as a slave.

Mundy soon learned his captors were Shawnee, and that they operated silver mines of their own there, both where Mundy had found the mineshaft and in the nearby Red River gorge. He, along with other slaves, was taken to the Red River valley region and made to work in the Shawnee silver mines for several hours each day.

One day, the Shawnee camp was raided by a large force of Cherokee. The invaders scattered the Shawnee, fired the village, and made captives of Mundy and several Shawnee youths. Mundy soon learned that the Cherokee had silver mines of their own, for they quickly put him to work in them. The Cherokee occasionally dug ore from Shawnee mines in secret, he also discovered.

Once, a party of Spaniards visited the Cherokee while they were camped in a wide valley. Leading three large ox-drawn carts, the newcomers brought mining tools and maps of the region. The Spaniards remained in the village with the Indians for several weeks, and with the aid of the Cherokee, found several of the old silver mines that had been abandoned and covered over during the de Soto expedition. From these mines, the Spaniards took great quantities of ore, gradually filling the ox carts with the treasure. From the Spaniards, Mundy learned something of the history of the mines in the area.

While exploring this region around 1542, de Soto's scouts heard of rich silver mines in the mountains. Local Indians told the soldiers the mines had been operated for centuries by the tribe. The Spaniards visiting the Cherokee village more than two hundred years later had detailed reports on the locations of these long-abandoned mines and the amount of silver that was taken out and shipped back to Spain as ingots. The Spanish and the Cherokee, with Mundy and a small number of other slaves, worked together to dig more of the ore from the nearby mines.

When the Spanish had gotten all the silver they could carry, they left the village and headed southeast. Several weeks later, a group of French soldiers visited the Cherokee village. Like the Spaniards before them, the French were welcomed. The French also knew of the rich silver mines and had come to ask the Indians if they could mine them. Mundy learned that the amicable relationship between the Cherokee and the French stemmed from an alliance committing the two to driving the British and Americans from the region. The silver from the rich Indian mines was financing the French army.

In 1754, the British general Edward Braddock was sent into the Kentucky wilderness, where he engaged the French and Cherokee in a savage battle. George Mundy, allied with the Indians, fought for the French in several skirmishes, and was eventually captured by Braddock's army. The young man was taken to Alexandria, Virginia. After being questioned about movements and affairs of the Indians, he was released. Mundy, with no means of support, wandered the streets of Alexandria begging for handouts. It was there he met Jonathan Swift.

Swift felt sorry for the young man who had endured so much and then been cast out to fend for himself on the sometimes wicked streets of the city. The former soldier invited the lad to live in his home and treated him as if he were his own son. In return, Mundy willingly served Swift as a valet and developed a fierce loyalty to him.

Some time after Mundy moved in, Swift had to sail for Cuba on business, and he left the young man in charge of his home. When Swift returned to Alexandria several weeks later, he and Mundy became close friends, and at that point, Mundy shared with Swift the story of the Kentucky silver mines.

Swift was enthralled by the tales of the wealth in silver that Mundy claimed could be found in the far-away Kentucky Appalachians, and his heart fairly burst with excitement as he thought of the fortune waiting in the remote wilderness of the far mountains.

Mundy told Swift that after the skirmish with the British soldiers, the Indians had abandoned the mines and the French had been driven from the area. There was enough silver, the young man claimed, to stock the treasuries of several nations. As Swift's mind reeled, Mundy offered to guide him to the mines.

Swift began preparing for a journey to the abandoned silver mines in far-away Kentucky. He sailed once again to Havana to secure the services of two competent miners he knew, named Gries and Jeffrey. Returning to Alexandria, Swift gathered around him several men with whom he had served in Braddock's army: Samuel Blackburn, Isaac Campbell, Abrom Flint, James Ireland, Shadrach Jefferson, and Harmon Staley.

Finally in late spring of 1759, financed by Swift and guided by young Mundy, the party left for the Kentucky Appalachians. On this and subsequent trips, Swift maintained a journal, and it is from his writings that much of the information concerning the silver mines has been gleaned.

With some difficulty, Mundy guided the men to an area in what is believed to be present-day Floyd County. On arriving, the young man seemed confused and cast around for a myrtle tree thicket that he said was near the entrance of one of the richest mines in the region. The following account appears in Swift's journal:

> On the first trip, Mundy got lost. We put our horses on the river called "Red." We put them in a place surrounded by cliffs and fastened to the entrance with grape vines. We crossed the river to the other side and wandered all day and came back from where we started from. The next day Mundy said he could go down the river to the Indian trace. He would know the way then. He went down the river two or three miles west and found the Indian trail. So we wandered all that day and next. Late in

the evening, Mundy hollered out, "Here is the myrtle thicket. I know the way now."

We went down a flight of Indian stair steps at the top of the cliff and crossed to the other side. We climbed up and went 200 yards on the second ledge and found the opening to the mine.

For many weeks, the party dug the plentiful silver from the mine. They made a crude furnace and smelted the ore, fashioning it into ingots. Soon the miners had more silver than they could carry on the horses and mules. Swift suggested they return to Alexandria, convert their silver to cash, and organize a second and larger expedition.

About a year later, another expedition was formed, including Swift, Mundy, Blackburn, Gries, Ireland, Jeffrey, and Staley, along with newcomers Henry Hazlitt, Joshua McClintock, and several Shawnee Indians.

On the second journey, according to Swift's notes, Munday took the men to a different mine somewhere in what is now Bell County. This mine proved to be even richer than the first, and they spent nearly seven months mining the ore and converting it into ingots. Winter was approaching, and Swift decided it would be wise to leave the wilderness and return to the east. As they had more silver than they could possibly take back, they hid hundreds of ingots in the mine shaft and in nearby caves and rock niches. The group arrived in Alexandria on December 10, 1760.

While resting in his adopted city, Swift contacted one Seth Montgomery, a British merchant who owned and operated a small fleet of trading vessels that plied the Atlantic between England and America. Montgomery formerly worked as an engraver for the Royal Mint of England, where his specialty was cutting dies and coining golden crowns, England's principal exchange medium in the new-world colonies. With his wealth, Swift bought into

Montgomery's trading enterprise, and the two purchased five more ships.

Once this new business was operating efficiently, Swift organized a third expedition into the Kentucky mountains. Montgomery accompanied the party on this trip, and they departed Alexandria on June 25, 1761.

The group journeyed by way of Fort Pitt (now Pittsburgh) where they were joined by more Shawnees and several Frenchmen. Swift had learned of increased Indian depredations in the wilderness and believed a large party of well-armed men would offer greater protection.

The expedition eventually arrived at the forks of the Big Sandy River near present-day Louisa in Lawrence County. Here the party split up. Half of them, led by Mundy, traveled up the west fork to locate new mines. The others, led by Swift, journeyed to the same mine they had worked the previous year.

Each group labored to extract ore and convert it into ingots. Apparently Montgomery, with his knowledge of dies and coinage, supervised the making of illegal British crowns. According to Swift's journals, thousands of the coins were fashioned and stored in barrels brought along for that purpose. Collectors now hold several of these coins.

Swift, Montgomery, and a few others departed for Alexandria, arriving on December 2, 1761. The rest of the party continued the mining and smelting operation. Swift and Montgomery took with them several mule loads of silver ingots and coins, and when they arrived at Alexandria, they immediately purchased an additional two ships for their fleet. Onto these ships were loaded goods bound for England from the colonies, and though it has never been proven, many suspect that barrels of English crowns molded in Kentucky crossed the ocean, too, and were used by the partners in business transactions. Hundreds of the illegal coins are also suspected to have been introduced into the colonies soon after Swift and Montgomery returned.

The two returned to Kentucky around the last week of March, 1762, bringing a large pack train of supplies. Arriving again at the fork of the Big Sandy, Swift traveled southward along the base of Pine Mountain to the Cumberland Ford in what is now Bell County. Here he organized the opening of several new mines and prepared to spend the winter.

The winter of that year, however, was unusually harsh, and the men were forced to quit the region. Several tons of silver bars and coins were loaded onto the pack animals, and the party returned once again to Alexandria, arriving on December 1, 1762. Along the way, according to Swift's journals, thousands of dollars' worth of silver had to be cached to make travel easier.

In Alexandria, Swift and Montgomery purchased more ships, expanding the size of their trading fleet to a small navy. Furs and other trade goods, along with several barrels of illegal English crowns, were loaded onto the ships and carried to England. Shortly after the vessels returned, Swift, Montgomery, and the others went back to Kentucky.

Regular trips to the Kentucky mountains to mine the silver continued until 1769. On the final expedition, the party left for the mines on October 9, and once they got there, split up the ore, ingots, and coinage that had previously been cached and returned to Alexandria on December 11. It was the last time Swift was to visit the mines.

According to Swift's journals, millions of dollars' worth of silver was taken from the mines while he operated them. On several occasions during return trips, some of the wealth had to be cached. Once, under attack by Indians, the travelers had to abandon large amounts of coins and ingots, hiding them in rock niches. On other occasions, pack animals became crippled and whatever portion of the silver they were transporting was hidden in nearby rock caves or buried near some prominent landmark with the intention of later retrieval. Swift's journal entry of September 1, 1767, reads:

...[W]e left between 22,000 and 30,000 dollars and crowns on a large creek running near a south course. Close to the spot we marked our names (Swift, Jefferson, Mundy, and others) on a beech tree with compass, square, and trowel.

No great distance from this place we left 15,000 of the same kind, marking three or four trees with marks. Not far from these we left the prize near a forked white oak and about three feet underground, and laid two long stones across it, marking several stones close about it. At the forks of the Sandy, close by the fork, is a small rock house with a spring in one end of it. Between it and a small branch we laid a prize under the ground; it was valued at 6,000 dollars. We likewise left 3,000 buried in the rocks of the rock house.

A later journal entry, recorded in Swift's rather cryptic style, gave directions to the mines in the Red River gorge area:

If you strike the creek below the furnace keep in the creek searching diligently for a big rock house on the left hand side about 100 yards from the smaller rock house the furnace is in, the creek makes a bend or turn to the south and there is the fallen rock in the creek near the bend. If you discover the furnace go to the middle mine, go up over a southeast course until you come to a remarkable hanging rock very high up with a gap in between it and a very large mountain, within 100 yards you will find a line of rocks the mine is in.

The last trip we came we saw our mine was so immensely rich it was decided by our party to abandon the mine for three years for me to go to England and get a party interested to come over here and work the mine on a large scale.

In 1770, Jonathan Swift left America for England. As stated in his journal, he intended to attract investors and skilled miners and engineers to return to the Kentucky wilderness with him and operate the silver mines on a grand scale. Swift had planned to remain in his home country for a while, but his stay turned out to be much longer than he expected. One evening while quaffing ale in a pub, he was overheard berating the king and his foolish colonial efforts in the new world. Swift was seized and thrown in jail for his vocal American partisanship, and there he languished for nearly fifteen years. While in prison, Swift began to lose his eyesight, and by the time he was released, he could not discern objects more than forty feet away.

When Swift finally returned to America, he discovered that many of his friends, including Mundy, had attempted a return to the mines the previous year and were never heard from again. They were believed either killed by Indians or perished in the unusually bitter winter. Swift had difficulty locating the others, but finally found Mc-Clintock. These two men, together with a ragtag party of several Indians and two Frenchmen, left Alexandria in 1790. They intended to travel along the old trails to the mines and recover some of the hidden wealth. Converted to working capital, this could be used to finance a larger expedition to reopen the mines.

Swift, half blind, couldn't find the landmarks he needed to relocate the silver mines. So rapidly was Swift's eyesight failing that a companion had to lead the once hale sailor, outdoorsman, and miner by the arm. Several times, the party found trees and rocks blazed with marks identifying nearby caches of coins or other wealth, but Swift could not see well enough to lead his men to the precise locations.

Though the small party searched many weeks for the mines and the buried caches of silver, they found nothing. When provisions finally ran low, Swift suggested they return to the east. In Alexandria, he lived out the rest of his life, alone and blind, and finally passed away in 1800.

While geologists and hard-rock miners have found silver in varying quantities in the Kentucky Appalachians, the many rich mines of Jonathan Swift remain hidden. Some suggest that when Swift and his men abandoned the mines, they went to great lengths to seal the entrances and camouflage them so they would look like the surrounding environment. Though hundreds have searched the rugged hills and mountains of eastern Kentucky, the Swift mines have eluded all.

Some who have studied the history of the Swift silver mines suggest they never existed and were a product of Swift's imagination, a cover for the alleged coin counterfeiting operation. Swift's silver, the argument continues, was actually plunder from his oceanic trading ventures, which supposedly were nothing more than a cleverly disguised piracy operation. According to the critics, Swift carted stolen silver chalices, plates, and jewelry into the wilderness, melted them down, and minted illegal coins from them.

Researchers have found no documentation linking Swift to piracy. Furthermore, it is not logical that Swift would travel hundreds of miles into the remote and rugged Appalachians to melt down stolen silver when he could more easily have done so only a few miles from Alexandria.

Most likely, the Swift silver mines did indeed exist, and produced an incredible fortune for the men who worked them. The evidence for the existence of these mines is plentiful and has been found in Bell, Estill, Jackson, Lee, Morgan, Powell, and Wolfe counties. Old furnaces have been discovered in these areas, and studies show they were used to smelt silver. Many caches of old mining tools have also been found, tools of mid-eighteenth century vintage. One cache of tools contained a hand-cast hammer bearing the inscription "JC Blackburn." Blackburn was one of Swift's miners. Several rock engravings bearing the names Swift, Mundy, and Jefferson have been found near the furnaces.

Historians for the most part agree the Swift silver mines existed. They are still lost today probably because they are in remote areas, they were likely concealed when abandoned, and the forest and undergrowth have encroached on the sites so they are almost impossible to identify.

The search for the rich silver mines continues, and the same passion for discovery and for great wealth that imbued the adventurous Jonathan Swift more than two centuries ago still beats in the hearts of modern-day treasure hunters.

Lekain's Fabulous Treasure Cache

In the year 1750, a half-breed Frenchman named Howard Lekain traveled up the Mississippi and Ohio Rivers from his Louisiana home in response to tales he had heard about the possibility of mining gold and silver in the Kentucky Appalachians. Lekain followed dozens of other Frenchmen who had gone to the area in search of wealth.

At that time, the French claimed all the territory west of the Allegheny Mountains. Because of this French dominance and because the French were on friendly terms with most of the Indian tribes in the region, Lekain and his countrymen passed easily through the area in their quest for silver and gold. So friendly did Lekain become with the local Indians that he eventually married into the tribe.

On one of his prospecting forays, Lekain discovered a very rich vein of silver near the present-day town of Carter, in Carter County. With the help of a dozen Indian workers, the Frenchman excavated a substantial amount of ore. In addition to the rich silver strike, Lekain found a significant gold deposit nearby. In the years that followed, Lekain built up a fortune as he mined and stored precious metals.

Once his mining operation was under way, Lekain built a furnace to smelt the ore into ingots. Besides the bars of silver and gold, he made some crudely formed coins of a Spanish design which he successfully used as currency in the region.

As years passed and word spread about the wealth that could be found in the Kentucky Appalachians, more and more Frenchman came to try their luck at mining. People from the eastern colonies also sought new lands in this area to farm and colonize. The encroachment of whites into their homeland and hunting grounds angered the local Shawnee Indians. Hostilities grew between the two cultures, and small raids eventually led to full-scale warfare.

Before long, whites could not move about the area without risk to their lives, and Lekain began to fear for his and his wife's safety. He decided to go back to Louisiana until the warring passions cooled.

Unable to transport his entire fortune of gold and silver, Lekain loaded as much as he could onto his wagon and made plans to cache the remainder in a safe place.

With the help of his Indian friends, Lekain packed ingots into six wooden kegs and coins into two one-gallon buckets. Then he examined several of the many caves in the area and chose one suitable for caching his fortune. The cave had a small opening and was located just across Tygart Creek from the settlement. From the cave entrance, one could see Cedar Cliffs rising above the creek. The narrow passageway wound down at a forty-five degree angle through a fifteen-foot layer of hard-packed clay and gravel and into a limestone formation. After about forty feet, the passageway opened into a chamber some thirty feet long and twenty feet wide with a ceiling averaging six feet in height. In the center was a large rock which had evidently fallen from the limestone ceiling.

With the help of his Indian laborers, Lekain hauled the kegs and buckets of ore into the chamber and put them against the far wall. He collected several of the limestone rocks that littered the floor of the cave and stacked them up around his treasure. Then he scraped dirt from the floor of the cave onto the mound of rocks, covering them entirely. To a stranger accidentally entering the subterranean chamber, the cache would look little different from the uneven floor of the cave. When this was done, Lekain, with the point of his knife, carved his name and the year—1774—on the side of the large rock in the center of the chamber. When the Frenchman and the Indians left the cave, they placed a large flat rock over the the opening.

By this time, back at the settlement, the wagon was loaded and ready for departure. Because an attack from the Shawnee was imminent, Lekain's Indian friends implored him to leave the valley as soon as possible. However, the Frenchman lingered near the cave another hour to sketch a map showing the location of the cave, noting prominent landmarks such as Cedar Cliffs, Ring Rock Spring, and Tygart Creek. Lekain also wrote a lengthy description of the treasure, the cave, and the area, all in French.

Before leaving, Lekain etched the outline of a snake on a nearby rock so that the head of the reptile pointed directly at the opening of the treasure cave.

Satisfied, Lekain and his wife climbed aboard the wagon and, accompanied by twelve Indians, headed north out of the Appalachian valley toward the Ohio River, where they hoped to get a boat and return to Louisiana.

On the evening of the second day of travel through the dense forest, the small party was attacked by the Shawnee. While Lekain's Indians fought off the attackers, the Frenchman and his wife fled through the woods into the darkness.

Weeks later, the two arrived in Louisiana. The Frenchman felt it prudent to wait until the Indian hostilities in the Appalachians subsided before going back to his mine, so he settled into subdued family life in his humid homeland.

The following year, a daughter was born to Lekain. While he relished the role of family man, he was anxious to return to the Appalachians and retrieve his treasure. Unrest in the region continued, though, and he feared for his safety. When Lekain's daughter was four, the Frenchman was struck with a fever from which he never recovered. He suffered for days lying abed, watched over by his wife, before passing away one night in his sleep.

Before he died, Lekain gave the map and directions to the treasure cave to his wife and told her to try to retrieve the fortune.

Lekain's wife had become too accustomed to the comfortable life in Louisiana to undertake a long journey to the rugged Appalachians. The map and the description were stowed away and forgotten.

When Lekain's daughter grew up, she married a man named Tinder. They had one child, a son they named Robert, and when Robert was grown, he accidentally discovered his grandfather's treasure map among some family belongings.

Robert Tinder lived in Kansas, and did not have the money to leave and search for the treasure the map said lay in the cave in the Kentucky wilderness. Tinder waited, and over time, saved money toward a journey to retrieve the treasure.

Sometime in 1819, a Kentucky settler accidentally found Lekain's treasure cave—but missed the gold and silver.

John Butler was farming part of the floodplain near the Meadow Fork of Buffalo Creek, an area now called Wesleyville. Butler and his wife built a crude log cabin on this site, gradually adding to it over the years as he tilled the rocky soil and grew corn and raised hogs and cattle. By 1840, Butler's log cabin had evolved into a fine home, a handsome accompaniment to his now-prosperous farm. Over the years, Butler added acres to his once meager holdings and became noted for his fine crops and good horses.

One winter morning, Butler found a dead colt near his barn. The animal had been partially devoured and there were two sets of mountain lion tracks leading away from it. Enlisting his fourteen-year-old son, Butler followed the lion tracks in the snow north for several miles across rocky terrain. Later in the day, as Butler and his son neared Tygart Creek, they discovered the lion tracks ended at the edge of a large flat rock on a hillside. On closer examination, Butler saw that the rock partially covered a cave opening just large enough to allow a supple panther to wriggle inside.

Butler and his son pried the rock away from the hole with a stout oak limb. Butler fashioned a crude torch of dry bark gathered from some hickory and cedar trees, and together the two entered the small cave to dispatch the livestock-killing lions.

On hands and knees, the trackers negotiated the first forty feet of the cavern before reaching a chamber where they could stand. Rifle ready, Butler held the torch high. Near the back wall crouched two young lions, their eyes aglow with the reflection of the flame. Butler shot them both.

After examining the dead lions, Butler and his son explored the small cave. The first thing he noticed was a large rock in the center of the floor that bore the inscription "LEKAIN, 1774." Butler assumed the carving was done by some wandering hunter.

Idly curious, Butler was staring at the mound of dirt heaped near the back of the cave when a shout from his son distracted him. The boy had discovered a shovel near the front of the chamber, and the two began searching the cave for other tools. As the torches burned low, Butler decided it was time to start the long hike home.

On leaving the cave, Butler and his son spent about an hour rolling rocks and boulders into the entrance to discourage any further use by mountain lions. They filled the entrance, then rolled a large boulder across the opening, completely covering it.

Some years later, Butler and his family moved to Kansas, where in a curious twist of fate, they became neighbors of Robert Tinder, the grandson of Lekain. Tinder later married Butler's daughter, and the couple eventually had two children.

As he grew older, Butler began to lose his eyesight and contented himself with sitting before the hearth telling stories of the old days in Kentucky. Tinder was visiting the Butler home one evening when the old farmer recalled tracking the mountain lions to the partially concealed cave near Tygart Creek. He told of killing the lions and finding a rock in the cave with the name "LEKAIN" scratched onto the surface.

Tinder listened intently and soon realized this was the same cave indicated on the old deerskin map in his possession! He retrieved the map, and as Butler described the region around the cave, found corresponding landmarks on it. Tinder then told Butler the story of his grandfather's buried treasure, a fortune in gold and silver that Butler had walked past as he explored the cave.

The desire to travel to Kentucky and find the treasure cave fired Tinder, but he could not afford to leave Kansas then. Years passed, and Tinder, then approaching sixty, was finally able to make the journey from the windswept fields of the prairie to the rocky remoteness of the Appalachian backwoods.

When Tinder reached the valley of the treasure cave, he met a farmer named Wash Stamper, who lived near Olive Hill. He told Stamper why he had come to the area and showed him the map and other documents penned years earlier by Howard Lekain. As Tinder spoke, Stamper recognized the landmarks indicated on the map—Cedar Cliffs, Ring Rock Spring, and Tygart's Creek. Stamper listened closely to Tinder's tale and told him he knew the exact location of the rock on which the snake had been carved, and that furthermore he knew the exact location of the cave of which Tinder spoke. Stamper, like everyone in this valley, was familiar with the story of farmer Butler tracking the mountain lions to their den, killing them, and then filling in the opening.

With little difficulty, Stamper led Tinder to the cave entrance, still sealed with rock and dirt and covered by the boulder. Tinder decided the rock and soil could be removed easily enough and hired several men for the job. By the afternoon of the second day, much of the fill was gone from the cave entrance and passageway.

The work was difficult because it rained throughout. A small stream of water flowed into the opening, turning the loose clay into an unstable slurry. About eight feet of passageway had been cleared and one of the workers was lowered by rope to the farthest extent of the excavation. As the worker tried to remove more of the packed clay and rock, the opening caved in, nearly killing the man. The rest of the laborers considered it folly to continue trying to open the dangerous passageway, and after a brief discussion, they all quit. During the evening, the rain washed more clay and rock into the opening, completely refilling the entrance.

Frustrated but undaunted, Tinder decided to sink a wide shaft straight down into the chamber of the cave from higher on the hillside. They easily excavated an opening about sixteen feet wide in the thick layer of soil, and reached the limestone formation that made up the bulk of the mountain. Several feet of the rock had been blasted and removed, for a total depth of twenty-five feet, when Tinder received word from Kansas that his wife was seriously ill and not expected to live. Work on the shaft halted while he made the long journey back to Kansas to begin a vigil by her bedside.

A year later, Tinder returned to the Tygart Creek area to resume excavating the shaft. His renewed efforts were set back by a lack of workers, funds, and competent engineering.

Robert Tinder died in 1903 still trying to locate his grandfather's cached fortune. He was buried near Tygart Creek. Members of the Stamper family still live in the area. According to them, people still come in search of Lekain's fortune, but there has been no concerted effort to gain entrance to the chamber where gold and silver still lie under a simple mound of rock and dirt.

The Lost Silver Mines of the Melungeons

Early in 1770, a strange and secretive group of travelers moved into and settled a portion of the Cumberland Mountain region of the Appalachians near the point where Kentucky, Tennessee, and Virginia share borders. Within a few months, the newcomers discovered silver and began to mine a very rich vein of the ore. The mining was carried on for several generations.

Most of the silver taken from the mines was made into coins which were used as a medium of exchange throughout the region. When the federal government began to pressure the so-called counterfeiters, the transfer of the coins became more difficult. Eventually the mines were closed, and the mysterious residents of the region turned to farming and distilling spirits. The mines, believed to be somewhere near Pineville, contain not only an incredibly rich vein of silver but also an estimated three million dollars' worth of coins and ingots said to have been cached in one of the passageways in 1794. The location of these productive mines has remained a mystery for nearly two centuries.

The odd settlers, who were the first non-Indians to penetrate the Cumberland Valley, were called Melungeons, and their origins are shrouded in mystery. Local legend, most of which has been gleaned from the Melungeons themselves, suggests a Portuguese ancestry, but this has never been verified.

One story is that sometime around 1768, several families chartered a boat to carry them from the port of Lisbon, Portugal, to America, where they hoped to establish a settlement. During the long, difficult voyage across the Atlantic Ocean, the ship's officers and crew tried to rob and kill the passengers, but the travelers fought back fiercely, subduing the sailors and throwing them overboard. They then comandeered the craft and guided it to the North Carolina shore, where they beached it. Fearing pursuit from allies of the ship's crew, the colonists retreated westward deep into the mountains, eventually reaching and settling the region just south of Pineville, Kentucky.

Few residents of the American colonies were aware of the arrival of this group of people in the country, and even fewer were aware of their settlement in the remote Cumberland River valley. Consequently, the migrants lived contentedly in relative obscurity for many years.

The name "Melungeon" has been described as a corruption of a foreign word, the meaning of which is lost to history. Though they have referred to themselves as "Portogee," at least one historian has suggested the Melungeons might be of mixed French origin.

Physically, the Melungeons appear more Mediterranean than northern European. They were described in a Tennessee Historical Society report of 1912 as having a swarthy complexion, straight black hair, black eyes, and heavy-set body structure.

So completely did the Melungeons dominate the area they settled that they eventually became a law unto themselves. During the early 1800s, a time when migrants from the eastern colonies sought new lands to settle in the Appalachian wilderness, the Melungeons repelled intruders with a fierce determination that often ended in the newcomers' deaths. They soon had a terrifying reputation, and the knowledgeable traveler avoided the region. On those few occasions when fearless and hardy families tried to start farms in nearby valleys, a horde of Melungeons would sweep out of the hills, steal cattle and other livestock, and set fire to barns and houses.

As time passed and more families came to settle in the region, law enforcement followed. The growing population and accompanying officers of the law subdued the warlike Melungeons, and the hostilities diminished. Eventually, the clan became less of a menace to homesteaders and turned to distilling whiskey and brandy and selling it in the area. For many years, the Melungeons were famed for their fine brandy, and it is believed their skill in producing it originated in their European homeland. Occasional raids and plundering forays continued, however, and the Melungeons remained a relatively serious threat as late as the onset of the War Between The States. It was not until around 1885 that area residents considered it safe to cross Melungeon territory.

Not long after settling in the Cumberlands, the Melungeons discovered silver. It is believed they found several abandoned mines that had once been operated by Spaniards, Indians, or both. The Melungeons excavated the silver for several decades. Their silver mines are believed to be located in the area of Straight Creek, a small tributary which joins the Cumberland River near the present-day town of Pineville.

As settlers began moving into the area and towns and communities started springing up, the Melungeons were quick to realize the value of coins as a medium of exchange. Using handmade dies, they fashioned their own currency and introduced it in the region in exchange for staples, cloth, and farming implements.

Locally-minted money was generally accepted in many of the more remote regions of this newly settled country. Silver was hard to come by, and shopkeepers were happy to obtain it in the form of coinage, no matter what the origin. Throughout much of the Appalachians, homemade coins fashioned from the ore of area mines commonly entered the local economy.

As Kentucky, Tennessee, and North Carolina were granted statehood and came under the laws of the United States, transactions involving locally minted currency became illegal, and the federal government sent agents into the mountains to confiscate such coins and see to it that production was halted. (Interestingly, the Melungeon coins actually had a higher silver content than the coins made at the United States mint!)

When the U.S. government shut down the local manufacturing of coins, the Melungeons abandoned their mines. A portion of the estimated three million dollars' worth of silver ingots and nuggets that had accumulated over the years and not been used to make Melungeon coins was divided up among the various families. The bulk of the wealth, according to legend, was stacked inside one of the mines. To inhibit prospectors, fortune-seekers, and the merely curious, the Melungeons sealed up the entrances to the shafts.

That the Melungeons did have access to a great wealth of silver cannot be disputed; local history fully documents it. In addition, James Adair, an Englishman who wrote of his travels through the Cumberland region in 1775, mentioned that the Melungeons (whom he described as "desperate vagrants") were seen carrying horseloads of silver into Georgia to purchase slaves.

Around 1900, a farmer searching for stray cattle in the valley of Straight Creek discovered furnaces which had apparently been used to smelt ore. The trees growing out of them suggested the furnaces had not been used in years, and residents of the area hadn't known they existed. Historians believe the Melungeons built these furnaces to smelt their ore. Nuggets of silver have also been found in the area, and some experts claim they actually came from one of the mines and were dropped during transport to the furnaces.

The fascinating history of the Melungeons has been researched over the past hundred years, but little more is known of them now than when the studies began. A relatively shy people whose society was rather closed, the Melungeons have successfully avoided scrutiny. The few who have been interviewed have revealed little.

The lost silver mines of the Melungeons, now covered with rock and forest debris in a seldom-traveled area near Straight Creek on the Cumberland Plateau, remain as elusive as the culture that mined them.

Buried Bank Robbery Loot at King's Mill Dam

The year before the War Between The States was fairly peaceful in most of central Kentucky, and hints of the impending violence were obscured by the tranquility and serenity of the Appalachians. The population in the western foothills of the range was growing steadily as settlers came from the east to establish small farms. Communities sprang up throughout the region, and as the population grew, new businesses and banks appeared among the buildings in the young settlements.

Nicholasville was one such community, comfortably nestled in the rolling hills near the Dix River some fifteen miles south of Lexington. It was toward this slumbering town that four sinister-looking men silently rode one early spring morning as the sun rose above the eastern mountains.

The riders, three just barely out of their teens and one about forty, gently coaxed their horses across the Dix River just above the King's Mill dam. The mill, powered by the diverted stream, ground area farmers' corn into fine meal for baking. Where the four men crossed the river, they could look downstream and barely see the outline of the mill through the slowly thinning fog.

Following a seldom-used trail, the four stopped just within the protection of the thick woods overlooking Nicholasville. As the sun climbed, merchants began to bustle about the streets readying their businesses for another day.

The attention of all four watchers focused suddenly on the bank as a black-coated, bowler-hatted, middle-aged man walked to the front door of the cut-stone building and bent to insert a key into the massive lock. Several minutes passed after the man entered the bank, and presently the riders saw the window curtains thrown open. After another five minutes, the oldest rider uttered a quiet command to approach the town.

Moving casually, yet with purpose, the four men passed through the community, stopping in front of the bank. The older rider glanced up and down the main street, and when he was satisfied the foot traffic was light and inattentive, he and two of the young men dismounted and handed their reins to the fourth rider, who stayed on his horse. Though proud of being given charge of the mounts, the young outlaw cast jerky, nervous glances all around as his three companions entered the bank.

In less than a minute, gunshots were heard from inside the building, and the three outlaws emerged, two of them laboring to carry a wooden chest. The third bandit mounted, and the others lifted the heavy chest so that the two riders could carry it between them. At once, they turned their horses and fled toward the forest from which they had come minutes earlier. The other two bandits had no sooner mounted and spurred their horses in the wake of their fellows when the banker came running into the street screaming that he had been robbed.

The first two riders had difficulty managing the heavy chest they carried between them. Twice they dropped it, and it was slowing their escape so much that the older man, fearing their pursuers, suggested they carry it to the Dix River, bury it somewhere along the bank, and come back for it later.

At the river bank, the four hurriedly dug a shallow hole, deposited the chest, covered it, and fled downstream just as a mounted posse broke through the woods in hot pursuit.

The fleeing bandits rode for the Dix River cliffs and sought shelter among the rocks. As the posse approached, the bandits opened fire. Dozens of shots were exchanged for several minutes, and then a silence fell over the area. Thinking the bandits killed, the posse members cautiously entered the rocks only to find the robbers had fled. The pursuers found no tracks leading from the hiding place and gave up the chase.

Back at Nicholasville, the banker told authorities that the stolen chest had contained several thousand dollars' worth of gold coins in one- and five-dollar denominations. He described the chest as being of fine cedar, bound with metal straps and corners.

Several years later, a man lay near death on a bed in a rooming house in Lexington. A consumptive, the man could scarcely breathe, and it was clear he would not live another night. The proprietress of the rooming house, along with a few of the boarders, tended to the sick man's needs as best they could, but their efforts were futile. Late that afternoon, the dying man beckoned the woman, and when she approached, he weakly pulled her toward him and whispered a confession. With the last of his energy, the man admitted his part in the Nicholasville bank robbery. He gave such clear and precise details as to leave no doubt that he had been there. He told the woman that, while fleeing from the posse, he had paused to bury the chest along the Dix River bank not far from the King's Mill dam. He told her the chest contained a fortune in gold coins, and he wanted her to have it as a reward for her kindness to him.

The confession was reported in area newspapers, and soon treasure hunters were digging every square foot of the Dix River bank near the old mill. Nothing was found, and the chest of gold remained lost until 1910, when it was finally discovered.

George Kelley, a local blacksmith and fishing guide, was diving for fish in the King's Mill Pond when he saw the treasure chest under about fifteen feet of water.

Kelley recognized the old chest for what it was immediately, but he was surprised to find it at the bottom of the pond. The chest was made of one-inch-thick cedar boards held together with metal straps and corners, and had clearly been designed to transport coins or bullion. The box had rotted so badly that some of the wood fell apart when Kelley tried to move it. After several dives and with considerable difficulty, Kelley finally got the chest to the nearest shore. Pulling the lid open, the blacksmith discovered some gold coins in the bottom of the chest. The others had apparently fallen through the many holes in the wood.

Because of the location and description of the chest and the pre–Civil War dates on the gold pieces, historians believe the strongbox was the one taken in the Nicholasville bank robbery about fifty years earlier.

When George Kelly found the chest and the coins, the decades-old story of the Nicholasville bank robbery was recalled by area newspapers, starting a steady stream of treasure hunters to the King's Mill pond over the next several weeks. Nothing more was discovered, for Kelley refused to say exactly where he had found the chest.

What of the other coins that supposedly had filled the old chest? George Kelley had a theory. The blacksmith believed the part of the tale about the outlaws burying the chest along the bank of the Dix River. He also believed that a sudden rainstorm and runoff eroded the river banks and uncovered the chest. Kelley thought that once the chest was uncovered, the force of the surging stream waters pushed it farther into the river, and gravity eventually pulled the old box to the bottom of the large pond. Over the years, the water and mud decayed the cedar boards.

As the wooden chest rotted and the wood decayed, Kelley theorized, the coins spilled out onto the bottom of the pond. Given the weight of gold and the softness of the muck, he believed the coins sank deep into the thick, silty bottom of the pond. The coins Kelley found in the chest when he pulled it to shore were all that remained of a vast fortune.

Under fifteen feet of water and who-knows-how-much muck at King's Mill Pond, an incredible fortune in gold coins may rest just beyond the reach of searchers.

General John H. Morgan's Buried Treasure

For many years, John H. Morgan was the pride of the Confederate Army. His record of command, leadership, and bravery was noteworthy, and it was inevitable he would some day be promoted to general. General Morgan conducted several successful raids for the Southern army, seizing needed horses, arms, and funds to support the Southern effort in the Civil War. They added to Morgan's stature as a military genius and encouraged influential politicians to regard him as a future contender for high political office.

Morgan always succeeded beyond expectation, earning lavish praise from his peers. While lower-ranking officers were placed in charge of confiscated horses, guns, and ammunition, General Morgan himself controlled a rapidly growing fortune in gold, silver, and currency.

As the end of the war approached, Morgan's career declined as a result of some poor military decisions. The tremendous wealth he gathered during the numerous raids was never entirely accounted for and is believed to be hidden along roads and trails the Confederate forces once traveled. It is estimated that Morgan accumulated nearly one million dollars in gold and silver bullion and both Union and Confederate currency during the time he commanded a Rebel battalion.

As this impressive fortune grew, Morgan had it packed and lashed onto several stout horses which, under heavy guard, stayed with his command. With each raid, with each sack of a town, with each addition of monies from county treasuries and town banks, the packs grew larger and the pack horses more numerous.

Morgan also extorted large sums of money from local businessmen and farmers who lived in and near the towns he raided. Accompanied by a well-armed contingent of cavalry, Morgan would ride up to a business or home and threaten to burn the structure unless a ransom was paid.

It is not certain when Morgan intended to deliver this rapidly growing fortune to the treasury of the Confederate army, for as he gathered more and more wealth, he became less and less inclined to part with it. He took great pride in his laden pack horses and bragged often to his contemporaries about transporting this treasure along with his army during his military campaigns.

As the Union army steadily advanced during 1863 and the Confederate forces weakened, Morgan suggested to General Bragg that several large cavalry raids in the north might divert pressure from the Rebel troops. At the same time, said Morgan, more money could be secured along the way to fund the Confederate cause.

At first Bragg was hesitant, but because the Confederates were both losing battles and running out of money, he finally relented and allowed Morgan to lead a command to the north. He cautioned Morgan, however, to keep his forces on the south side of the Ohio River. Morgan agreed, but had no intention of following Bragg's orders. In fact, the general looked forward to raiding and looting the cities of the north.

With a command of 2,460 men, Morgan advanced from Tennessee into Kentucky on July 1, 1863. All along the route, Morgan's army looted and pillaged towns, farms, communities, and travelers. It is said that Morgan even robbed the collection boxes at local churches. While these new funds were intended to aid the Confederate cause,

Morgan and a few of his staff always seemed to spend a great deal of the money on themselves. Morgan and his followers dined well on fine meals and expensive wines, attended by servants.

During the campaign, Morgan's army struck Salem, Kentucky, raiding and looting like bandits. The cavalrymen were so intent on acquiring goods and destroying the town that they paid little attention to the orders of their commanding officers. There was fighting, killing, raping, burning, and drunkeness, and it became clear that Morgan was losing control of his command. After the Salem raid, Morgan had trouble maintaining discipline.

During that raid, hundreds of rifles were confiscated along with thousands of dollars. The guns and ammunition were shipped south to Confederate troops in Tennessee and Virginia, and Morgan added the money to his growing wealth.

On July 12, Morgan led his forces into Versailles, Kentucky. Attacking the small town on that warm, still morning, Morgan personally led a raid on the county treasury and pocketed in excess of five thousand dollars.

Disobeying Bragg's orders, Morgan crossed the Ohio River, and his force swarmed into Ohio, raiding and looting the towns of Jasper and Piketon. As on previous raids, Morgan's undisciplined soldiers vented their fury on these towns, behaving more like a mob than trained cavalrymen.

The continued breakdown of discipline and vigilance brought tragedy on Morgan's army. On July 18, a portion of Morgan's command was intercepted, attacked, and captured by Federal forces, leaving the general only nine hundred soldiers. Massive Union forces were closing in on Morgan from several directions. Morgan, normally a brilliant military tactician, ignored warnings of the impending attack. The only precaution he took was to add extra guards to his pack train.

On July 26, the Ninth Michigan Cavalry launched an attack on Morgan's army at Salineville, Ohio. Thirty Confederate soldiers were killed in the first few minutes of battle, fifty more were wounded, and two hundred were captured outright. Realizing a crushing defeat was inevitable, Morgan, along with several fellow officers and his heavily guarded pack train, fled the battle scene, traveling south toward the Ohio River. Slowed by the cumbersome load, Morgan and his group were captured near West Point, Ohio. None of the treasure was in his possession when he was overtaken, and it is believed the wealth was buried somewhere along the escape route.

Morgan and his fellow officers were held at the state penitentiary at Columbus, but the general had no intention of remaining a prisoner for long. Within days of being jailed, Morgan organized an escape plan. Using tableware for digging tools, he and his men excavated a tunnel and escaped on the evening of November 26, 1863. Traveling at night, Morgan and his followers eluded their pursuers and reached the safety of the Confederate lines far to the south.

After his capture, Morgan's prestige began to wane. Though he was now largely ignored and avoided by Confederate leaders, he did manage to obtain command of a force of twenty-five hundred cavalrymen for a raid on Kentucky.

Departing from a location near Pound Gap, Virginia, Morgan led his raiders at a rapid pace some one hundred fifty miles into Kentucky, arriving at the town of Mount Sterling on the morning of June 8, 1864. Following a brief battle, the small town was easily taken, and Morgan, apparently learning nothing from previous raids, turned his troops loose to sack the town. While his men were looting, burning, and drinking, Morgan himself organized and participated in robbing the Mount Sterling bank of eighty thousand dollars.

On June 11, the raiders entered Cynthiana and encountered a large contingent of Federal forces. Fighting viciously, Morgan's men defeated the Union soldiers and burned the town to the ground as the general confiscated money from local businessmen. Several more Confederate soldiers were killed, wounded, or captured, and Morgan's force dwindled to fewer than a thousand men.

Morgan led his victorious but battered force to a field just outside of Cynthiana and ordered a temporary camp set up to rest men and horses while he planned new strategy. The next morning, as the Rebels were just beginning to stir, five thousand Union cavalrymen swept onto the field, firing into the confused mass of Confederate soldiers. Caught unaware and unprepared, the Rebels fought halfheartedly, and within thirty minutes, dozens were killed and the remainder captured. During the short battle, Morgan and two enlisted men dug a shallow trench and buried the currency and bullion taken in the plunder of Mount Sterling and Cynthiana. Then Morgan and several men fled the scene of battle and, after several days' hard riding, reached Abingdon on June 24.

This last defeat at the hands of the Union forces ruined Morgan's reputation and career as a military man. He was now completely ignored by Confederate leaders. Several prominent generals called for his court martial for looting and extortion and requested an investigation into what became of all the gold, silver, and cash he had acquired during his raids and never turned over to the Southern treasury. A request for the eighty thousand dollars Morgan took from the Mount Sterling bank was drafted and delivered to the beleaguered general.

No one knows whether Morgan would have capitulated and returned any of his buried fortune, for he was killed during a Union attack on the Confederate headquarters at Greenville, South Carolina on September, 14, 1864.

If Morgan left maps or directions to the buried Civil War loot, they have never been found. At least a million dollars' worth of gold, silver, and currency is believed to have been cached in several places along routes Morgan traveled and at the battle site outside of Cynthiana, Kentucky. To date, not a penny of the treasure has been recovered.

Secret Silver Mine of the Cumberlands

The Cumberland Mountains of Tennessee have long puzzled geologists. Their research of the area strongly suggests that precious minerals are most unlikely to be found there. In spite of the scientists' qualified and authoritative declarations about the geology of the region, there are many persistent tales about the mining of silver deep these mountains.

The Cherokee Indians, who lived here long before the white man came, were known to have taken a fortune in silver from the Cumberland Mountains. One tale of treasure has a small party of Cherokee returning to the Piney Creek region of the range sometime in the late 1860s. The Indians, riding in two sturdy wagons pulled by mules, came from the Indian Territory (now Oklahoma) where they had been sent more than twenty years earlier. Before they left, the tribe elders had hidden their silver in the area and covered the entrances to their mines, planning to return someday for the fortune.

The small group of visiting Cherokee hid in the Piney Creek canyon during the day and left in the dark of night. Nearby residents who noticed the deep wheel ruts made by the departing wagons guessed that the vehicles carried a heavy load, and speculated that the Indians had recovered the tribe's hidden silver and taken it back to Oklahoma.

Attempts to backtrack the wagon trail to the secret mine failed.

One local intrigued by the tale of Indian silver mines in the Piney Creek area was a curious character named Leffew. Leffew lived with his wife and children deep in the wooded Cumberland Mountains not far from Piney Creek. He was a farmer, making a living for his family by growing corn and raising hogs and chickens on a hardscrabble mountaintop not far from Spring City.

Farmer Leffew was a tall, gaunt man with large hands calloused by years of hard outdoor work. His skin was leathery and tanned and always in need of washing. Those who chanced to visit the small Leffew farm in the woods remarked that it suffered badly from neglect.

Leffew's neighbors thought him peculiar, and most were uncomfortable around him. The rare times the farmer ventured into nearby settlements, he was generally avoided because of his ragged and unclean appearance. Leffew was often seen talking to himself, gesturing wildly, and sometimes screaming at demons only he could see. The old farmer also suffered from a severe nervous tic that caused his left shoulder to jerk sharply forward every few seconds, suggesting a grotesque dance and lending a bizarre touch to an already strange character.

Sometime early in the 1870s, Leffew began to neglect his farm and family more than usual, often disappearing for days at a time into the deep and gloomy canyons that spawned tributaries of Piney Creek. His frequent extended trips worried his wife and children.

One day Leffew arrived at the front door of his cabin and told his wife he had just discovered an old silver mine deep in Piney Creek gorge. From a dirty leather pouch that hung from his thin neck, he pulled a large nugget of almost pure silver and held it up as proof.

The next day, Leffew took his nugget into town and showed it to any who cared to see it. In a fit of behavior quite uncharacteristic for the eccentric old farmer, Leffew bought several rounds of drinks for everyone at a local tavern.

In a short time, Leffew, who normally drank not at all, began to feel the liquor. Proud of his new-found wealth, he boasted loudly of his secret mine. While bragging, Leffew let slip that the silver mine was in the Piney Creek gorge, not far from a prominent landmark known as Big Rock.

This announcement had an unwanted effect. Several men, coveting Leffew's silver, began searching for the mine. Leffew was followed each time he went into the woods, but being crafty in the wild, he eluded his trackers and vanished into the deep canyon of Piney Creek. For months, men tried to trail Leffew to his mine and always failed.

One afternoon, a young black man appeared at a mercantile in Evansville. He claimed Leffew had recently hired him to help dig the silver ore, and said Leffew had sent him to purchase some dynamite and mining supplies. The young man carefully loaded his purchases onto two mules and then led the pack animals out of town toward Piney Creek. It was the last time anyone ever saw him alive.

Several weeks later, his partially decomposed body was found on the bank of Piney Creek near where it joined one of its tributaries. The man had been shot through the head, and though few cared to say so too loudly or often, most believed Leffew had killed the young man to preserve the secret of the silver mine. To this day, the small canyon near where the body was found is known as Dead Negro Hollow.

In time, a rough-looking gang of men began to hang around the small Leffew farm. The farmer clearly disliked these desperate-looking characters and would caution his wife and children to remain in the cabin while he met with them out in the woods, beyond hearing. Though his wife asked him several times who they were, Leffew remained silent.

It soon leaked out, however, that the men were part of a gang of counterfeiters who allegedly minted phony silver coins in hiding deep in the mountains. Many townspeople suspected that Leffew had become part of the gang.

One afternoon after a brief, stormy meeting with several members of the gang at his farm, Leffew told his wife he was going to the mine and would be back the next day. After two days passed and her husband didn't come, Mrs. Leffew enlisted neighbors to help search for him. Another day went by, and the sheriff was called in. He organized yet another search, which was called off after a week when no trace of the farmer could be found.

About a year later, three young boys were hunting raccoons near Vinegar Hill when they made a grisly discovery. Hanging from the limb of a tree was the dried and shriveled body of a man. The corpse dangled from leather suspenders wrapped tightly around the victim's neck. The body had evidently been there for a long time, as the skin had dried around the skeleton. Clothing, boots, and other articles nearby suggested the skeleton had been Leffew.

Several years later, a local farmer named Thurmond, searching for stray cattle in the Piney Creek gorge, got lost. While climbing a steep wall of the canyon, he found an opening in the rock wide enough to allow the passage of a man. Several mounds of rock fragments outside the opening seemed to indicate that some excavation had taken place. Thurmond had heard of the secret mine of Farmer Leffew but never took it seriously. He wondered if he had accidentally discovered it.

Thurmond went on looking for his lost cattle, intending to some back another time and examine the opening in the rock more closely. Though he tried several times in later years to relocate the mysterious hole, he never could.

During the 1920s, a man named Warrick heard the story of the Leffew mine and decided to search for it. Warrick had lived in the region all his life, as had his father before him, and knew the country around Piney Creek. For months, Warrick spent several hours a day searching the Piney Creek gorge, always optimistic that he would eventually find the silver. Late one afternoon, the tired and begrimed Warrick arrived at his sister's home and announced to her he had discovered it!

Each day for several weeks thereafter, Warrick journeyed to the secret site near Piney Creek and excavated a small handful of silver ore. Each evening on his way home, he visited his sister and related the day's activities. Warrick's sister often asked to see some of the silver ore he had dug, but he steadfastly refused to show it to her. Finally, she accused Warrick of fabricating the story of his discovery.

One Sunday morning as Warrick and his sister were walking home from church, he told her he wanted to show her something important. He led her several yards off the trail near a place called Warrick Fork and showed her a large boulder. With some difficulty, Warrick rolled it to one side, revealing a shallow hole. Inside the hole were several leather pouches, each filled with nuggets of the purest silver.

Warrick explained to his sister that this was where he cached the silver dug from the mine. He told her that if anything ever happened to him, he wanted her to have his fortune.

Several more months passed, and Warrick continued to dig the silver from the secret mine and cache it beneath the large boulder. One morning, like so many other mornings, Warrick gathered his mining tools and headed out to Piney Creek. He cheerfully hailed his sister as he walked by her house on his way to his mine. It was the last time anyone ever saw Warrick.

To this day, no one knows whether Warrick met with foul play or simply decided to leave the country. After two weeks of fruitless searching, Warrick's sister and another relative went to the boulder to retrieve Warrick's cache. When the boulder was rolled aside, they found the shallow hole empty.

The Spring City region of the Cumberland Mountains in Tennessee is not much different today than it was when Leffew lived there in the late 1800s. Heavily forested and thinly populated, the region is infested with rattlesnakes and ticks, and moonshine stills are rumored to operate in the shallow caves and narrow canyons of the area.

In spite of the rugged and forbidding environment, occasional searchers for the secret silver mine of the Cumberland Mountains still come to this section of the Appalachians.

Tasso's Field of Confederate Gold

Tasso, Tennessee, lies just outside the western boundary
of the Cherokee National Forest and about five miles
northeast of the town of Cleveland in the Appalachian
foothills. Scattered across a farmer's field by the railroad
tracks just south of Tasso may lie Civil War relics and a
fortune in gold and silver coins, the bizarre remains of a
great explosion that disabled a Rebel train during the War
Between the States.

The Cherokee Indians who originally settled this
region called their small community Chatata, which
means "clear water." When the Indians were removed in
the early 1830s, white settlers took over their land. They
retained the Cherokee name, and Chatata soon became a
productive agricultural center in southeastern Tennessee.
Around 1858, the railroad came through, connecting
Chatata with the larger towns of Cleveland and Chatta-
nooga to the southwest and Knoxville to the northeast.

During the Civil War, Chatata residents went about
their business of planting, tending, and harvesting corn
and other crops, trying to live as normally as they could
under the circumstances. They saw hundreds of soldiers,
both Union and Confederate, pass through and around
their town, but for the most part, the small community was
spared the misery of so many other settlements during that
violent and bloody conflict.

The forces of both armies used the nearby railroad tracks, and it was not uncommon to see a Yankee troop train pass through in the morning and a Rebel one in the afternoon.

In the spring of 1864, Company C of the Confederate Army of Tennessee was camped by Chatata. The company had been ordered to scout the area and gauge the strength of any Union forces it encountered. If it could, the company was to attack and kill or capture any Yankees they found.

One morning, the commanding officer of Company C, a young captain, got word that a Union troop train was approaching from the southwest. The train was said to carry two hundred soldiers, a supply of guns and ammunition, and three cannons. The officer decided to try to wreck the train and get the weapons.

He also learned that the Union train was being pursued by a Confederate train. The Rebel train consisted of a locomotive and five cars. Most carried men and horses, but the second car behind the locomotive held a large payroll in gold and silver coins destined for a Confederate camp about ten miles up the line at Charleston. The payroll car also held guns, ammunition, sabers, and other military equipment.

The two trains were close enough to exchange gunfire as they traveled, and at least one Yankee was killed.

The commanding officer summoned Private Isaac Griffith and ordered him to set an explosive charge the Union train would detonate as it passed over. Once the train was disabled, the mounted Rebels were to swoop down on the scene and kill or capture any surviving Yankees. To spare Chatata any damage, Private Griffith was told to set the charge several hundred yards south of the town.

Pressed for time, Griffith hurriedly attached the explosives to the railroad bed at the designated point. Once satisfied with the placement of the charge, Griffith leaped onto his mount and sped to his fellows, who had gathered on a low hill nearby to await the train.

Moments later, the mounted Rebs heard the trains approaching and the guns firing. As the Union locomotive came into view, a huge cheer rose from the expectant troops. Their cheering turned into horrified silence as the Union train passed over the charges without setting them off. As it roared on away, the Confederate locomotive smashed into the charge, generating a gigantic explosion that destroyed the engine and the next two cars. The rest of the train jumped the tracks.

When the smoke cleared, the stunned Rebels saw pieces of the train, military equipment, and fellow soldiers scattered several dozen yards on either side of the railroad tracks. The payroll had been transported in canvas sacks piled within a wooden crate. The crate was blown to bits by the explosion, and coins were hurled across the surrounding countryside.

The screams and groans of the wounded and dying reached the ears of the mounted Rebels, who quickly mobilized. As the company advanced to aid their stricken comrades, they were suddenly attacked by a large Yankee force that charged out of the nearby woods. The Confederates, completely unprepared for the onslaught, fled for their lives, unmindful of orders barked by their frantic captain.

Several Rebels were killed or wounded as they raced across the fields, but most of them escaped into the woods. A few were taken prisoner.

The Union troops, ignorant of the gold payroll, glanced over the accident scene and quickly abandoned the area.

Attracted by the sound of the explosion and the initial billow of dark smoke, Chatata residents ran to the scene and gave what help they could to the surviving Confederate soldiers. The gold and silver coins and military supplies lay unnoticed in the nearby fields.

With the passing of generations, the accidental demolition of the Confederate train faded from the memories of area residents and soon became only a minor footnote in the history of the region. After the Civil War, Chatata grew and prospered and became one of several pleasant and attractive communities in the scenic foothills on the western side of the Appalachian Mountains.

In 1905, residents of Chatata changed the name of the town to Tasso. The name was that of an Italian gentleman who often rode the train through the small town. When the train stopped to let off and take on passengers, Tasso would stand on the rear deck of the caboose and sing opera to any who cared to listen. The townspeople often gathered in large crowds to hear him. They must have loved his singing.

In 1970, the destroyed Confederate train was brought back into people's awareness by a Tasso youth's remarkable discovery. On a hot afternoon with locusts whirring in the trees, sixteen-year-old Ben Casteel was playing along Chatata Creek where it runs parallel with the railroad tracks for several yards. He noticed something slightly out of place in the muddy bottom of the shallow stream and investigated. To his surprise, he pulled a Confederate saber from the thick mud. Though rusted and dirty, the saber was in good condition. Upon examination, it was determined to be part of the shipment of military goods carried in the blown-up train. The discovery of the saber revived the story, and people soon were searching the area for more of the relics—and for the gold and silver coins.

Since the saber, many other relics have been found: mess kits, silverware, parts of boots, brass buttons, and belt buckles. No coins have been found, but a researcher who has examined the site has an explanation. He also claims to know where to find the coins.

Gold and silver, he says, are relatively heavy metals. When coins lie on soft and often muddy soil, as at this site, they gradually sink below the surface. The area near the railroad tracks is also flooded once or twice each year. When the ground is saturated with water, the individual soil grains separate easily, permitting any dense object to sink. The local flooding is also believed to have added at least two and perhaps as much as four feet of silt to the field since the explosion well over a hundred years ago.

The individual gold and silver coins, the expert says, are probably between five and ten feet below the surface.

Locating the coins would mean removing a considerable amount of topsoil, an idea not encouraged by local farmers. One enterprising treasure hunter has suggested a series of narrow trenches to be dug one at a time near the explosion. Each trench would be excavated to ten feet and the unearthed soil carefully examined with metal detectors. The trench would then be refilled and another dug, causing minimum disruption and damage.

If it could be agreed to by all concerned, this method might yield a bountiful harvest of gold and silver coins and Confederate Army relics.

Buried Union Army Payroll

In the spring of 1902, the town of Rogersville, Tennessee had just survived the worst storm to strike the area in a decade. High winds had destroyed several homes, and removed shingles and toppled chimneys from others. Crops were ruined, and huge trees had blown down, with their broken and torn roots splayed out like so many spider legs.

Several days after the storm, three boys were hunting rabbits through the debris. At a deadfall, one of the boys, Bobby Venable, saw a hole where a large tree root had been pulled out. Hoping to grab a rabbit, the boy knelt at the hole and thrust his arm inside. His fingers touched pieces of cold metal! The youth pulled one out and was surprised and excited to discover it was a silver coin. In fact, the hole was full of coins, all U.S. silver dollars.

The three boys enlarged the hole and found a metal cooking pot partially filled with the coins. The pot had evidently been tipped over when the roots were pulled from the ground, spilling some of the coins.

The boys filled their pockets and game bags with the coins and went home, intending to keep the discovery secret. Their parents soon found out, though, and encouraged the youths to turn the coins over to authorities and let them try to find the rightful owner. The silver dollars had a face value of $1,512.

It was not clear who owned the land on which the coins were found, and an investigation lasted weeks.

Meanwhile, several newspapers reported the discovery, and the news spread nationwide.

Bobby Venable received a letter with a New York postmark from an elderly man who had read about the discovery. The writer, who had served in Tennessee in the Union army during the Civil War, told how the coins came to be buried there.

Sometime in 1864, he was promoted to corporal and assigned to a Union escort carrying a huge payroll in silver coins for four hundred troops stationed near the Tennessee–North Carolina border. As the escort approached Big Creek near Rogersville, it was attacked by a company of Confederate troops.

Badly outnumbered, the Union escort retreated into the nearby woods, looking for a place to turn and fight. Once inside a perimeter of trees, the officer in charge ordered his men to dismount and return fire. For several hours, firing from behind tree trunks and fallen logs, the Yankees held off the attacking Rebels. But as the Union soldiers fell one by one to Confederate bullets, the outcome became clear.

Not wanting the payroll to fall into enemy hands, the commanding officer enlisted one of his men to help him hide the silver. That man was the corporal who wrote young Bob Venable thirty-eight years later.

The officer and the corporal unloaded payroll sacks and other supplies from the mules and went from tree to tree digging shallow holes. Into each, they put two or three of the canvas sacks and a few supply items, until all of it was hidden. The former corporal recalled digging one hole large enough to hold a cooking pot. He put several sacks of coins into it and hastily refilled the hole. Once the payroll and supplies were hidden, the officer told the corporal they would return for the cache if they survived the attack.

Minutes after returning to the fight, the officer took a bullet through the head and died. Only a handful of Union soldiers remained alive, and the corporal fled into the woods, far from the sounds of combat.

The writer said he wandered days, finding neither food nor water, before happening on an isolated farm. The farmer and his wife took him in, fed him, and gave him a new set of clothes. Having had his fill of the war, the corporal went home to New York, where he lived in hiding for many years because he was a deserter.

He wrote that he and the officer buried portions of the payroll silver in at least a dozen different locations, always at the base of large trees.

Venable first shared this letter with his two friends, and then made it public. Hundreds of treasure hunters came to Rogersville to dig for the hidden payroll. Soon the forest near Big Creek looked like a shelled battlefield because of the many small excavations.

Near the original find, several relics were discovered, no doubt remnants of the battle: bridle bits, tools, a stirrup, and several buttons from both Yankee and Rebel uniforms.

None of the remaining payroll silver was ever found.

After several weeks, the tide of treasure hunters began to ebb and Rogersville gradually returned to normal. Nothing more was heard from the former Union corporal, and the incident was forgotten.

Perhaps another severe storm will one day strike the Rogersville area, blowing shingles from the roofs and felling large trees in the forest. Perhaps another cache of silver dollars will be discovered and the search renewed.

The Cave of Gold
Above Elk River

The more remote parts of the Tennessee Appalachians are rugged and almost impenetrable, made up of deep, dark hollows, steep ridges, and infinite treacherous caves. Natural hazards such a rattlesnakes, cottonmouths, ticks, and poison ivy abound in the wild region. Rumor says there are whiskey stills in the deep recesses of the mountain range, but most residents don't want to talk about that.

Isolated parts of the range are overgrown with dense thickets of briars and tangled undergrowth. It is easy to get lost in there, and once lost, hard to be found.

Somewhere in this forbidding environment, a great Spanish treasure was reportedly left more than four hundred years ago—a treasure of hundreds of golden ingots and artifacts that required twenty mules and an armed escort to transport. It is a treasure hoard that to this day remains hidden in the Tennessee Appalachians.

As rugged and dangerous as parts of these mountains are today, they were even more so before the plows and axes of white settlers cleared the hillsides and lowlands for corn and other crops more than a hundred years ago. In time, much of the region was tamed and settled.

One afternoon in 1886, an old Cherokee arrived at the small community of Pelham. He was dirty, disheveled, and road-weary, and apparently hadn't had a solid meal in weeks. His clothes were torn and the soles of his pitiful shoes had long since worn through. The old man said he had walked all the way from the Cherokee Reservation in eastern Oklahoma.

Going from house to house and farm to farm, the Indian offered to trade work for food. Two days later, a local farmer hired him to chop wood and do other chores. The old Indian proved a hard and efficient worker who labored from dawn until far past sundown. He never seemed to tire and seldom stopped except to get a drink of water. The old Cherokee slept in the farmer's barn.

During the two weeks he labored on the small farm, the farmer and the Cherokee came to know one another, and one evening over dinner, the Indian explained why he had come to eastern Tennessee.

In halting and clumsy English, the Indian said that many of the older Cherokee in Oklahoma knew of a hidden Spanish treasure near the "hills of Mannanetcha," the divide between the Elk and Duck Rivers.

Many generations earlier, the Indian said, a Spanish mule train was attempting a particularly broken and difficult part of the mountain range when it was set upon by Cherokee.

The Indians attacked early one morning, when the pack mules had been loaded and the Spaniards were getting breakfast. The escort was caught by surprise and killed within minutes.

When the Cherokee ransacked the mule packs, they found gold—in the form of hundreds of ingots, several sacks of coins, and other items such as chalices and candleholders. Since the Cherokee sometimes used gold to make ornaments, they stored the treasure in a nearby cave.

In succeeding years, the Cherokee periodically visited the cave to retrieve gold for making bracelets, necklaces and ceremonial jewelry, but by and large the treasure remained intact.

The old Cherokee who had come to Pelham said he carried directions to the cave in which the treasure was stored, but refused to show them. He did say that the golden hoard was hidden in a limestone cave somewhere on a steep mountainside in the area. The cave had a very low opening, and even from only a few yards away, was difficult to see. According to the directions, a freshwater spring issued from the mouth of the cave, cascading down the mountainside to the Elk River below.

The Indian said the entrance to the cave was probably covered thickly with forest vegetation and would be hard to locate. He planned to find the stream where it met the Elk River and follow it up the side of the mountain to its source.

Near the entrance of the cave, the Indian said, a cross was carved into an exposed rock. When the Cherokee attacked the hapless mule train, they had noticed the symbol of the cross embossed on weapons, armor, and saddlebags, he said. After they hid the gold, they copied the symbol onto a nearby rock to mark the cave's entrance.

As the story of hidden treasure spread through the area, several neighbors offered to help the old Indian in his search. He refused them all.

After two weeks of recuperation from his long journey, the Cherokee had regained much of his strength. He bid his employer goodbye and went into the nearby mountains.

A Pelham resident spotted the old Indian leaving and decided to follow him. The man had been intrigued by the story of the hidden Spanish treasure and thought of searching for it himself. He followed the Cherokee into the Elk River canyon, but there lost him after only a few hundred yards.

For several days, no one saw the Indian. Then he reappeared, but he carried no treasure. He said he had followed several small springs to their sources on the mountainside, but none of them issued from the treasure cave.

After resting a few more days, the Indian left once more for the Elk River valley. He was never seen again. Some speculated that the old man had found the treasure and departed, his pockets filled with riches. Others suggested he failed in his search and went back to Oklahoma. Still others thought the old man might have perished, alone in the harsh mountains.

Intrigued by the old Indian's tale, several locals tried to find the treasure cave over the next few years. In 1893, a group of searchers found a rock near the Elk River chiseled with a large cross. The carving was quite weathered, as if it had been made hundreds of years earlier. The discovery of the cross renewed interest in the hidden gold, and soon the hills and canyons were alive with treasure hunters.

The cave was never found.

Where there are caves in the Appalachians, the mountains are normally made of thinly bedded, highly jointed, and porous limestone rock. This kind of rock is easily eroded by percolating ground water that seeps down through it. Sometimes ground water is trapped in the limestone aquifer for centuries and eventually drawn back to the surface through wells. Sometimes the water may flow for hundreds of miles deep below the surface as an underground river. Occasionally this stored ground water escapes to the surface as a spring.

Earthquakes and occasional shifts in weakened and aged rock formations can change the course of the underground water, cutting off springs in some areas and starting others elsewhere.

Given the geology of the Tennessee Appalachians, the spring of which the old Cherokee spoke may no longer flow from the treasure cave as it did over four hundred years ago.

The low entrance to the treasure cave probably still looks out across Elk River valley, though. Thick foliage and dense undergrowth may have made the entrance hard to find, and hunters and outdoorsmen may have passed close to it over the centuries and never noticed it, but just inside this small cave in the Mannanetcha Hills may still lie a vast fortune in Spanish gold ingots and artifacts.

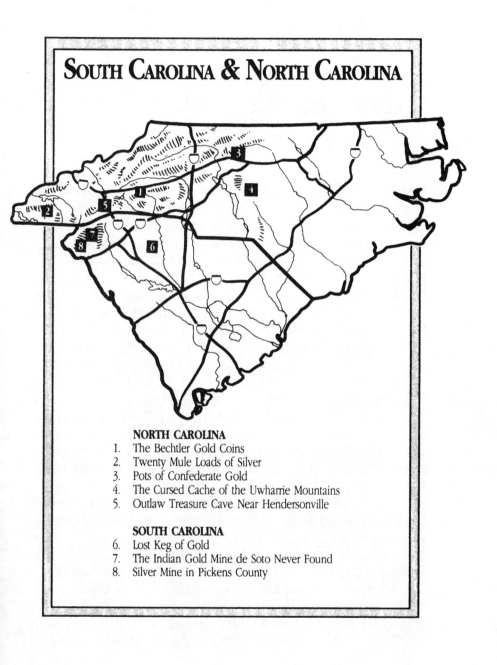

SOUTH CAROLINA & NORTH CAROLINA

NORTH CAROLINA
1. The Bechtler Gold Coins
2. Twenty Mule Loads of Silver
3. Pots of Confederate Gold
4. The Cursed Cache of the Uwharrie Mountains
5. Outlaw Treasure Cave Near Hendersonville

SOUTH CAROLINA
6. Lost Keg of Gold
7. The Indian Gold Mine de Soto Never Found
8. Silver Mine in Pickens County

The Bechtler Gold Coins

Between 1831 and 1840, a small, privately-owned mint operated in the remote town of Rutherfordton. Its owners mined, processed, and coined nearly forty million dollars' worth of gold over a nine-year period. The coins, cast into denominations of $1.00, $2.50, and $5.00, were in general circulation in western North Carolina, northern South Carolina, and much of northern Georgia.

As United States-minted specie became available, these locally made coins were gradually withdrawn from the area economy. Collectors now possess hundreds, perhaps thousands, of the coins, and many more of them, perhaps millions of dollars' worth, are still in Rutherford County. So is the rich mine from which the gold came.

Few are aware of it, but most of the gold mined in the United States between 1790 and 1840 came from western North Carolina and parts of South Carolina and Georgia. North Carolina supplied most of the gold coined by the U.S. mint in Philadelphia during that period, and according to a 1948 U.S. Geological Survey report, there were about three hundred gold-producing mines in North Carolina alone. Rutherfordton, in the western part of the state about forty miles southeast of Asheville, was known as America's gold mining capitol during the early 1800s.

Although most of the gold used for minting U.S. coins came from western North Carolina, U.S. money was, in fact, quite scarce in the region. Because of that, some area residents made their own from locally mined gold. These maverick coins were in common use throughout the region and were generally accepted.

In 1830, a German immigrant named Christopher Bechtler and his son, August, arrived in the small community of Rutherfordton. The Bechtlers had been metallurgists and jewelers in Europe, and they hoped to put their skills to use in the famous gold fields of the Carolinas.

The Bechtlers found a promising outcrop in Rutherford County near Rutherfordton, settled, and soon discovered a rich deposit of gold-bearing quartz on their new land. As they mined the ore, the Bechtlers decided to open their own mint. They built a roller and a stamp press, and began producing a high quality specie in denominations of $1.00, $2.50, and $5.00. Area residents came to prefer the Bechtler coins, and they began to be used almost exclusively throughout the region.

The Bechtlers preferred minting their own coins to selling raw and smelted gold to the Philadelphia mint. Hauling the heavy ore from western North Carolina to eastern Pennsylvania was a long and arduous journey and took time that could have been spent digging gold. Robbers occasionally lurked along the old ore trail, and more than one hauler was killed for his rich load. Selling the gold to a broker or middleman meant reduced profit. Thus, Christopher and August Bechtler decided to optimize their profit by continuing to fashion their own gold into what came to be known as "Bechtler coins." They also charged a small fee to mint the gold brought in by other area miners. In a few years, the two men became very wealthy.

For nine years the Bechtler mine and mint prospered. It has been estimated that forty million dollars' worth of coins (at today's market value) were made. Most of them went into the area economy.

But the Bechtler mint was not destined to endure. In 1840, the United States opened a mint in Charlotte, about seventy-five miles east of Rutherfordton. With U.S.–minted specie now more available in the region, the Bechtlers were pressured by the federal government to cease their private manufacture of coins. The family didn't object, since by that time it had already amassed a fortune. Western North Carolinians, however, often insisted on using the Bechtler coins. They were preferred by most area merchants and residents, and for well over twenty years, the coins were the most common form of currency in this part of the Appalachians.

During the War Between The States, Bechtler coins were also in demand by the Confederate government. One historian noted that Confederate purchasing contracts often specifically called for payment in Bechtler gold rather than U.S. gold or paper money. Metallurgical analysis showed that the Bechtler coins had a higher gold content than did the U.S.minted coins! They were also more plentiful in the area and more acceptable to merchants and suppliers who had been happily using them for years.

As the Civil War raged, even after North Carolina joined the Confederacy, the western section of the state was spared much of the violence that disrupted the rest of the South. Though most of the conflict occurred elsewhere, many families in and near the Carolina Appalachians buried large caches of Bechtler coins so they would not be confiscated by roving bands of either Yankee soldiers or Rebel bandits who terrorized the countryside.

Within months after closing down his mine, Christopher Bechtler, along with a trunk filled with gold coins, disappeared. He was traveling by wagon to nearby Buncombe County to pay off a large debt. He was last seen at the Parris Gap toll gate, where he stopped to visit with the operator for about an hour. A few days later, Bechtler's wagon was found overturned in a deep ravine about three miles west of the gap. His two horses had been killed and their carcasses lay near the ruined wagon. Christopher Bechtler and the trunk of coins were never seen again.

His son August closed down the mine shortly thereafter. August abandoned the settlement near the mine and moved into Rutherfordton, where he opened a shop and made jewelry, firearms, and occasionally, in response to local demand, a few coins, using some of the original rollers and dies. Beset with serious health problems, August Bechtler passed away a few years later, leaving his business and his fortune to his closest relative, a cousin who had come to live with him five years earlier. The cousin, also named Christopher and sometimes referred to in the region as Christopher Junior, ran the business for several years. Then he closed it down and moved away, not saying where he was bound.

The Bechtler coins gradually disappeared from circulation over the years, to be replaced by federal specie. As the coins became a part of the region's history, the Smithsonian Institution saw fit to create a display of them. Coin collectors considered them valuable both intrinsically and as historical artifacts. Researchers have recently learned that several current Rutherfordton residents still hold hundreds, perhaps even thousands, of the Bechtler coins. Interviews have revealed that many of the town's citizens own several hundred of the old coins, which were handed down in their families. These collections of Bechtler coins could be worth from several hundred thousands to well over a million dollars on today's collector market.

The Bechtler coins still turn up from time to time. One long-time Rutherfordton resident reported finding hundreds of the coins in a secret hiding place in the concrete-lined chimney of an old house that Christopher Bechtler had lived in. The coins were picked out of a square, hollow cement chamber. It has also been suggested that many coins hidden during the Civil War were never retrieved and still lie buried in the area.

Some of the minting equipment once used by the Bechtlers is still around. The rollers and the stamp press, both valuable artifacts, are held by local residents. The original dies used in the manufacture of the coins served as door stops for a Rutherfordton family for twenty years. When World War II broke out, the lady of the house donated them to the government during a scrap-metal drive!

The location of the original Bechtler mine, with its rich, seemingly inexhaustible supply of almost pure gold, was well known for generations. When Christopher Bechtler closed it down in 1840, the vein of gold was reported to be as rich and abundant as the day it was discovered. August reopened the mine for a brief time during the mid–1840s, then shut it down for good.

Around the turn of the century, the open shaft, regarded as a hazard, was covered over and fenced off. Over the years, the town's residents largely forgot the mine, using it as a garbage dump.

One Rutherfordton old-timer actually entered the mine around 1945. He claimed he and his father were lowered into the shaft on a rope, and once inside they walked around the excavation for several minutes, discovering artifacts, furniture, and mining apparatus. The old-timer recalled that the air in the mine was bad and smelled strongly of gas. He also reported the shaft was almost knee-deep in water that was seeping in through the fractured rock. He and his father left quickly, and to his knowledge, no one has gone down the old shaft since.

Today, the old Bechtler mine is a victim of progress. Contruction projects and real estate developments have covered the area where it was believed to have been, completely cutting off access to the rich ore that lies below the ground.

Rutherfordton is today a pleasant community attractively sprawled in the shadows of the Carolina Appalachians. It's a typical small American town, and few that walk the streets and travel the highways of this village of some thirty-five hundred souls know that it was once a place where fortunes in gold were mined and minted.

Twenty Mule-Loads
of Silver

In far western North Carolina near the Nantahala
Gorge, fast-flowing rivers and streams have carved impressive canyons into the fractured, folded, and uplifted rock that makes up this portion of the Appalachian Mountains. It was there, one day in 1896, that an aged Cherokee Indian inadvertently revealed to a young white boy the existence of a long-hidden secret cache of twenty mule-loads of silver somewhere near Silver Creek.

The young boy was W.I. Grant, born in a small log cabin alongside Wesser Creek in 1881. Grant's father raised corn and hogs on the narrow bottomland by the creek and made a fair living during a time that was hard on most people in the area. With several children, the Grants had little food to spare, and many a meal was postponed. Regardless, the family never turned a hungry traveler from the door.

One day in 1893, a trader arrived in the region of Wesser Creek with a wagonload of goods. The Grant family had no money to make purchases, but they did feed a meal to the merchant and his Indian helper. At first, the old Indian stayed in the yard, not realizing he was welcome in the home of white people, but Mrs. Grant called him inside and invited him to sit at the table and dine with the rest of the family. Though not plentiful, the food was delicious, and the Grants were happy to share their slim fare with their guests.

As the trader and Grant's father caught up on the news of the day, the youngster, W.I., devoted all his attention to the Indian, and the Indian seemed pleased by the child's interest.

The Indian told young Grant that he was called Bigfoot and was a member of the Cherokee tribe. Bigfoot was large for an Indian, towering nearly six-and-a-half feet. He was about fifty, well-muscled and strong, and always carried a big rifle. His feet were the obvious source of his name.

After the meal, the trader thanked the Grants, left a few goods and trinkets in appreciation, and he and Bigfoot rode away in the wagon.

Several days later, the huge Indian appeared at the front door of the Grant cabin. He presented a dressed deer carcass to Mrs. Grant, and told her the deer was a token of his gratitude for the meal and the hospitality given him on his earlier visit. With a slight bow, he excused himself and disappeared into the nearby woods. Bigfoot seemed to know the Grants had barely enough food to feed their large family and that the shared meal must have taxed their meager resources.

About a week later, young Grant was working in the cornfield with his father when he saw Bigfoot approach, carrying several wild geese by their necks. He handed the cleaned fowl to the older Grant and merely said, "Food." With a smile and a nod, he turned and once again retreated into the forest.

Bigfoot made several more sudden and quiet appearances, bringing gifts of deer, geese, grouse, and sometimes fish. The Grants always thanked him for the food and began to ask the Indian to dine with them each time he came.

One evening, Bigfoot told the Grants he had left the trader because he preferred to live in the woods instead of getting by like a white man. The Grants told the big Indian he was welcome on their farm any time, and Bigfoot soon became a regular visitor, always bringing food and occasionally toys he had carved for the children. He played with all the youngsters, but W.I. was his favorite.

Young W.I. Grant was fascinated by Bigfoot's huge rifle, and he would often run his hand over the smooth, shiny barrel and poke his finger into the bore. Bigfoot told the lad that when he was older and stronger, he would show him how to shoot the gun, and as the boy grew, the two spent much time together in the woods. Bigfoot taught Grant to read animal sign, set traps for small game, and find the finest herbs and greens in the forest. Bigfoot continued his regular visits to the Grant farm over the years and became almost a part of the family.

One day, Bigfoot and the boy were sunning themselves on a large rock overlooking Wesser Creek. They had caught some fish, and as the afternoon wore on, the two relaxed, enjoying the late summer weather. While young Grant reclined on the rock, Bigfoot molded bullets for his rifle, heating the metal over a small flame and pressing it into shape using a hand-forged tool he always carried.

Bigfoot looked thoughtfully around at the canyon, the woods, and the sky, and with a deep sigh told the boy that one day all the deer, geese, and fish would be gone. He added that the Indians would someday be gone as well.

Worried, Grant asked what he meant. Bigfoot explained that the area was rapidly filling up with white men, and that when white men arrive, all the game and the Indians are killed off or run out.

When Grant asked why, Bigfoot replied that white men were greedy, wanting most of all the silver that was found in these hills. He showed young Grant the bullets he was molding and told him they were not made from lead, but from pure silver.

The lad asked where the silver came from, and Bigfoot pointed to a nearby ridge. The Cherokee had had a secret silver mine for hundreds of years, he said, in the mountains on the other side of the ridge near Silver Creek. He said the mine was rich with the precious metal, but when white men started moving into the area, the Cherokee closed it down, knowing the white man's unbridled greed for such things. When the boy asked for more details, Bigfoot cut him off sharply and told him it was forbidden for members of the tribe even to talk about the silver.

When he finished making his bullets, the Indian handed several to Grant and told him to keep them hidden and bring them out only when he was a grown man and he, Bigfoot, was no longer around.

About a week after Bigfoot had described the secret silver mine of the Cherokees, young Grant, then fifteen, walked to Silver Creek and climbed over and through the ravines and hillsides in search of the mine. He found nothing that remotely resembled a mine, but he did discover two primitive smelters that had obviously gone unused for many years. Grant knew he was in the right area and rightly guessed that the Cherokee used the smelters to process their ore. The youngster was determined to quiz Bigfoot about the silver mine on his next visit.

When Bigfoot came the next week, he was drunk and still sipping from a half-full jar of strong homemade whiskey. He and young Grant went into the woods and laid down beneath a large tree. As Bigfoot grew more and more inebriated, Grant took advantage of his state and asked pointed questions about the silver mine.

Presently, Bigfoot began to laugh and talk incoherently about the trick the Cherokee had played on the white man. When Grant asked him what he meant, the Indian told an intriguing tale.

Many years ago, he said, white men had heard about the silver mine of the Cherokee and came to the Silver Creek valley in search of it. Like Grant, all they found were the remains of the old smelters. The Cherokee, according to Bigfoot, took all the silver from the mine and secreted it inside a large hollowed-out rock some distance away.

For many days and nights, the Indians worked in the mine, digging out the silver and smelting it with their crude equipment. Bigfoot said they dug twenty mule-loads of the ore before moving it. While many Indians dug the silver, several others hollowed out an opening in a boulder large enough to hold all of the silver. Once the bags of ore were placed in the hollow boulder, a large slab of the same kind of rock was placed over the opening.

The Indians swore to each other to keep secret the true story of the silver and to punish by death any violation of the oath. They let the white men believe they had merely covered the mine, leaving the silver inside, and let them search for it. Over the years, Cherokees who knew of the treasure-filled boulder would occasionally retrieve some ore to make bullets and jewelry.

When Grant asked Bigfoot where the hollowed-out rock was, the drunken Cherokee pulled an old, weathered, grimy deerskin map from his pocket and handed it to the youth. The map contained Indian symbols, and though it was hard to read, Grant could make out some familiar landmarks. While the boy was reading the map, the big Indian fell asleep in a stupor.

For nearly two hours Grant studied the map, memorizing the marked trails, mountain peaks, ridges, and streams. Presently, the Indian awoke and saw the boy holding the map. Bigfoot asked Grant if he had told him the story of the hidden Cherokee silver. The boy replied that he had, and handed the map back to him.

Bigfoot held out an open palm and told the boy to keep the map. He said he had broken a tribal code by revealing the information and would likely be killed for it. He told Grant to hide the map and never let anyone know he possessed it, or he, too, would be killed. The boy promised to hide the map and keep the secret.

Bigfoot bid the lad goodbye and staggered into the woods. Two weeks later, his body was found about a mile from the Grant cabin. The big Indian's throat had been cut from ear to ear, and a knife had been thrust into his chest up to the hilt.

The death of Bigfoot had a devastating effect on young Grant. Because he and the Indian had been close friends, the boy grieved for many weeks, but the resilience of youth finally won out, and life returned to normal. True to his promise, Grant told no one about the treasure map and kept it hidden.

Many years later when Grant was grown, he dug the map out of its hiding place and undertook a search for the silver cache. Following the directions on the old, cracked deerskin, Grant went right to the boulder, lifted the covering rock, and saw the many leather sacks filled with silver lying in the hollowed-out chamber. Grant spent an entire afternoon sitting on top of the boulder wondering what to do with this vast fortune. In the end, he covered it up and left it where it was.

Years later, when asked how he could walk away from such a great wealth, he replied without hesitation that it was simply not his treasure. It belonged to the Cherokee, he said. They mined it, they labored hard and long to move it to the hollowed-out rock, and they guarded it over the years. At first, he said, he was afraid the Indians would somehow find out if he removed some of the silver and he would die a horrible death like his friend Bigfoot, but in the end, he believed it was simply not rightfully his to take.

The map, Grant said, was in an old trunk filled with belongings, and he intended to leave it there.

In the fall of 1954, W.I. Grant passed away at age seventy-three. A friend of Grant's who knew the story of the Cherokee silver asked his widow about the map. She had no idea where it was. When the friend told her Grant had said he kept it in an old trunk, she explained apologetically that the trunk and everything in it had been burned right after the funeral.

Unless some Cherokee still live who remember, the secret of the great cache of silver somewhere on Silver Creek near the Nantahala Gorge died with W.I. Grant. Many remember there was a silver mine, but few know that the great wealth of precious metal was removed and hidden in a huge hollowed-out boulder. Most of that twenty mule-loads of almost pure silver is still there.

Pots of Confederate Gold

Toward the end of 1864 it was becoming painfully clear to the Confederate Army that the war was winding down and they were losing. Some Southern generals, foreseeing the inevitable outcome, came to be more interested in salvaging what was left of the Confederate treasury than in winning battles. To that end, much of the Southern army's wealth, intended to purchase arms, ammunition, and riding stock, was hurriedly hidden in various places below the Mason-Dixon Line. Some of this wealth was later retrieved, but most of it, perhaps several million dollars' worth of gold and silver coins, remains hidden.

One such cache was an incredibly rich store of gold held in a temporary treasury headquarters in Richmond, Virginia, during the war. When it became clear that the days of the Confederacy were numbered, military leaders decided to hide the gold so it would not fall into the hands of Union forces. Captain J.W. Duchase, commander of Company C of the Fourth Mississippi Infantry stationed in Richmond, was charged with removing the South's store of gold coins to another state and burying them in predetermined locations.

Duchase was roused from his sleep around two o'clock one crisp autumn morning in 1864 and told to report to headquarters. There he found officers and aides frantically preparing to abandon the area in the wake of the news that the Yankees were closing in.

Duchase, along with his entire company, was ordered to report to the railway station at 6:30 that evening. Each man was to bring three days' worth of rations, at least forty rounds of ammunition, and full marching gear.

That evening, Captan Duchase and the seventy-eight fighting men from Mississippi who made up his infantry company assembled at the station platform. The train had four boxcars and three flatcars. The boxcars contained arms, ammunition, and other material the Confederate leaders thought prudent to ship out. The end flatcar held a three-inch-bore fieldpiece, some other armament, and a detachment of gunners. The two remaining flatcars were loaded with iron cooking pots, each filled with gold coins, each lid tightly fastened with wire.

As Duchase waited near the train, he was delivered a set of orders and told to open them when he arrived at his assigned destination, Greensboro, North Carolina.

Duchase's notes on the incident explain what occurred next:

> We traveled all night and reached Greensboro the next day at 4 P.M. There I opened my orders and found the following instructions: 'You are to proceed the following night to McLeansville by way of the North Carolina Railroad. After leaving McLeansville, you will bury these pots in groups of three on each side of the R.R. and not over one hundred paces from the right of way. In case there are houses nearby, proceed further. Also, plot the burial places as nearly as possible.'

Duchase and his men followed the orders to the letter, burying the pots in lots of three. In all, they covered about sixteen miles along the railroad tracks between Greensboro and Company Shops (later renamed Burlington).

Their mission complete, Duchase and his infantry company rode the train into Company Shops, turned the train around, and returned to Greensboro. From Greensboro, they went by another train toward Richmond to submit the information on the locations of the buried

Confederate gold and to aid in the defense of that city against Yankee attack. Along the way, however, the train was derailed by a Union blockade, and most of Company C was captured. Duchase and one lieutenant escaped, but they lost the description of the burial locations in doing so.

The two men lived in hiding for several weeks and were forced to steal and beg food from the isolated farms they found in the area. Union troops eventually found Duchase and his companion. The two men, near starvation, were huddling under a fallen log. They surrendered to the Yankees, were interrogated, and waited out the remainder of the war in a prison camp.

When the South surrendered, Duchase, along with thousands of other captured Rebels, was freed. He went to Mexico and got involved in mining and real estate. He prospered over the years from several successful ventures, married a Mexican woman, and raised a family. Duchase sometimes thought of returning to North Carolina for the Confederate gold he had buried. The former infantry captain believed he remembered enough of the area between Greensboro and McLeansville to locate the treasure easily. Business concerns and family matters, however, occupied his time, and he could not travel. While living in Mexico, Duchase wrote extensive notes in a journal about the war in general and his assignment to conceal the Confederate gold in particular. His descriptions of where he hid the gold-filled iron cooking pots were clear and precise.

More years passed. Duchase's wealth grew, and his desire to return to the United States waned. His notes on the war, along with the account of the buried Confederate gold, were given to a man named P.H. Black, a former Greensboro resident who met Duchase in Mexico in the 1890s. When Duchase learned Black was from North Carolina, he told him the story. Before Black left Mexico, Duchase gave him all his notes about it.

Duchase died in Mexico around the turn of the century, having never left since he first arrived in 1865. P.H.

Black died in North Carolina in the 1930s, and no one knows what became of Duchase's notes. Nor does anyone know whether Black ever tried to retrieve any of the gold. If he did, he did not find all of it.

During the 1880s, Burlington grew into an important settlement in that part of the Appalachian piedmont. In the fields and meadows along the old North Carolina Railroad tracks, farmers met the growing demand for cotton and corn.

Late one summer afternoon in 1910, a black farmhand was plowing in a field about three miles west of Burlington. The horse-drawn plowing was tedious and the day was hot. Both man and horse were tired and looking forward to quitting time when the steel plow struck something hard, breaking its point. The farmhand dug into the ground and retrieved a rusted iron cooking pot wrapped tightly with thick wire. He wrestled the heavy pot to the surface, and when he removed the wire and the lid, he was surprised to find it filled to the top with twenty-dollar gold pieces. The farmhand was about a hundred paces from the old railroad tracks.

Not knowing the true value of the coins, the farmhand took several into Burlington the next day and traded them for dimes. The twenty-dollar gold pieces aroused local curiosity, and the laborer was asked about his discovery. Before sundown of that same day, the corn field was swarming with men digging the rich soil for other pots. Within two feet of the first iron pot, the landowner found two others. Though he never told anyone the value of his discovery, from that day on he was a wealthy man.

The three pots of gold were found in the corn field by luck and accident. Others may have been recovered, but if so it has never been recorded. Most likely, hundreds of the iron cooking pots, each filled with gold coins, are still buried near the old railroad tracks. For well over a hundred twenty years, a king's ransom has lain hidden in the fields under a few inches of North Carolina soil.

The Cursed Cache of the
Uwharrie Mountains

In west-central North Carolina about fifty miles
south of Greensboro lie the Uwharrie Mountains, an ancient subdivision of the Appalachians. Geologists have
written that the Uwharries might be the oldest range on
the North American continent and at one time reached
altitudes surpassing any found today in the Rockies.

Because of their great age, the Uwharries have eroded
over time, the once-majestic peaks now worn down into
no more than rounded knobs, hills, and ridges.

Anthropologists and archeologists tell us that some ten
thousand years ago, these mountains were populated by
an Indian tribe that left complex burial mounds suggestive
of elaborate rituals and ceremonies. Why the early Indians
abandoned the region, no one knows, but they inspired a
rich lore of folktales and legends of demons, spirits, ghosts,
and witches, all of which allegedly haunt the range to this
day.

In 1835, a man named Francis J. Kron came to the
Uwharrie Mountains. From somewhere in Europe, Kron
had arrived on the east coast several years earlier, had
repeatedly run into trouble with the law, and had finally
moved westward. He eventually came to the Uwharrie
Mountains, traveling alone and on foot. For months, Kron
lived deep in the woods, appearing on rare occasions at
small area settlements to purchase supplies.

Kron was a dark-complected, sharp-featured, angular man with shoulder-length black hair. Though he claimed to be a doctor, it is doubtful he ever received a medical education from any established institution. A few of the local residents, though, let Kron doctor their ailments. They reported his methods of treatment were bizarre, using wild herbs and strange powders, and sing-song chanting in a language no one understood. Many of the area residents began to believe that Kron was evil and that he was somehow linked with the mountain demons, spirits, and curses of the old folktales.

Within a few years, Kron married a local woman, a wealthy widow, and immediately purchased a plantation near what is now the town of Albemarle. Kron built a mansion, bought numerous slaves to work on his farm, and prospered.

A few months after the wedding, Kron's wife disappeared and was never seen again. No explanation was ever offered. Visitors to the Kron mansion were never greeted and often left without seeing a soul on the farm. Stories of bonfires and odd ceremonies on the Kron plantation spread throughout the area.

Around 1879, Kron hired a man named Dan Compton to do odd jobs around the plantation. Compton lived in one of the old slave cabins and took his meals with the hired help. Once, Kron ordered Compton into a dark room deep in the mansion and showed him a large keg standing in the center of the room. The top of the keg was nailed shut and heavy steel bands were secured tightly around the oak staves. Kron told Compton to roll the keg into the middle of one of the large fields.

The keg was heavy and unwieldy, but Compton managed to wrestle it from the house and roll it to the prescribed site, accompanied by the evil-looking Kron. As he rolled the keg along the ground, Compton noted that it jingled as if it were filled with coins. About halfway to the field, Compton pleaded with Kron to let him to rest. The plantation owner granted the handyman a few moments to catch his breath, and   Compton sat on the tipped-over keg, he noticed a small space between two of the oak staves. He saw that the keg was filled with gold coins. Compton assumed Kron intended to bury the keg of coins.

When the two men arrived at the designated site, Kron told Compton to set the keg upright and pile some boards around it. Nearby were three torn-down slave shacks, and from them Compton took dozens of pieces of milled lumber, stacking them around the keg as ordered. When Compton finished, Kron ordered the handyman to leave and never return to the site.

That evening, Compton was awakened by the sound of loud chanting. From the doorway of his cabin, he could see a huge bonfire out in the large field where he had rolled the keg of gold coins. He could just make out human figures leaping and swaying to some primitive rhythm.

Slipping on pants and shoes, Compton crept closer to the fire, keeping to the trees at the edge of the field. When he stopped some fifty yards from the blaze where he could observe the goings-on, he saw Kron and several Indians he had never seen before dancing naked around the huge fire and chanting in a language he had never heard.

In the middle of the blaze, the wooden staves of the keg were burning away and the gold coins were beginning to melt. Ochre streams of molten metal flowed lazily from the pyre, and then cooled into shapeless masses. As the gold melted, the screams and chants of the dancers grew louder and more passionate. Frightened and appalled, Compton fled from the scene. Reaching his cabin, he snatched up his few possessions and left the Uwharries, never to return.

Years later on his deathbed, Compton related for the first time the story of that strange autumn night of 1878. Asked why he had never told it before, he said he was afraid of Kron, afraid that he was some kind of demon and had the power to call down a terrible curse on him. Magic and witchcraft were a powerful part of the beliefs of many people in those days, and Compton, who was susceptible to such notions, never returned to the plantation for any of the gold he was certain still lay in the field.

The old Kron place was just northwest of present-day Morrow Mountain State Park. The field on which Kron held the strange rituals lies between a small unnamed creek and the Louder Ferry Road. Immediately south of the field is Hattaway Mountain. Somewhere near the center of that field, beneath a few inches of soil, likely lies a shapeless mass of gold worth millions of dollars.

Outlaw Treasure Cave Near Hendersonville

For years caves have been favored haunts of outlaws. Caves were normally far removed from settlements and thus afforded isolation; caves offered simple yet effective protection from the elements—they were cool in the summer and warm in the winter; and caves were ideal places to hide loot.

One such cave exists in Henderson County. History reveals that this cave often served as a temporary home for renegades and as a repository for stolen gold, silver, and currency. History has not, however, revealed whether any of the hidden treasure has been recovered from this cave.

The story of the Henderson County treasure cave came to light with the discovery of the diary of Lieutenant J.W. Hadley, a Union officer. Hadley's company fought Confederate forces during the famous Battle of the Wilderness in 1864 in eastern Virginia. Early in the fighting, Hadley was wounded and captured and, along with hundreds of other Union prisoners, shipped by rail to Columbia, South Carolina, where he was interned in a prison camp.

The prison camp was a makeshift assemblage of poorly constructed shacks in a disease-ridden swamp. Each day, men died from dysentery and malaria. Hadley and three companions plotted to escape the dreadful confinement.

One night, the four men fled the prison, and once out of range of pursuit, undertook the long journey northward, hoping to encounter Union forces. For days the men slunk through the woods, keeping to low areas and dense brush to avoid being seen. Sometimes they hid from roving patrols of Rebel soldiers.

Where they could get them, the men fed on wild berries and small game. The difficult travel, the hunger and the hiding, slowed the fugitives' journey, and an unusually cold autumn overtook them as they crossed the border into North Carolina.

With the frigid temperatures, wild berries were scarce, and the men resorted to stealing frost-killed vegetables from gardens on the outskirts of small communities. In one raid on a garden patch, the four men were surprised by the arrival of three women who had come to harvest greens. The women were armed, and while the fugitives were held at gunpoint, the youngest ran back up the trail in search of help.

Presently, a tall bearded old man returned with the young woman. He was carrying a rifle and had a vengeful gleam in his eye. He noted the ragged and torn Union blue uniforms on the haggard men and told them he had no use for Yankees or thieves. Hadley and his companions dropped to their knees and pleaded for their lives, swearing they intended no harm and only wanted to get food and leave the region as soon as possible.

The old man took pity on the starved, ragged soldiers. Though he was a bred-in-the-bone Southerner who believed in the Confederate cause and had lost two sons to Union bullets, the man lowered his rifle and invited the fugitives to his cabin, where he saw to it they were fed a proper meal.

During dinner, the host suggested to Hadley it might be prudent to hire a guide to lead them to Union sanctuary. He said he knew a man who might deliver them to Knoxville for a hundred dollars in gold coins. Hadley agreed, the man was sent for, and he arrived at the cabin late the next day. The newcomer was a quiet, thin, dark man whose black bowler hat shadowed his face. After listening to the fugitives' tale of escape and flight, he agreed to let Hadley pay him the hundred dollars on arrival at Knoxville since none of the escapees had any money. He told the four he would return with horses after sundown the next evening.

The following night, a quiet knock at the cabin door preceded a deep voice announcing that all was ready and they must depart at once. When Hadley and his companions assembled outside the cabin, the guide told them they would be blindfolded and that they would soon understand the reason for the precaution. Each was helped onto a horse, and they were led into the woods. As they rode along, Hadley made mental notes of the journey. He recalled later that while he didn't know which way they went on leaving the cabin, they were on horseback for about an hour, and he recalled that they crossed two shallow creeks near the end of the ride. Eventually the guide called a halt, and the four blindfolded men were helped off their horses. After a brief hike up a moderately steep gravel slope, they were led to a guide-rope. Following the rope, the men came into what was unmistakably a large cave. After several more minutes of walking, they were ordered to halt and their blindfolds were removed.

Hadley saw they were in a large torch-lit chamber. He could hear water dripping some distance away and occasionally heard voices coming from some far passageway. Against one wall of the cave were piled several saddlebags and chests.

The guide handed each man a blanket and told them to sleep, as they would depart early in the morning. They would have this chamber to themselves, he said, but they were not to leave it. He told them a guard was stationed in the passageway with orders to shoot anyone who tried to escape.

During the night, Hadley found it difficult to sleep. He threw off his blanket, removed one of the burning torches from a niche in the cave wall, and explored the chamber. When he arrived at the pile of saddlebags and chests in the far corner, he regarded them with interest. Hadley noted the chests were of the type railroad companies used to transport gold, silver, and currency. Bending to one of the saddlebags, he unfastened the straps and peered within. His heart pounded as he saw what must have been hundreds of gold coins. He opened several more of the packs and found gold or silver coins in each. He guessed the chests held a fortune in gold and silver as well. Hadley began to understand the reason for the blindfolds—he and his companions were being held in a cave used by bandits to store treasure! Hadley returned to his blanket but could not sleep.

Early the next morning, six rough-looking men entered the chamber. Each was carrying a heavy saddlebag which was added to the pile against the far wall. Pretending sleep, Hadley listened to the conversations of the new-comers and learned that they were robbers and smugglers and that the cave was a indeed a repository for their booty.

A few minutes later, the guide came and told the four fugitives it was time to leave. The six newly-arrived men would go with them to Knoxville, he said, since they were all headed that way anyway.

Hadley and his companions were once again blindfolded and led from the cave. Outside, they were ordered to rest near a grove of trees while their hosts sealed the entrance. As he waited, Hadley managed to adjust his blindfold so he could see what the workers were doing. The bandits piled boulders in front of the low cave entrance, covering it and making it look much like the rest of the talus-covered slope. When this was done, the outlaws gathered in front of the camouflaged entrance and swore an oath of secrecy about the location of the treasure cave.

Presently all were mounted and riding north. After about a mile, the guide told the soldiers they could remove their blindfolds. After doing so, Hadley glanced about for prominent landmarks, but all he could see was the dense grove of beech trees where they had stopped and a small creek across which was a thick oak forest. The rest of the journey was uneventful, and a few days later, they reached the outskirts of Knoxville and a Union Army camp.

The bandits held one of the fugitives hostage and told Hadley and the two others to go into the camp and get the promised hundred dollars. Hadley and his companions were escorted to the tent of a company commander, where they told the incredible story of their capture, escape, and flight through the Southern countryside. After some initial disbelief, the officer accepted Hadley's tale and told his aide to bring him a hundred dollars. There was no gold in the camp, and the aide came back with paper currency. The commander told Hadley to offer the bandits the currency and sent him off in the company of two armed soldiers.

The bandits were understandably nervous when Hadley returned in the company of the armed escort, but when they saw the fee was in paper money instead of gold they were furious. Hadley explained there was no gold in the camp and pleaded for the outlaws to take the money. The discussion grew heated, and one of the bandits pulled a gun and fired at a trooper, killing him instantly. While Hadley and the hostage ducked for cover, the outlaws fired at the second trooper, who took shelter behind a tree. Frustrated, the outlaws reined their horses around and dashed back to the south.

Hearing the commotion, the company commander assembled two dozen troops and set out in pursuit of the outlaws. About five miles from the hostage exchange site, the soldiers overtook the fleeing desperadoes and a gunfight ensued. After a half hour of exchanging gunfire, all of the outlaws and three of the Union troopers lay dead. When the outcome was reported to Hadley later in the day, he realized that all the men who knew where the treasure cave was had died with the secret.

When the war ended, Hadley returned to Henderson County to seek the treasure cave. With some difficulty, he found the small farm where he and his companions were first discovered. He looked up the old farmer who had fed them and arranged their escape, and thanked him for saving their lives.

Hadley was sure the treasure cave was still sealed and the gold and silver coins lay untouched deep within the large chamber where he had first sen them. He set up a small camp near the cabin and spent the next several weeks walking and riding through the forest in search of the cave. With no visual landmarks to guide him, Hadley had trouble retracing the route he had followed blindfolded two years earlier. After successive failures, he finally gave up and went home.

Hadley returned to Henderson County many times over the next twenty years, but each trip was no more successful than the one before it, and he never found the elusive cave. On his deathbed, Hadley said he was certain the cave had never been reopened and the treasure was still intact.

Others have tried to follow Hadley's directions to the hoard, but to date none of it has been recovered.

Lost Keg of Gold

Deep in a forgotten gold mine in the Union County region of the South Carolina Appalachians rests an old nail keg half-filled with gold mined from a rich vein. The keg of gold, along with its owner, were buried in an 1858 cave-in, and all attempts to retrieve the fortune have failed.

Two years before the Civil War, life in the Piedmont region of South Carolina was slow and uneventful. An easy peace lay across the mountains, the valley, and the area farms. As it would for years to come, cotton reigned. Large landowners with plenty of slaves were wealthy and powerful.

Asa Smyth was one such landowner. He had three thousand acres of rich farmland that, with the help of his hundred slaves, produced healthy crops of cotton each year. Smyth was hard on his slaves, just as likely to whip them as to look at them. One of the slaves, a tall, strong, older man Smyth called Blue, was a particular favorite because he was a natural leader and just as hard a taskmaster as his owner. Smyth elevated Blue to foreman and charged him with the daily operation of the cotton farm.

In the winter, when the fields lay fallow, Smyth worked his slaves in the nearby Hopkins Mine. The mine had operated for several years and been productive, but poor management had caused it to close down. Smyth took out a lease on the mine, and when his cotton was in, he put his slaves to work digging gold.

Smyth and Blue would wake the slaves before dawn and, following behind in a horse-drawn wagon, run them the two miles to the mine where they would work until sundown. Many slaves died in the mine, but neither the owner nor the foreman showed any mercy.

Each morning as Blue was readying the slaves, Smyth loaded an old nail keg into the wagon. Gold dug from the mine went in the keg. Soon it was too heavy for Smyth to lift into the wagon by himself, and Blue was enlisted to help. As more gold was added to the keg, it got so heavy that Smyth began keeping it at the mine. Deep in the gold mine and alongside one of the main shafts, Smyth had his slaves dig a chamber which he referred to as his "room." The low-ceilinged little room was sparsely furnished with a wooden table and chair. Here Smyth would sort and weigh his gold before adding it to the store in the keg.

Smyth oversaw the work done by the slaves, recommending the excavation of new shafts and supervising the cleaning and processing of the gold. At the end of each day, Smyth would have Blue line up the slaves and check their hair to make certain no gold was caught—or cached—in it. This done, the slaves were marched back to the plantation.

March of 1859 was wetter than normal. It rained hard every day. Parts of the Hopkins Mine flooded and Smyth put several slaves to hand-pumping the knee-deep water out of several shafts. To compound the problems, one of the main shafts suffered a minor cave-in.

As March wore on, Smyth was still adding gold to his growing fortune—the keg was now a little more than half full. While sorting the gold one afternoon in his room, Smyth called for his foreman, who came running. Smyth, standing ankle deep in water, told Blue he was feeling chilled and sent him to the wagon for his coat. When the foreman reached the wagon, parked about a hundred feet from the mine entrance, he heard a loud rumble and felt the earth shake. He turned back toward the entrance and saw a great cloud of dust roll from the shaft and disperse into the clear outside air.

Blue ran to the entrance, calling through the thick dust hanging in the shaft. Several slaves came stumbling and crawling out of the shaft and told him a cave-in had destroyed a large section of the mine, killed many of the workers, and completely buried the chamber where Smyth was counting his gold.

Blue leaped into the wagon and drove rapidly to the plantation, where he told Smyth's wife, Sara, of the accident. She told the foreman to get some of the neighbors and try to reach the chamber to see if Asa could be rescued.

Within hours, about two dozen people had gathered at the entrance of the old Hopkins mine. An exploratory party of several men entered the shaft but came out after only a few minutes, telling the gathering crowd that the cave-in had destroyed most of the mine and no one could have possibly survived.

Over the years, several attempts were made to excavate the collapsed rock and debris from the old Hopkins Mine to retrieve Asa Smyth's keg of gold. While tons of material have been removed from the first hundred feet of the original shaft, most of the passageways remain filled. Asa Smyth's chamber, according to Blue, was about a thousand feet deep in the mine, and the room that held the keg of gold and Asa Smyth's bones was blocked by tons of debris.

An excavation company tried to reopen the mine in the early 1930s but was defeated by the tons of rock it would have to remove. The workers were also constantly threatened with new cave-ins.

Somewhere deep in the old Hopkins Mine in a room carved out of mountain rock, like a mausoleum, a nail keg half-filled with gold lies next to the bones of Asa Smyth.

The Indian Gold Mine
de Soto Never Found

One of the most fascinating and enduring lost mine
legends in South Carolina tells of a rich lode of gold known
to the local Indians and at one time sought by the famed
Spanish explorer Hernando de Soto. The mine, probably in
present-day Pickens County, was never found by the intrepid de Soto, and for centuries it was apparently a primary
source of the gold used by several area Indian tribes to make
fine jewelry, ornaments, and icons.

As de Soto traveled and explored the southern Appalachians, he thought always of his mission to locate,
excavate, and ship back to Spain any and all kinds of
precious metals. When he stumbled across a gold or silver
mine operated by Indians, he would often enslave the
members of the tribe and force them to dig the ore for
Spain. If the Indians resisted, de Soto would kill several of
the tribe's leaders as an example. Thus, the gold-hungry
Spaniard subjugated, tortured, and killed hundreds of Indians in his quest for wealth for the Spanish king.

At an Indian village called Nepetaca in what is now
southern Georgia, a young Indian who was about to be
tortured by de Soto's men pleaded for mercy, telling his
captors he knew of a wealthy gold mine in the mountains
several marches to the north. The mine was supposed to
be a three-day ride from a large Indian village called
Cofitachiqui, which was ruled by a queen.

The soldiers brought the young man to de Soto, and the explorer listened with interest to the story. He decided to go to Cofitachiqui, and ordered his men to get ready to leave immediately. De Soto had one of his priests baptize the young Indian, gave him the Christian name of Peter, and incorporated him into his army.

The Spanish force left Nepetaca in March, 1540, and for several weeks traveled north through the plains, forests, and swamps of the humid lowlands. Provisions were running dangerously low, hunting was poor, and the progress and morale of the party was deteriorating rapidly. Whenever the Spaniards sighted an Indian village, they would prepare to raid it for food and women only to find each time it was infested with smallpox brought to the region by an earlier Spanish explorer, Vasquez de Ayllon. De Soto's army gave each such village a wide berth.

Several times, de Soto was ready to abandon the quest for the mine, but young Peter always reassured him that the waiting riches would make the toil and sacrifices worthwhile.

But after weeks of weary marching and being forced to eat dogs and horses, an angry and frustrated de Soto ordered the young Indian killed. Juan Ortiz, de Soto's chief interpreter, argued for Peter's life, saying that the boy's knowledge of the local language would prove useful and could mean the difference between life and death. De Soto relented, and four days later, the young Indian led the party of Spaniards to the outskirts of Cofitachiqui.

The village lay spread along the flood plain of the Savannah River about a dozen miles downstream from present-day Augusta, Georgia, on the South Carolina side of the River. The village housed large families in its many circular earthen structures, and had been spared the smallpox epidemic that had decimated tribes farther south. The inhabitants of Cofitachiqui were friendly, cultured, and courteous.

As de Soto and his men rode into the village, they were warmly greeted by the Indians and invited to a welcoming feast. The Spaniards were brought gifts of fresh-water pearls, fine furs, and food.

Looking around at the Indian population, de Soto noticed much gold. Many of the Indians were wearing armbands, rings, and ornate headpieces made from it.

During the feast, the queen of the village came to the Spanish leader. De Soto wrote in his journals that the queen was tall, almost statuesque, light of color, and very attractive. De Soto called the queen *la Señora,* and he thanked her when she personally welcomed the Spaniards and invited them to set up camp near the village.

Playing the role of the grateful guest, de Soto agreed to remain for a few days, but uppermost in his mind was gold. A casual walk through the Indian village revealed that the dwellings and temples were filled with gold icons and ornaments. De Soto even saw ceremonial ax blades and spearheads made from the precious metal.

He asked for and was granted an audience with *la Señora*, and during their conversation, he asked where the wealth he saw in the village had come from. The queen would not be specific, but did tell the Spaniard that for many generations the Indians had excavated gold from a mine in the mountains to the north. She claimed the mine had an unending supply of the precious ore and would provide the metal for her people for centuries to come.

That evening, greed overtaking gratitude, de Soto made plans to kidnap *la Señora* and force her to guide him to the mine.

At dawn the following day, the Spanish soldiers swarmed into the village, sacked the temples, and seized the queen and several of her followers. De Soto told *la Señora* that she was to guide him and his army to the rich gold mine in the north or they would all be tortured and killed. The queen and her followers agreed to show the Spaniard the mine, and the party began to wind its way through the low foothills of western South Carolina toward the higher reaches of the mountains looming miles ahead of them.

Progress was slowed dramatically when spring rains struck the second day of the journey. Torrents fell for days on the Spanish army and its captives, making travel nearly impossible at times. Flood waters washed out trails, and the company got lost more than once. Rivers were often too high and swift to ford, forcing the travelers to wait days to cross. The horses were slowed by the soft muck of the trails.

Word had spread to Indian villages north of Cofitachiqui that the queen had been taken by the Spaniards, and each time the army approached a village, they were met with hostility and sometimes attacked. Several soldiers were killed, food again became scarce, and de Soto's confidence began to suffer.

The journey that was to take only days dragged into weeks. The Spaniards were weary and frustrated, and de Soto was beginning to worry about dissension. The soldiers were tired of difficult marching and going days without food. The men guarding the queen and her subordinates grew more careless each day, and one evening, *la Señora* and her followers saw their chance and escaped.

De Soto, having lost his hostage and guide to the rich gold mine, became discouraged and surly. Fearing he would soon lose control of his army, he ordered them to abandon the quest. Turning their backs on the Appalachian Mountains, the party of explorers marched west toward the lowlands, reaching the Mississippi River many weeks later.

Scholars, prospectors, geologists, and students of this tale of a lost gold mine in the South Carolina Appalachians have often debated whether the lode really exists, but some facts support that it does. First, there *was* an abundance of gold in the village of Cofitachiqui. Second, the Indians had little reason for lying about the source of the ore, for to them it was used merely for ornaments and ceremony and had no value as a medium of exchange. Third, gold has been found elsewhere in the South Carolina Appalachians. There are impressive deposits in both Pickens and York Counties.

De Soto was probably only a day or two from the famed Indian gold mine of the Appalachians, but the hardship of his journey, coupled with the escape of his prisoners, caused him to abandon the quest.

The incident was the first of the difficulties and bad luck that would plague the Spanish leader. While his party did cross the wide Mississippi River and find gold in the Ozark and Ouachita Mountains to the west, de Soto's health was starting to deteriorate. Many of his soldiers deserted, several with fortunes in gold and silver gained in the expedition. Eventually de Soto became delirious and had to be carried on a litter. The Spaniard, an important early explorer of the southern United States, died somewhere near the Arkansas–Louisiana border while trying to get back to Spain.

The lost mine of the South Carolina Appalachians was said to be a rich source of almost pure gold for the local Indians, who were probably members of the Creek tribe. When the area was abandoned during the infamous Trail of Tears resettlement, the mine was closed and probably covered over. Many have searched for it over the past century and a half, yet it remains lost.

Silver Mine in
Pickens County

Gold lured de Soto to explore western and north-
western South Carolina, and according to the tales and
legends passed down over the centuries, gold was indeed
plentiful. Silver, however, was equally abundant, and like
the fabled gold, eludes modern-day treasure hunters.

One legend of lost silver from this region tells of a small
exploration party of Spaniards, most likely a detachment
from de Soto's army under the leadership of Juan de
Villalobos, that dug ore from a hillside by an Indian village
near the present-day junction of Anderson, Oconee, and
Pickens counties.

The Spaniards asked permission from the Indians to
mine the silver. It was freely granted. During the following
few weeks, the Spaniards bartered their possessions to the
Indians for food. The vein of silver the Spaniards followed
into the rock was so rich that excavating it left them no
time to hunt for food. Soon, though, the newcomers ran
out of items to trade to the Indians.

The leader of the Spanish mining expedition ordered
the Indians to hunt and fish for his men, but they refused.
Enraged, de Villalobos enslaved them, tortured and killed
many, forced the rest to work in the mine, and stole their
stores of food.

During the roundup of slaves, several Indians escaped
into the woods and fled to a neighboring village. There the

refugees told what had happened, and the Indians plotted to attack the Spaniards, free their brothers, and drive the intruders from the country.

Weeks went by, and the Spaniards grew complacent. Never threatened, they saw little need to post guards.

One night, by the light of a full moon, a large force of Indians crept through the woods to the Spaniards' bivouac and slew them all in their blankets. They carried the bodies deep into the mine shaft and covered the entrance. The Indians thereafter regarded the site as evil and cursed, and they moved their village far away. The story of the rich silver mine was told and retold over successive generations, becoming part of the tribal folklore, but the location of the mine eventually faded from the memory of the Indians and remains a mystery.

In 1670, an expedition led by a Dr. Henry Woodward arrived at the village of Cofitachiqui on the Savannah River. Woodward, a wealthy British physician, explorer, and ambassador to the New World, befriended the Indians he found in the large settlement and earned their trust. So completely was he incorporated into the tribe that he was given lodging, food, and a prominent place on the village council.

Woodward was familiar with the story of de Soto's visit to Cofitachiqui more than a hundred years earlier and the ill-fated search for the gold mine. Woodward asked several of the Cofitachiqui residents about the tale and was assured every word of it was true, and that, in fact, gold was still being taken in great quantities from the mine.

While living in Cofitachiqui, Woodward also noted an abundance of silver jewelry, icons, and ornaments. When he asked about the source of this ore, he was told that it came from a mine very near the legendary gold mine.

During his stay, Woodward learned approximately where the Indians' gold and silver mines lay, but as he was preparing an expedition to the area, he took sick and died within days. Many believe that the Indians, learning of

Woodward's plans to search for their mines, poisoned his food.

In 1760, during the French and Indian War, a company of British soldiers was returning from a skirmish with hostile Cherokee when they camped on the banks of Little Wilson's Creek adjacent to the Keowee Trail. While encamped, several soldiers noticed some intriguing color in the local rock formations and dug out chunks as souvenirs.

The war kept the soldiers occupied for months thereafter, and when the conflict wound down, the company disbanded and its members dispersed. Later, several men who had dug pieces of the brightly colored rock from the stone matrix near Little Wilson Creek discovered that it was almost pure silver! The former soldiers organized successive attempts to find the original site of their discovery, but always failed. The silver is believed to have been found near Pointing Rock, which is just south of Old Stone Church near Little Wilsons Creek in the western corner of Pickens County.

Around 1815, a Cherokee family was known to have mined pure silver near the settlement of Shainrock, now a ghost town not far from present-day Clemson. The Indians would sometimes sell the silver to travelers and passers-by, but during the 1820s they disappeared. They may have been killed for their presumed wealth and their bodies hidden in a mine, but the truth was never known. Years later, visitors to Shainrock reported finding nuggets of raw silver as well as small clots of the smelted ore. No one has found the source of the Cherokee family's silver, though many have searched.

During the late 1850s, two separate mining companies sank shafts in the area, seeking a vein of silver they suspected was just below the surface. Both reported failure.

Just a year after the two companies withdrew from the region, a small contingent of miners from Charleston arrived, established a well-provisioned camp, located some silver, and successfully mined it for two years.

Operations ceased when the War Between The States broke out. It is not known what became of the miners, but after the war, the abandoned shafts were not reopened, and no one ever came forward to renew the claim.

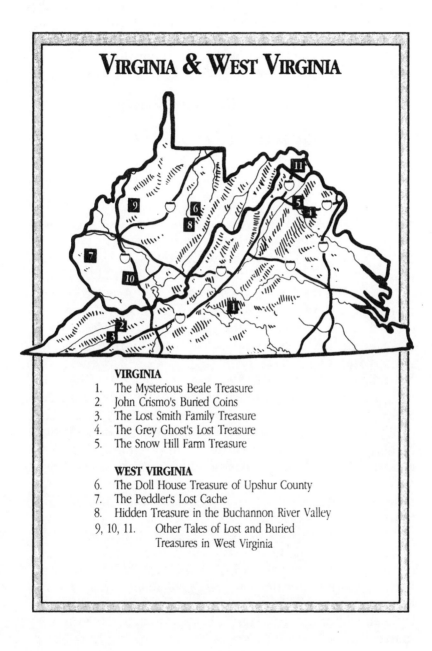

VIRGINIA & WEST VIRGINIA

VIRGINIA
1. The Mysterious Beale Treasure
2. John Crismo's Buried Coins
3. The Lost Smith Family Treasure
4. The Grey Ghost's Lost Treasure
5. The Snow Hill Farm Treasure

WEST VIRGINIA
6. The Doll House Treasure of Upshur County
7. The Peddler's Lost Cache
8. Hidden Treasure in the Buchannon River Valley
9, 10, 11.   Other Tales of Lost and Buried
              Treasures in West Virginia

The Mysterious Beale Treasure

The best known and most sought-after lost treasure in the state of Virginia is the mysterious and elusive Beale cache. This buried fortune is said to consist of nearly 3,000 pounds of gold, 5,088 pounds of silver, and $13,000 worth of jewels. The Beale treasure has been the subject of books, magazine articles, and television programs, and one network news broadcast said the search for the Beale treasure was one of the longest and costliest in the history of the United States.

Specific directions to the fabulous Beale treasure can be found in three separate codes devised by Beale himself, as far as is known. Only one has ever been deciphered. The other two complex codes, though having been examined by cryptoanalysts and studied by computer and decoding experts, remain unbroken, and the location of the great treasure is as much a mystery today as it was when Thomas Jefferson Beale and eight friends buried it in Bedford County in 1819 and 1821.

Little is known of Beale's life. What is known is that early in 1817, he and twenty-nine other Virginians journeyed westward to New Mexico and Colorado. Two conflicting stories, neither proven, give Beale's reasons for leaving Virginia. One tale is that he shot his neighbor in Fincastle, Virginia, in a fight over a woman. Believing the man dead and fearing he would be hung for the deed, Beale fled west. The second tale, considerably less colorful, is that Beale gathered up friends for a buffalo-hunting and fur-trapping expedition to the western plains and mountains.

Whatever the reason, Beale and his companions eventually found themselves in south-central Colorado, searching for a pass into the higher reaches of the Rocky Mountains, where they planned to hunt beaver. As the party climbed the foothills of the great range, one of the men discovered a thick vein of gold in some exposed rock. Deciding that mining the ore would profit them more than trapping and selling furs, the men spent the next few years systematically excavating the precious metal from the rock matrix of the mountainside. They found silver nearby, and mined great quantities of it, too.

After eighteen months, they had an impressive stockpile of gold and silver. The men, all good friends, agreed to split the fortune evenly. They held a meeting and decided to send Beale and eight others back to Virginia to bury the rich hoard in a safe place. The others would keep working in the mines while awaiting the return of the Beale party.

On a bitterly cold afternoon in late November, Beale and his companions, along with two wagon loads of gold and silver nuggets, arrived at Goose Creek in Bedford County, Virginia. The party followed a narrow and seldom-used trail which paralleled the creek and led into a gap in the foothills of the Blue Ridge Mountains near Peak of the Otters. Once in the pass, Beale looked around until he found what he wanted—a place where he could bury the treasure. Snow began to fall, and the men worked swiftly, digging a square pit six feet deep. As the wind swirled the snow around them, the miners lined the floor and walls of this man-made vault with flat stones they found nearby. Into this chamber they placed the gold and silver from nearly two years' work in the Colorado mines. The nuggets were packed into iron cooking pots, the covers tightly secured with wire. The men filled the hole to the top with dirt and covered it with rocks and forest debris.

Beale and his party rested several days after the long journey from the west. They bought supplies and fresh riding stock, and started back in early December. They rejoined the other miners in the Colorado foothills nearly a month later.

Mining continued, and after almost two more years, another load of gold and silver was ready to be shipped east and buried with the previous cache. Beale was again chosen for the trip. The partners agreed to keep mining until they had enough gold and silver for a third and final trip to Virginia, where they would unearth the rich cache, divide it, and return to a normal life as wealthy men.

One morning in the third week of November in 1821, the wagons were loaded to capacity with the ore. Bidding farewell to those who remained to work in the mines, Beale and his companions began the second long journey back to the Blue Ridge Mountains.

Reaching the cache a little over a month later, Beale and his companions added the second load of gold and silver. When the hole refilled and camouflaged, Beale and his fellows decided to write a description of the secret location and its contents and leave it in the area for the others to find, should something happen to them. Over the next several days, Beale and a few of his partners devised a series of incredibly complex codes. They produced three sheets of paper, each covered with a series of numerals. These three papers have since been called the Beale Code, and have mystified researchers for well over a century.

Cipher Number One allegedly tells how to find the fabulous treasure and remains unbroken to this day. Cipher Number Two describes the complete contents of the treasure vault. Cipher Number Three supposedly lists the names of the thirty men who were to divide the treasure equally.

When the ciphers were completed, they were placed in a metal strongbox fastened with a stout lock. By agreement of the nine men who buried the ore, the locked box was given to one Robert Morris, a man they all knew and trusted. Morris, a quiet gentleman who ran a respectable inn at Lynchburg and often kept valuables for travelers, readily agreed to keep the strongbox for Beale and his friends.

At Morris's invitation, the miners stayed several days at the inn, resting. The day they left for Colorado, Beale told Morris that if someone did not return within ten years to claim the strongbox and its contents, he, Morris, was to open it. Beale also told Morris that within a few weeks he would mail him the information he would need to interpret the codes in the strongbox. Beale and his eight companions rode away from the inn a short time later, disappearing into the dense forest to the west. Morris never saw any of them again.

About two months later, Morris received a short letter from Beale that had been mailed from St. Louis. The letter reiterated what Beale had already told Morris—that the contents of the strongbox would be meaningless without the decoding keys. He said the necessary keys were in a sealed envelope with Morris's address on it. The envelope, according to Beale, was given to a friend in St. Louis with instructions to mail it to Morris in June, 1832. Morris never again heard from Beale, nor did he receive the envelope ten years later.

Although the designated time had elapsed, the trustworthy Morris refused to open the strongbox, thinking that someone from the Beale party would eventually return to claim it. Years passed and Morris soon forgot about the strongbox, which he had hidden away under some clutter in an old shed adjacent to the inn. One day, about twenty-three years after Beale had left the strongbox, Morris chanced upon it while searching the shed for a harness.

When Morris broke open the box, he first saw lying atop the contents a letter addressed to him. In elaborate detail, the letter told of the expedition to the west, the discovery of the gold and silver, and the subsequent trips to the Blue Ridge Mountains to bury the treasure. The letter ended by asking Morris to use the code to find and dig up the treasure. Morris was to divide it into thirty-one equal parts—one for each of the original participants and one for Morris himself.

Morris examined the three pieces of paper which bore the Beale Code. Each was written over with an apparently random series of numbers, ranging from single to quadruple digits. Intrigued, the innkeeper spent many hours trying to decipher the curious arrangements of numbers, but couldn't make any sense of them. For the next several years, Morris tried to decipher the complex Beale Code, but he eventually gave up.

Some time later, when Morris was convinced no one would return to claim the strongbox and its contents, he showed the codes and letters to a friend, James Ward. For months Ward pored over the three pieces of paper and eventually broke Cipher Number Two.

Purely by accident, Ward discovered this code was based on the Declaration of Independence. When finally deciphered, it read:

> I have deposited in the county of Bedford about four miles from Buford's Inn in an excavation or vault six feet below the surface of the ground the following articles belonging to the parties whose names are given in number three herewith. The first deposit was ten hundred and fourteen pounds of gold and thirty-eight hundred pounds of silver. This was deposited November, 1819. The second deposit was made December, 1821, and consisted of nineteen hundred and seven pounds of gold and twelve hundred and eighty-eight pounds of silver. Also jewels obtained in St. Louis in exchange to save transportation and valued at thirteen thousand dollars. The above is packed securely in iron pots with iron covers. The vault is lined with

stones and the vessels lie on solid rock and are covered with other stones. Paper number one describes the exact location of the vault so no difficulty will be had in finding it.

Ward, suspecting the other two codes would likewise be deciphered by using the Declaration of Independence, eagerly tackled them, but was soon disappointed to learn that they apparently had separate and independent keys. Ward was particularly interested in breaking Cipher Number One, which allegedly gave directions to the treasure site, but could make no sense of it whatsoever. *(The code, containing 520 numbers, is reproduced in its entirety at the end of the story.)*

Ward worked on the two unbroken codes for several months before giving up. With Morris's permission, Ward made the codes public.

Ever since the Beale Code was made known, hundreds of people—cryptographers, computer programmers, historians, treasure hunters, adventurers—have tried to decipher it. For many years, the Blue Ridge Mountains in and around Bedford County were fairly teeming with those who thought they had an inside track on the treasure. To date, however, the first and third codes remain unbroken, and the fabulous treasure is still hidden.

Although the Beale treasure is Virginia's best-known and most sought, many believe it is nothing more than an elaborate hoax and that Thomas Jefferson Beale never existed! Skeptics have suggested that innkeeper Morris and his friend Ward fabricated the entire story. They point out that Thomas Jefferson, the third president of the United States and author of the Declaration of Independence, on which one code was based, had a penchant for writing in numerical codes and ciphers. It may also be worth noting that a man named Beale brought word to the east of the fantastic gold finds in California during the early 1800s.

If the Beale treasure is a hoax, two things remain to be explained. First of all, what would have been the purpose of such a trick? There appears no obvious or profitable motive for such a sophisticated and elaborate hoax. Both Morris and Ward shunned any kind of publicity, and neither profited from his association with the Beale treasure. Secondly, the sheer intricacy of the codes makes it seem unlikely to have been devised merely as a prank.

The Beale treasure probably does, in fact, exist and in exactly the amounts indicated by Beale himself in Cipher Two. Many who have researched the Beale story over the years have agreed on the authenticity of the events, the treasure, and the codes.

Beale Cipher Number One:

71, 194, 38, 1701, 89, 76, 11, 83, 1629, 48, 94, 63, 132, 16, 111, 95, 84, 341, 975, 14, 40, 64, 27, 81, 139, 213, 63, 90, 1120, 8, 15, 3, 126, 2018, 40, 74, 758, 485, 604, 230, 436, 664, 582, 150, 251, 284, 308, 231, 124, 211, 486, 225, 401, 370, 11, 101, 305, 139, 189, 17, 33, 88, 208, 193, 145, 1, 94, 73, 416, 918, 263, 28, 500, 538, 356, 117, 136, 219, 27, 176, 130, 10, 460, 25, 485, 18, 436, 65, 84, 200, 283, 118, 320, 138, 36, 416, 280, 15, 71, 224, 961, 44, 16, 401, 39, 88, 61, 304, 12, 21, 24, 283, 134, 92, 63, 246, 486, 682, 7, 219, 184, 360, 780, 18, 64, 463, 474, 131, 160, 79, 73, 440, 95, 18, 64, 581, 34, 69, 128, 367, 461, 17, 81, 12, 103, 820, 62, 116, 97, 103, 862, 70, 60, 1317, 471, 540, 208, 121, 890, 346, 36, 150, 59, 568, 614, 13, 120, 63, 219, 812, 2160, 1780, 99, 35, 18, 21, 136, 872, 15, 28, 170, 88, 4, 30, 44, 112, 18, 147, 436, 195, 320, 37; 122, 113, 6, 140, 8, 120, 305, 42, 58, 461, 44, 106, 301, 13, 408, 680, 93, 86, 116, 530, 82, 568, 9, 102, 38, 416, 89, 71, 216, 728, 965, 818, 2, 38, 121, 195, 14, 326, 148, 234, 18, 55, 131, 234, 361, 824, 5, 81, 623, 48, 961, 19, 26, 33, 10, 1101, 365, 92, 88, 181, 275, 346, 201, 206, 86, 36, 219, 320, 829, 840, 68, 326, 19, 48, 122, 65, 216, 284, 919, 861, 326, 985, 233, 64, 68, 232, 431, 960, 50, 29, 81, 216, 321, 603, 14, 612, 81, 360, 36, 51, 62, 194, 78, 60, 200, 314, 676, 112, 4, 28, 18, 61, 136, 247, 819, 921, 1060, 464, 895, 10, 6, 66, 119, 38, 41, 49, 612, 423, 962, 302, 294, 875, 78, 14, 23, 111, 109, 62, 31, 501, 823, 216, 280, 34, 24, 150, 1000, 162, 286, 19, 21, 17, 340, 19, 242, 31, 86, 234, 140, 607, 115, 33, 191, 67, 104, 86, 52, 88, 16, 80, 121, 67, 95, 122, 216, 548, 96, 11, 201, 77, 364, 218, 65, 667, 890, 236, 154, 211, 10, 98, 34, 119, 56, 216, 119, 71, 218, 1164, 1496, 1817, 51, 39, 210, 36, 3, 19, 540, 232, 22, 141, 617, 84, 290, 80, 46, 207, 411, 150, 29, 38, 46, 172, 85, 194, 36, 261, 543, 897, 624, 18, 212, 416, 127, 931, 19, 4, 63, 96, 12, 101, 418, 16, 140, 230, 460, 538, 19, 27, 88, 612, 1431, 90, 716, 275, 74, 83, 11, 426, 89, 72, 84, 1300, 1706, 814, 221, 132, 40, 102, 34, 858, 975, 1101, 84, 16, 79, 23, 16, 81, 122, 324, 403, 912, 227, 936, 447, 55, 86, 34, 43, 212, 107, 96, 314, 264, 1065, 323, 428, 601, 203, 124, 95, 216, 814, 2906, 654, 820, 2, 301, 112, 176, 213, 71, 87, 96, 202, 35, 10, 2, 41, 17, 84, 221, 736, 820, 214, 11, 60, 760.

John Crismo's Buried Coins

Early one autumn morning in 1887 on a remote ranch near Pecos, Texas, a young cowhand was trying to wake his bunkhouse companion, an elderly cowboy named John Crismo. When Crismo did not respond to his call, the boy walked over to his bunk and tried to shake him awake. The old man was dead.

The foreman was summoned, a burial was arranged, and as the owner of the ranch searched Crismo's belongings for the name of a relative, he chanced upon an old and well-worn diary. It held fascinating details of buried treasure, a treasure that may today be worth nearly four million dollars, and yet still lies buried beneath a few inches of soil and rock on a lonely mountainside in western Virginia.

The ranch owner pored over the often unintelligible handwriting in Crismo's diary and over several weeks pieced together the story of the buried fortune.

In 1846, when the United States declared war on Mexico, a very young John Crismo enlisted in the army in his home state of New York. Before leaving for foreign soil, Crismo got engaged to a local girl, and they agreed to marry when his enlistment was over. While Crismo was in Mexico, however, his betrothed fell ill, dying only days before he returned.

He never recovered from the loss of his sweetheart. He visited her grave, then mounted his horse and rode out of New York, never to return. For years, the young man roamed the wilderness of Pennsylvania and Ohio, keeping to himself and living like an Indian deep in the woods, craving neither the sight nor company of other humans.

When the War Between The States erupted, Crismo, wishing to return to combat, rode eastward into Pennsylvania, enlisted in the Union army, and was assigned to a cavalry regiment that was immediately ordered to Virginia.

Crismo's unit made several raids on farms and communities in western Virginia, taking livestock, food, and arms and often filling their own pockets with stolen money. In time, the cavalry force became little more than a gang of bandits robbing and looting its way across the Appalachian landscape.

One day, the unit was sent to patrol an area in southwestern Virginia, in Tazewell County. The men, about twenty-four in number, camped on the side of a mountain that overlooked a long narrow valley, flat and richly productive. At one end of the attractive valley was a mansion, and the prospect of finding something valuable at the fine home appealed to the raiding troops.

The valley and everything in it belonged to the eccentric James Grierson. Grierson, who had inherited a fortune, made another from cotton and livestock. The old bachelor owned thirty slaves and was thought the wealthiest man in western Virginia. He was reputed to be worth nearly a million dollars, a staggering amount at the time.

When the war broke out, Grierson, concerned about the safety of his fortune, withdrew all of his money from the area banks and converted it into gold coins. With the help of his favorite slave, Grierson packed the coins into canvas bags and buried them behind his barn.

Anticipating a successful raid, the cavalrymen rode into the valley and overran Grierson's farm, taking the owner prisoner and hanging him by his wrists from a tree limb in the yard. Throughout an intense and sometimes brutal interrogation, Grierson steadfastly refused to reveal where he'd buried his fortune, and the Union raiders soon realized that the old man preferred death to giving up his wealth. Grierson apparently did not survive his interrogation.

While Grierson was being tortured, Crismo befriended the old slave who knew where the plantation owner's fortune lay. With some cajoling and the promise of freedom, Crismo convinced the slave to show him where Grierson's wealth was buried. The slave took Crismo behind the barn, dug about two feet down, and pulled up one of the heavy sacks of gold coins. Crismo looked at it and told the slave not to tell any of the other cavalrymen about the treasure.

Several days later, the cavalry unit was assigned to another area several miles away. Once they had established camp and were awaiting further orders, Crismo returned to the Grierson farm under cover of night, and with the help of the old slave, dug up all the gold coins buried behind the barn. The two men loaded the gold onto a pair of horses and hauled it to where the cavalry had camped before raiding the Grierson plantation. A short distance from the old campground, Crismo and the black man dug a large hole, deposited the coins, and covered the cache with rocks and forest debris. Then they started for the new cavalry encampment. On the way, Crismo handed the old slave a fistful of gold coins he had taken from one of the sacks, and gave the man his freedom.

Crismo told none of his companions about the Grierson fortune when he returned. That night, by the dim light of the fire, Crismo sketched in his ragged diary a crude map showing about where the gold coins lay. In his rough and clumsy grammar, he added descriptions of the terrain and landmarks. The next day, the cavalry unit left Tazewell County for a new assignment in the eastern part of the state.

As the war went on, the regiment fought in several skirmishes, and in one, Crismo was seriously wounded. After a lengthy recovery in a field hospital, he was granted an honorable discharge and sent on his way. He first thought of returning to Tazewell County and digging up the gold, but continuing military action there would have made that difficult. So Crismo took his few belongings and traveled westward instead, roaming the country and regaining his health while biding his time until he could return to Virginia for the gold.

For many years, Crismo wandered the sparsely settled regions west of the Mississippi River, eventually finding his way to Texas. Traveling from town to town and taking odd jobs, the former Union cavalryman barely earned enough to survive. His few diary entries during this time suggest that the wound Crismo had suffered was giving him some serious problems and causing great pain. His writings also suggest that he was not mentally sound at that time.

Years passed, and Crismo eventually landed a job as a cowhand on a ranch near Pecos, Texas. Though much older than most cowboys and quite infirm, he proved a consistent and loyal worker up to the day he quietly passed away in his sleep.

In the years that followed, Crismo's diary passed through several hands and eventually wound up in the possession of a Pecos County man who decided to seek out the buried cache of coins. Using the clumsily-drawn, faded, and somewhat vague map, the searcher arrived at a small Virginia settlement called Aberdeen. Just north of the hamlet, the man located the long narrow valley that had once been part of the extensive Grierson plantation. The land was now state property, having reverted to government ownership when Grierson passed away leaving no heirs.

Just north of the old Grierson plantation was a prominent mountain, undoubtedly the one on which Crismo and his cavalry unit camped before attacking the farm. After exploring the mountain for several days, the searcher discovered what must have been the old campground. He found two Union army-issue canteens, numerous shell casings, and other items suggesting a temporary cavalry bivouac. While Crismo's directions were clear enough to this point, his diary entries never actually said on which side of the camp he buried the fortune. For weeks, the treasure hunter searched. He finally gave up and went back to Texas.

Crismo's diary was relegated to a high dusty shelf in a storeroom and in time was lost. The disappointed searcher never tried again to find the treasure.

Others have searched for John Crismo's buried coins. So-called experts, using metal detectors and dowsing rods, have combed the mountainside near the old cavalry camp, trying to find the four-million-dollar cache. No one knows what became of the diary, and the treasure remains hidden to this day.

The Lost Smith Family Treasure

In the years before the Civil War, Abraham Smith and his two sons, Eli and Samuel, owned and operated one of the largest and most successful plantations in western Virginia. Not far from the farm, near the Clinch Mountains, was a large salt works in which the Smith family had an interest. The vast works supplied much of the salt for this part of the South and was a primary source for the Southern army as well.

Early on the morning of October 2, 1864, Abraham Smith learned that a large Union cavalry contingent, led by the ruthless General George Stoneman, was rapidly approaching the valley. Smith decided to hide the family fortune lest it be found and seized by the Yankees. He hurriedly gathered up approximately fifty-eight thousand dollars' worth of gold and silver coins and jewelry, and with the help of his sons, buried it in the middle of a partially completed roadbed that led to the salt mines near Saltville.

Stoneman, with orders to destroy the salt works and thus disrupt Confederate army supply and cause economic havoc in the area, led his Union force into the valley late that morning, just after the Smiths finished burying their fortune.

Stoneman expected little resistance in the valley, and was therefore surprised when a large combined force of citizens and Confederate soldiers met him. Southern scouts had warned area residents of the approaching Yankees. The hastily assembled force of farmers, laborers, and Rebel soldiers engaged the Union cavalry in a fierce battle. After nearly an hour of fighting, Stoneman called for a retreat. The untrained but enthusiastic Southerners pursued the famous cavalry leader and his troops back through the Cumberland Pass and clear into Kentucky.

After the skirmish, Eli Smith could not be accounted for. He was not among the dead and wounded lying in the valley, and was thought captured by the Yankees and executed along the trail during the disorganized retreat. Though searchers looked for Eli's body for several days, it was never found.

A few days after the battle, Abraham and Samuel Smith returned to the roadbed only to find that the cached jewels and coins had already been dug up and removed, presumably by Union soldiers.

The shock of losing his son and his entire fortune all within the space of a few days was too much for the elderly Abraham Smith, and his health and will to live deteriorated rapidly. Within a year and a half of the battle at the salt works, the old farmer passed away, a broken man.

A few years later, his son Samuel received a strange letter. It was addressed to the late father, but was dated nearly two years earlier, and was from a Corporal Allen E. Brooks, formerly of Stoneman's cavalry unit. Its message surprised and shocked Samuel—it told what had happened to his brother Eli and the buried cache of Smith treasure.

The letter read:

> Kind Sir: I am in pain and upon my deathbed, but I feel I must divest my conscience of a burden that has kept constant company with my soul since shortly after we fought over the salt works there. Your son, Eli, fearing he would be hanged, made a deal with my first sergeant, Jack Harrington, to share your fortune with him, an amount of some $46,000 in gold

and silver coins, $12,000 in jewelry and several gold watches. In return your son was to be helped to escape into Tennessee. Your son was not killed during the fighting, Harrington murdered him later on the pretext that he was escaping. With my help, Harrington removed the cache and hid it in a saltpeter cave, about a quarter of a mile distant from the little town church. Harrington was accidentally killed in a blast while we were destroying the saltpeter caves before we abandoned the area. I took a minie ball at the Battle of Seven Mile Ford and have been unable to travel since. I had planned to return to Saltville and reveal the location of your money to you. But I am dying and I want you to know that I took no part in the murder of your son. Respectfully, Corporal Allen E.Brooks, late of the Fortieth Mounted Infantry, Army of the U.S., General Stoneman Commanding

Using the letter from Corporal Brooks as a guide, Samuel Smith tried several times to find the treasure. The saltpeter cave was a natural cave in Poor Valley, between Allison's Gap and Saltville. Many caves in the area had been blasted shut and otherwise destroyed by Stoneman's troops during the battle of the salt works, and removing the debris from all of them would have been a formidable and expensive task for Samuel Smith. His efforts to find the treasure proved vain, and he eventually gave up and moved away.

Most who have researched this tale believe that the Smith treasure is hidden in a cavern known locally as Harmon's Cave. All attempts at finding the fifty-eight thousand dollars' worth of gold and silver coins and jewels, however, have failed. There are several other caves in this region, and in one of them, it is likely that the Smith fortune still reposes on the floor of some deep chamber.

The Gray Ghost's Lost Treasure

General John Singleton Mosby was one of the better known and more colorful leaders of the Confederate army during the War Between The States. A University of Virginia graduate and practicing lawyer, Mosby joined the Southern army as a private at the outbreak of the war. After serving as scout for General J.E.B. Stuart during the Peninsula Campaign and earning recognition for valor at Bull Run and Antietam, Mosby was promoted to colonel. In 1863, he organized and led a guerrilla unit called Mosby's Raiders. With this team of fearless fighting men, he conducted a campaign of harassment and predation against Union forces in Virginia and Maryland that made his name legendary. Union soldiers, who had no success in pursuing Mosby and his raiders, began calling him the "Gray Ghost," a name by which he is still known.

In the spring of 1863, Mosby captured three hundred fifty thousand dollars' worth of gold, silver, jewelry, and coins during a desperate flight from Yankee pursuit and buried it secretly in Fauquier County in the Appalachian Piedmont.

Mosby and his raiders had attacked the Fairfax courthouse, where they surprised and captured Union General Edwin H. Stoughton. Though a general, Stoughton was never seen as much of a leader by most Union officers. The overweight and overbearing general had too much appetite for fine foods, wines, and women, and he lacked enthusiasm for combat. When Colonel Mosby and his hand-picked guerrillas entered the courthouse, they found Stoughton surrounded by casks of wine and great stores of food. Stoughton had apparently taken over the courthouse as his private quarters for the duration of the war, and in spite of the bloody conflict around him, the hedonistic general saw to it that he himself wanted for little during those trying times.

Though Stoughton was guarded by two captains and thirty-eight enlisted men, the practiced raiders took him with ease. Mosby also captured fifty-eight horses, several carriages, numerous crates of victuals and drink, and about three hundred fifty thousand dollars' worth of gold and silver plate, coins, jewelry, and tableware that Stoughton's soldiers had looted from Southern homes. Colonel Mosby had all the valuables gathered up and placed in a large canvas bag.

Learning that large Union forces were in the area searching for him, Mosby had his guerrillas hurriedly load the booty into the carriages, and with Stoughton and his men as prisoners, they fled southwest toward the town of Culpeper, where General Stuart awaited them.

Mosby's Raiders, along with the captives and cargo, raced through the rolling hills of the Appalachian Piedmont, a low eroded plateau that offered a transition from the rugged highlands to gentle lay of the coastal plain.

When the guerrilla force crossed into Fauquier County, one of Mosby's scouts raced back to the colonel with the news that a Union cavalry contingent was bearing down on them from the northeast. Because the captured goods were slowing the retreat to Culpeper, Mosby decided to ditch the barrels of wine and the crates of food. He also elected to bury the large canvas sack of treasure.

By Mosby's later recollection, the raiders halted briefly about midway between the towns of Haymarket and New Baltimore to unload the excess baggage. While his soldiers quickly dumped the cargo from the carriages, Mosby, accompanied by his trusted sergeant James F. Ames, carried the large sack some distance from the trail and placed it in a hastily dug hole between two tall pine trees. After filling the hole, Mosby notched several tree trunks with his knife so the site could be easily identified on a return visit.

Mosby expected to retrace his trail within a few days and dig up the treasure, but the war kept him busy and carried him farther and farther from Fauquier County.

When the war was over, Mosby returned to his law practice and settled in western Virginia, far from where he fought during the war. He never returned to the piedmont to retrieve the treasure.

Mosby, as well as members of his crack guerrilla unit, often told of burying the treasure along the rocky trail during the flight from the Fairfax courthouse. Though many knew about the fortune, only Mosby and Ames knew the exact location. Sergeant Ames, however, would never reveal the secret. During the war, he was captured by General George Armstrong Custer and hanged at Fort Royal.

When asked why he never returned for the treasure, John S. Mosby, the famed Gray Ghost and Confederate War hero, would always evade the question and change the subject.

Of course, the question of the buried treasure would return. It was raised again in 1916 when Mosby was eighty-three and near death. Responded the Gray Ghost,

> I've always meant to return to the area and look for that cache we buried after capturing Stoughton. Some of the most precious heirlooms of old Virginia were buried there. I guess that one of these days someone will find it.

The cached canvas sack of gold, silver, jewelry, and other items hidden by Mosby on that spring day in 1863 would be worth several million dollars today. Many treasure hunters have tried to retrace Mosby's retreat from the Fairfax courthouse to the rendezvous with General Stuart at Culpeper, but none could ever be certain of the route.

The Snow Hill Farm Treasure

Sometime in the late 1760s, a Scotsman named
William Kirk brought his wife to Fauquier County to settle.
The couple was soft-spoken and rarely found in the company of others. Their reclusiveness was a small mystery to
the townspeople of New Baltimore, who would have been
shocked to learn of the notorious background of this polite,
kindly, and well-dressed man.

Years earlier, William Kirk had been an infamous
pirate. His years of freebooting brought him adventure and
great wealth, but as he grew older, he realized his violent
days at sea were numbered. By anyone's standard, Kirk was
a wealthy man, made rich by looting the merchant vessels
that plied the ocean between North America and Europe.

Taking his wealth, Kirk retired from pirating and lived
quietly in a small town on the Carolina coast. Here he met
and married his wife, and settled into respectability, determined to keep his lawless past a secret. In time, Kirk and
his wife decided to move to the higher lands of the Virginia
Piedmont. Through an intermediary, he arranged to buy
Snow Hill Farm, a relatively prosperous plantation in Fauquier County about a mile south of the New Baltimore
settlement. Kirk proved as adept at running a large farm as
he had been at piracy. He hired several men to work on his
plantation and soon turned it into a prosperous enterprise.

All the while, Kirk and his wife fed local curiosity about their lives by rarely going to town, preferring instead to send one of the hired men.

Kirk distrusted banks and hid his wealth in places known only to himself. The ex-buccaneer never told his wife about any of his secret caches. Afraid someone might accidentally discover one of them, he would occasionally dig them up and rebury them elsewhere. According to documents in the Fauquier County courthouse, Kirk possessed an estimated sixty thousand dollars in gold and silver coins, a tremendous fortune for the time.

Kirk and his wife apparently lived a quiet and happy life on Snow Hill Farm for about eighteen years. His health finally began to deteriorate from several serious bouts of pneumonia, and William Kirk died in his sleep in 1779. Before he did, he drafted a will leaving his entire estate to his wife. The will alerted her to the cached wealth. She searched for months after his death, but never found any of it.

Though she lived in relative comfort for many years, the work and responsibility of running Snow Hill Farm became too much for the Widow Kirk, and she eventually sold the property to a man named William Edmonds. Edmonds continued to farm the plantation much as Kirk had, and the property passed down through a succession of his heirs.

In the 1870s, the Edmonds descendants ran most of Snow Hill Farm on shares, paying several sharecroppers a part of the profits of their harvest and letting them live on the land. One day, one of the tenant farmers was breaking ground in a field when the plow hit something hard in the dirt. Thinking he had struck a rock, the farmer stopped the mule and went to work to remove it. His plow had hit a large porcelain crock. Removing the lid, the astonished farmer found the crock filled with gold and silver coins.

Not sure what to do with his find, he returned to his modest home and sent his youngest son to tell the plantation owner of the discovery. Between the time the lad was sent and the owner arrived, the farmer thought better of announcing his discovery and hid the crock, keeping only a handful of the coins in his pocket. When the owner arrived, the farmer showed him the few coins he had set aside. The plantation owner was unimpressed with the discovery and let the farmer keep the few coins.

A few weeks later, the landowner began to wonder what the sharecropper had actually found. It seems he purchased a nearby farm for eight thousand dollars in cash and spent another two thousand dollars on equipment and supplies.

Many New Baltimore residents of the time believed the sharecropper had chanced upon a cache from William Kirk's fortune, booty taken long ago in pirating escapades. The story of the discovery soon spread throughout the piedmont and people came to Snow Hill Farm to search the fields for other likely caches. Over the years, several coins minted in the eighteenth and nineteenth centuries have been found on the old plantation, but no large caches.

Some fifty thousand dollars of the original William Kirk pirate fortune could still be hidden somewhere on Snow Hill Farm, and if it were found, could well be worth ten to twenty times that amount today.

If the original boundaries of the Snow Hill Farm when it was purchased by Kirk in the 1760s could be determined, it would be easy to grid the property and systematically explore it with a sophisticated metal detector. Simple enough—if the present owners would permit it, and if the treasure has not already been discovered and removed.

The Doll House Treasure of Upshur County

From the Appalachian Plateau region of West Virginia comes one of the more bizarre tales of hidden treasure, a tale of a strange and reclusive Spaniard, an even stranger miniature house, and three hundred thirty thousand dollars of alleged bank robbery loot.

The Appalachian Plateau, which takes in most of northern and western West Virginia, is an elevated tract of nearly flat to gently folded land ranging in altitude from a thousand feet along the western edge to more than three thousand feet where it meets the Allegheny Front in the east and south. Ancient glacial abrasion and the more recent erosion by flowing water have sculpted the plateau into gentle hills and deep valleys.

Into one of these valleys in 1889 came a dark little stoop-shouldered man. Giving his name as Alfonso Marzo, the man approached a farmer named Shahan about purchasing some land on which to build a cabin. Marzo, who claimed he was from Spain, offered gold. Shahan and Marzo haggled briefly, then struck a deal, and the Spaniard became the owner of a few acres near the railroad tracks about a mile from Shahan's house.

Carrying all his possessions in a large canvas sack and a suitcase-sized metal trunk, Marzo moved onto his new property and built a house. It was a queer little home, a dramatically scaled-down version of a normal frame house that looked like a miniature such as one would build for young children to play in. The neighbors dubbed it the "doll house."

Though Shahan and other local residents tried to be friendly, Marzo remained distant. He shunned visitors and actually fled into the woods at the approach of strangers. Marzo rarely visited town to purchase supplies, and on the few times he did venture into a settlement, he conducted what little business he had and left as quickly as possible.

Marzo gave Shahan the impression that he was a blacksmith, but he didn't seem to have any of the tools of that trade. Other than building the doll house, Marzo was never seen to work.

Marzo lived on his property for nearly four years, then suddenly and mysteriously disappeared. The Spaniard left no word with anyone—he simply vanished. All that remained to remind anyone of him was the odd doll house, still seen occasionally by passers-by.

Several years elapsed, and Shahan was surprised to receive a letter one day from Marzo. It was dated August 17, 1911, and was postmarked Madrid, Spain. The letter read,

> My Dear Sir: I am imprisoned in this city and knowing your honesty and personality, I beg to beseech you to herewith whether you want to come here to take away my equipages seizure in order to seize upon a trunk containing a secret in which I have hidden a document indispensable to you to come in possession of 330,000 dollars that I have in the United States. As a reward, I will yield to you the third part of the aforementioned sum.
>
> Fearful that this letter don't arrive at your hands, I will want your answer and then I will say you my secret with every detail and to subscribe with my name.

As here is a newspaper that publish all the
cablegrams whose addressee are unknown
which it is allowed to me to read and I cannot
receive here in the gaol your reply, you must
send a cablegram to the address indicated at the
end.

Notwithstanding, your cable not reach to me,
this will be sufficient to know that you accept
my proposition.

Waiting eagerly to read your missive.

I only inscribe
V. ex-banker

Above all, please answer by cable, but not by
letter, as following:

Alfonso Marzo
Ysabel Catolica ZO- Madrid
Yes—Julius

While much of Marzo's letter is vague and difficult to
interpret, probably a result of the Spaniard's poor command of the English language, some points are clear. First,
Marzo apparently knew where three hundred thirty thousand dollars lay hidden and had secreted a document
somewhere which gave directions to the cache. Was the
trunk the letter mentioned the same one he brought to the
West Virginia valley? Second, Marzo was apparently willing to share a third of the alleged wealth with Shahan.
Third, the Spaniard said he was a prisoner in Madrid,
although he gave no explanation.

Shahan had trouble understanding the cryptic letter
and was not quite certain what to make of it. In any case,
he did not reply to the Spaniard and never received any
more correspondence from him.

One element of Marzo's mysterious letter has puzzled
researchers for years: If the three hundred thousand dollars
did, in fact, exist, where did it come from and how did it
come to be in the Spaniard's possession?

Perhaps Marzo's fortune can be tied to an incident that occurred elsewhere in the state several weeks before his quiet arrival at the Shahan farm. Somewhere east of Upshur County, a bank was robbed, and the little documentation that exists suggests that about a third of a million dollars was taken. Coincidence?

And what of the doll house? No satisfactory reason has ever been given for the building of the strange little structure. Did it have anything to do with the three hundred thirty thousand dollars? A story told around Upshur County following the arrival of Marzo's letter was that the Spaniard had indeed robbed the bank and fled with his stolen loot to the Appalachian Plateau, where he buried it beneath the doll house.

This tale sent many area residents to the valley in which Marzo had lived, searching for the miniature house. They could never find it. Farmer Shahan, who seldom visited the Marzo property when the Spaniard was there, rode over shortly after receiving the letter. The doll house was gone. There was no evidence that it had fallen down or burned; it had simply disappeared without a trace. Try as they might, neither Shahan nor any of his neighbors could remember just where the mysterious doll house had sat on the property.

Attempts to trace Alfonso Marzo back to Spain failed, and what became of him remains a mystery. As far as anyone knows, the Spaniard never returned to the Appalachian Plateau to reclaim any of the treasure thought buried on his small plot of land.

Documents on the old Shahan farm locate it near the junction of Bear Camp Run and the left fork of the Buckhannon River in the southeastern corner of Upshur County. Somewhere not far from the original Shahan cabin, the mysterious doll house treasure still lies buried.

The Peddler's Lost Cache

Moishe Edelman was an unlikely source of buried treasure, but over the course of several years, the old immigrant peddler apparently buried several thousands of dollars' worth of gold coins in a secret location in West Virginia, intending someday to retrieve them. Edelman, however, suffered a fatal heart attack and died before he could enjoy any of the fruits of his hard work and systematic saving. Before he died, Edelman stammered out the directions to his buried fortune to the physician who was attending him in a Cleveland, Ohio, hospital.

Moishe Edelman, known to his customers as "Mose," was born early in the 1880s in a Jewish ghetto in Russia. As a boy, Moishe was weak and sickly and often complained of chest pains. In his teens, Moishe fled Russia and made his way to England, where he could not find decent work. The young man often labored eighteen hours a day at menial jobs that paid little, but because he was frugal, he saved enough money to buy a steamer ticket to the United States.

When Moishe arrived in America, he worked at various low-paying jobs and eventually became a peddler. In the beginning, the young man toted a large canvas sack filled with household wares such as were needed by the people of the remote and rural parts of the Appalachians in Virginia and West Virginia. Burdened by the heavy bag, the dedicated merchant traveled on foot from house to house and farm to farm, selling his goods. Travel was usually difficult in the rugged, sparsely settled Appalachians during that time, and the weather was often disagreeable, but Moishe persevered. Between 1916 and 1930, he walked thousands of miles of back-country roads in the hills and valleys of the Appalachian Plateau.

Because Moishe had miserly habits and no family or other apparent expenses, his savings grew. By 1930, he had amassed what in those days amounted to a large fortune. The immigrant peddler's distrust of banks led him to convert his money into gold coins and bury them on a riverbank somewhere in Lincoln County in western West Virginia.

As Moishe grew older, carrying a heavy pack through the rugged mountain country exacted an increasingly heavy toll on his frail frame. He finally bought an inexpensive secondhand automobile. Moishe occasionally would stay in a hotel, but more often than not, he lived in his old car.

In June 1933, Moishe drove to Ohio to purchase a new line of household goods from a dealer he knew. While loading merchandise into his car, the peddler was felled by a sudden heart attack and rushed to the local hospital. After several days of intensive care and many consultations with the attending physician, Moishe realized that his weakened heart would not recover and that he would soon die.

One morning when the doctor stopped by Moishe's room, the peddler reached out and grasped the physician's lab coat and pulled him closer. Feeling weaker with each passing moment, the dying man haltingly whispered to the doctor that he had something important he needed to tell him. With difficulty, Moishe told him how he had acquired wealth and then buried gold coins many times along a remote creek bank in West Virginia. When he told the doctor he wished to give him directions to the fortune, the physician grabbed a notepad and pencil and quickly jotted down the peddler's final words:

Go along the hard road until you reach Fry, a small community between Logan and Huntington, West Virginia. Go toward the settlement of Leet across the mountain from Fry. At Leet, Laurel Fork Creek empties into the Big Ugly River. Go up Laurel Fork for a mile or two until you reach a large rock. Directly across the road from the rock, in a small bend of the creek, thousands of dollars are in four chests. Dig along the bank.

A few moments later, Moishe Edelman, peddler, was dead.

The doctor believed Edelman was sincere, and that the information he gave was not a raving caused by delerium.

Several weeks later, the doctor took several days off to travel to Lincoln County, West Virginia, where he searched for Moishe Edelman's buried treasure. The physician was amazed to discover how remote and rugged the area was, and how many miles of creek bank might conceal the peddler's gold coins. Several spots along Laurel Fork Creek fit Edelman's description, but after digging a series of holes at several sites, the doctor came away with nothing. Discouraged by his poor luck and the immensity of the task, and burdened by the obligations of his medical practice, the physician packed up and returned to Cleveland after a few days.

Moishe Edelman's description does include a lot of territory. Perhaps someday a treasure hunter with a reliable metal detector and a bit of luck may uncover the old peddler's buried money.

Hidden Treasure in the Buckhannon River Valley

During the height of the Civil War, a soldier whose name has been lost to history dropped by the Wilson farm in a sparsely settled portion of Monongalia County. The soldier and Wilson were old friends, and the farmer and his wife asked their guest to stay the night.

Wondering why his friend was not with his military unit, Wilson asked several pointed questions. The soldier said he was on temporary leave, and then unfolded an amazing tale of a hidden treasure for which he was searching. The vast fortune lay in a lost cave in the upper reaches of the Buckhannon River Valley, about fifty miles to the south in Upshur County.

The soldier had just returned from Upshur County where he had been thwarted in his search by roving bands of outlaws and opposing military detachments, both making travel through the remote and unprotected West Virginia wilderness difficult, if not impossible.

After the evening meal, when the soldier and Wilson were alone, the guest opened a large leather traveling bag and took out an eighteen-inch-square parchment map. He showed Wilson where the map said the treasure was buried. The soldier told Wilson about a party of miners who had been taking bags of coins and ingots of silver east when they were set upon by a roving band of Indians. Fleeing, the miners hid in a cave and buried the ingots and coins in the far corner of a large chamber. In the dark of night, the miners silently crept from their hiding place and continued their journey east, intending to come back someday for the fortune. The miners, according to the young soldier, never returned and the treasure still lay in the cave. His map was made by one of the miners, who drowned in a rain-swollen river while trying to return to the cave.

The map, he said, was useless without its key, held by a close friend just to the west, in Marion County.

Wilson shared the soldier's enthusiasm for the hidden treasure. The two agreed to become partners, get the key, and search for the treasure together. The soldier, however, was overdue in reporting back to his cavalry unit and said that he needed to be on his way. Leaving the map with Wilson, the soldier gave directions to the Marion County resident with the map key. He asked Wilson to wait for him to return, but to pursue the search on his own if he was not back within a reasonable time after the war ended. With that, the soldier bid farewell to his friend and rode away into the woods. The farmer never saw him again.

Wilson waited nearly two years after the end of the war for his partner's return. Finally, he decided to go to Marion County and get the key. Wilson packed a wagon, hitched up two stout horses, and at the last minute, invited his grandson along. The trip through the rugged and often dangerous wilderness was long and hard, an unforgettable experience for the younger Wilson.

Decades later, when Joseph M. Wilson was himself a grandfather, he easily recalled the arduous trip through the Appalachian backcountry. It rained often and they had difficulty crossing streams. The wagon occasionally bogged down in the mud and the two had to slog through muck and high water to help the horses pull free. The younger Wilson also recalled that at one point during the return trip, his grandfather told him he now had the key and could go directly to the cave and find the treasure. Unfortunately, once they returned home, the old man became very sick and died.

Because he was so young, Joseph Wilson had little inkling of the potential worth of the buried treasure that the map and key supposedly led to. Several years later, when he had developed an appreciation for the value of money, he recalled his grandfather's quest. He also recalled that his grandfather was a very conservative man, not one to waste time. That he had traveled across two counties to get the key to the treasure map suggested to young Wilson that the old man had thought it important.

Joseph Wilson's family moved to another valley, but when he was old enough, he went to his grandmother's home and asked about the map and the key left by his late grandfather. After searching through several drawers, old trunks, and bundles of papers, he found the map. Carefully unrolling it, young Wilson noted that it was a very old, stiff parchment. The inscriptions on the map were finely written in ink, and while clear and easy to read, were vague about the amount and type of treasure. Nothing on the map told the origin of the treasure or who buried it.

Diligent searching failed to turn up the key. The grandmother, who could neither read nor write, confessed she might have burned it along with some other papers she considered worthless.

After several weeks of studying the map, the younger Wilson determined that the treasure had long ago been hidden in a cave close to the old Seneca War Trail where it crossed the upper Buckhannon River in Upshur County. According to the map, the trail could be seen from the cave's low entrance.

Without the key, Joseph Wilson searched for the treasure cave several times but never found it. After several years, he gave up, and in 1891 turned the map over to one Lucullus Virgil McWhorter, a native of the town of Buckhannon. McWhorter was one of the few educated men living in the area at the time. During the early 1880s, McWhorter had conducted a detailed study of local Indian artifacts and campgrounds. Wilson gave McWhorter the map because he seemed keenly interested in local history.

Wilson also told McWhorter what he knew of the origin of the map, and of the lost key. McWhorter was interested in the tale of buried treasure and tried to find it several times himself, with no success. In 1915, McWhorter published an account of the lost treasure cave.

Though many others, using the old parchment map or copies of it, have searched for the lost treasure cave, none have found it. Researchers have diligently pursued an explanation for the origin of the treasure, and many believe that it is part of a shipment of silver ingots from one of the famed Jonathan Swift mines. *(See "The Lost Jonathan Swift Mines," page 76.)*

Members of the Swift party often passed through the Buckhannon River Valley on their way to and from the mines in Kentucky, and Jonathan Swift himself makes several references to the area in his journals. One particular entry by Swift may shed some light on the hidden treasure.

While establishing a temporary camp along what many think was the Buckhannon River, the Swift party was suddenly attacked by Indians. Quickly strapping the packs of ingots and equipment onto their mules, the miners fled along the Seneca Trail, eventually taking refuge in a cave near the headwaters of the stream. While several men guarded the entrance, others buried the bars of silver. Relieved of their heavy load, the miners waited until darkness and then escaped, intending someday to return and retrieve the wealth secreted in some dark chamber of the cave.

It may also be worth noting that Swift occasionally referred to rich silver mines in the Buckhannon River Valley which he and his men excavated during 1761. It may very well have been silver taken from one of these mines that was cached in the lost cave.

Many mining tools, all of the them quite old, have been found in the Buckhannon River Valley, and they may have belonged to the Swift party. In addition, at least two very old mine shafts have been discovered. The shafts had been covered up in a careless attempt at concealment, but years of erosion have exposed the openings.

Few people these days have reason to travel to the relatively isolated upper reaches of the Buckhannon River in Upshur County. The local tales and legends of lost mines and buried treasures are relatively unknown to outsiders, and so there have been few organized attempts to find the lost cave. Continued research and organized, systematic exploration of the area might someday yield one of the country's largest treasure caches.

Other Tales of Lost and Buried Treasures in West Virginia

Cavern of Gold by Bear Fork Creek

Two friends were deer hunting near Bear Fork Creek in Gilmer County in the early 1950s when they accidentally discovered a thick seam of gold in a remote cavern.

The two had taken a few days off from their jobs as coal miners. Happy to be away from the mines and out in the peace and solitude of the forest, the friends approached the hunt with enthusiasm. Around mid-morning of their second day in the woods, they had spotted fresh deer tracks and followed them for nearly two miles when they chanced upon a cave.

Neither of the men had ever been in a cave, and they decided to explore this one. Carrying crude torches made from grasses and tree limbs, the two crept cautiously into the dark passageway. Sixty yards into the cave, they noticed one wall painted with Indian signs and symbols. While one examined the markings, the other discovered a long, thick line of color transecting the opposite wall. On closer inspection, the hunters discovered the color was a vein of gold.

The two friends returned to their homes and jobs the following day and began to make plans to return to the cave to excavate some of the rich ore. Several months passed before they could coordinate their vacation time so they could go back to Gilmer County, find the cave again, and dig out some of the gold.

Eventually they returned to Bear Fork Creek, where they set up camp. On the morning of the following day, the two friends began their search. Armed with digging tools, they trudged up and down hills and through valleys, trying to retrace the route they had followed tracking the deer months earlier. After three days of fruitless searching, they admitted they had no inkling where the cave might be. They had failed to take note of pertinent landmarks and features in their haste to get home after their discovery. The two men thought they could walk right to the cave of gold, but in the several months since their trip, they had apparently forgotten much of what they saw. Disheartened, they returned home.

Apparently known to the Indians of long ago, the cave of gold remains lost.

Hidden Gold in Jefferson County

Colonel Joseph Van Swearingen, a retired veteran of the Revolutionary War, bought a small farm and settled into the community of Bellevue in Jefferson County. Swearingen had been a soldier for nearly forty years and had grown weary of the profession. He looked forward to living out the rest of his life in leisure, growing a few crops on the acreage he purchased.

During his years in the military, Swearingen had accumulated impressive wealth, much of it booty he had taken in wartime. Though no one knew exactly how much money the old soldier had, the Bellevue townsfolk saw the colonel as an extremely wealthy man.

One day while in a nearby town on business, Swearingen visited a fortune teller who predicted he would die within the year. Normally not one to believe in such things, Swearingen began to think of his mortality, and decided to hide his fortune. Somewhere on his farm, Swearingen had a field hand dig a pit, and into the pit he put an iron kettle filled with gold and silver coins. He told no one where it was buried, and as far as anyone knows, left no written record of it either.

Within the year, Swearingen died—at the exact hour and day predicted by the spiritualist. Swearingen left no heirs, and the small farm soon fell into disrepair. Stories of his buried wealth spread throughout the area, and occasional treasure hunters would set up camp for a few days at the old farm while they searched for the buried coins. The cache was never recorded as having been found.

The Lost Fort Seybert Treasure

Old Fort Seybert lay in the heart of Indian country, and relationships between the fort's inhabitants and the Shawnee were strained at best. In 1758, growing tensions gave way to violence, and the Shawnee launched a vicious attack on the fort, killing most of the soldiers and capturing many civilians living in the stockade. The Shawnee decided to keep the white prisoners as slaves and roped them together and marched them from the fort toward the Indian village several miles away.

Before leaving the fort, the Indians had the settlers gather up all their valuables and put them in a large iron kettle. When the kettle was filled, the Indians inserted a wooden pole through the handle and had two of the male captives carry it to the Shawnee village. The big pot full of gold and silver coins and other valuables was heavy and hard to manage. The two men assigned to it wrestled with the cumbersome load, sometimes falling and spilling the contents.

To reach the Shawnee village, the party of Indians and captives followed a well-used trail up one side of South Fork Mountain. As the trail grew steeper, the men carrying the treasure-filled kettle had even greater difficulty. Finally, the Shawnee chief, tired of the clumsiness of the white men, ordered them to leave the pot and signaled the group to

391

continue the march. When the column was out of sight, the chief had two of his braves scrape out a hole and bury the pot and its contents. This was done in a few minutes, and the Indians rejoined the group and continued on to the village.

Several weeks later, the Shawnee village was attacked by a large rescue party. The Indians were routed and the captives returned to safety. After their release, several of the former prisoners tried to find the pot of coins, but saw no evidence of a recent excavation. Since the Shawnee were driven from the area never to return, they probably didn't have a chance to retrieve the treasure.

If the route from Fort Seybert to the Shawnee village could be retraced, a persistent and fortunate treasure hunter with a good metal detector might find the buried kettle of coins.

Abandoned Union Payroll Near Chapmanville

In Fayette County during the War Between The States, a contingent of Union soldiers was escorting a large payroll—a wagon full of gold coins—to a Yankee encampment in the area. As the party traveled along the winding trails through the dense woods, scouts told the commanding officer that a Confederate patrol was rapidly approaching from the east.

The Union officer ordered the escort into a full gallop in the hope of outdistancing the Rebels, but after trying to elude the enemy for about five miles, it became clear that they would soon be overtaken. Anticipating a skirmish, the officer halted the wagon and ordered the canvas bags that held the Union payroll taken from the wagon and buried a short distance from the trail. While troopers hastily dug a pit in which to hide the gold, the officer noted the surroundings in his journal. He wrote that the payroll was hidden on the west side of the Buyandotte River, near a small settlement named Chapmanville.

Once the hole was filled, the soldiers remounted and rode on. About an hour later, the Confederates overtook the Union soldiers and opened fire. The Yankees sought cover and returned fire, but they were disorganized and greatly outnumbered. The fighting lasted about two hours, and when it was over, all of the Yankee soldiers lay dead.

The Rebel soldiers searched the wagon for the money and found it empty. Suspecting the gold had been buried shortly before the engagement, they retraced the Yankees' trail for several miles, without finding the payroll.

Returning to the site of the skirmish, the Confederates stripped the Union soldiers of anything of value and left the corpses to rot in the sun. An unknown soldier took the commanding officer's journal and later tossed it into a trunk and forgot it. In the early 1930s, someone discovered the old journal and searched unsuccessfully for the buried coins.

The directions in the journal claimed the gold was buried at a point where the old road and the Buyandotte River came within twenty yards of one another. Since the war, however, the road has been all but obliterated by a more modern thoroughfare, and the river has shifted its course.

If the Union payroll of gold coins was not uncovered by the shifting river and washed downstream, the Civil War cache is probably still lying just a few inches beneath the soil near Chapmanville.

References

Anderson, Nina and Bill Andrews. *Southern Treasures*. Chester, Connecticut: The Globe Pequot Press, 1987.

Andrews, Ernest M. *Georgia's Fabulous Treasure Hoards*. Hapeville, Georgia: E.M. Andrews, 1966.

Atchley, D. Van. "West Virginia's Lost Gold Mine." *Western And Eastern Treasures* (December 1978): 50.

Bailey, Jay. "John Swift's Lost Silver Mines—Fact or Fiction." *True Treasure* (January-February 1970): 58-64.

Belcher, D.R. and Wade Chastain. "New Clues To The Carolinas' Incredible Spanish Treasure." *Treasure Search* (April 1983): 6-10.

Boren, Kerry Ross. "Lost Silver Crowns Of The Appalachians." *True Treasure* (November-December 1972): 28-33.

_____. "Lost Mines And Buried Treasures In The Trans-Allegheny." *Treasure World* (June-July 1975): 11-13.

Bradley, Bob. "Civil War Loot In Tennessee." *Lost Treasure* (June 1978): 50.

Brown, Dee. "Legends of Confederate Gold." *Southern Magazine* (November 1987): 49-51, 88-90.

Clark, Jafar. "Confederate Gold In North Carolina." *Lost Treasure* (March 1978): 61-62.

Dangerfield, Dan. "Where Are The Melungeon Mines?" *Lost Treasure* (October 1978): 28-29, 49-50.

Duffy, Howard M. "Snow Hill Pirate Trove." *Lost Treasure* (November 1976): 31.

_____. "Confederate Treasure." *Lost Treasure* (May 1977): 45-46.

Everman, William J. "Lekain's Lost Silver Cache." *True Treasure* (October 1974): 40-41, 48-50, 52.

Harris, Charles S. "The Civil War Treasure Of Tasso, Tennessee." *Treasure Search* (Summer 1973) 32-35.

Harvey, Davis E. "Lost Alabama Silver." *Lost Treasure* (December 1976): 23-24.

_____. "Georgia's $250,000 Treasure Tunnel." *Western And Eastern Treasures* (October 1977): 24-25.

Henson, Michael Paul. "West Virginia Treasure Cave." *Treasure Search* (March 1975): 54-55.

_____. "Kentucky's Five Barrels Of Silver." *Treasure* (May 1975): 68-69.

_____. "Lost Silver Mine In West Virginia." *True Treasure* (September-October 1975): 13-15.

_____. *A Guide To Treasure In Virginia And West Virginia*. Deming, New Mexico: Carson Enterprises, 1982.

_____. *A Guide To Treasure In Kentucky*. Deming, New Mexico: Carson Enterprises, 1984.

_____. "$330,000 West Virginia Cache." *Treasure* (October 1986): 24, 59.

_____. "Clues To The Swift Silver Mines." *Treasure* (December 1987): 24, 51.

_____. "West Virginia Treasures." *Lost Treasure* (February 1980): 8-14.

Hudson, C.M. "Drowned Man's Gold." *Lost Treasure* (July 1978): 36.

Hughes, Brent. "Find The Cave—Find The Gold!" *Lost Treasure* (May 1988): 20-22.

Hunt, Burl. "Crismo's Captured Coins." *Lost Treasure* (June 1979): 57-58.

Hunt, Charles B. *Natural Regions Of The United States And Canada*. San Francisco: W.H. Freeman and Co., 1974.

Malach, Roman. "Bone Cave Gold." *Treasure Search* (June 1985): 18.

_____. "Lekain's Coins." *Treasure* (January 1986): 28, 74.

Masters, Al. "Treasure In West Virginia." *Treasure World* (November 1975): 25.

_____. "Multi-Million Dollar Treasure Of Red Bone Cave." *Lost Treasure* (September 1979): 27-29.

Milberger, Joe F. "Bellfaun's Gold In A Pot Of Clay." *Western And Eastern Treasures* (May 1977): 42-44.

Raitz, Karl B. and Richard Ulack. *Appalachia: A Regional Geography*. Boulder, Colorado: Westview Press, 1984.

Ronoto. "The Doll House Treasure In West Virginia." *Western And Eastern Treasures* (February 1979): 18-20.

Rush, J.William. "Find Bechtler's Lost Carolina Fortunes." *Treasure* (January 1979): 56-59, 61.

Steely, Michael S. "Silver Arrowhead Points To Legendary Swift's Mines." *Treasure* (September, 1984): 8-10.

Townsend, Tom. "Lost Gold Of The Uwharries." *Lost Treasure* (November, 1976): 55-56.

Traywick, Ben T. "Mystery Silver Mine." *Lost Treasure* (February 1988): 16-18.

Van Dyke, R.E. "Elkhead Hoard." *Treasure* (October, 1985): 51-52.

Wade, Forest C. *Cry Of The Eagle: History And Legends Of The Cherokee Indians And Their Buried Treasures*. Cumming, Georgia: F.C. Wade, 1969.

Ward, John K. "Dix River's Buried Bandit Loot." *Lost Treasure* (October, 1977): 33-36.

Weber, Glenn. "Missing $115,000 In Confederate Gold." *Treasure World* (June-July 1973): 29.

Williams, Jerry. "Asa Smyth's Keg Of Gold." *Treasure Search* (April, 1985): 48-49.